THE
COMPLETE
WEDDING
HANDBOOK

THE COMPLETE WEDDING HANDBOOK

GENNA HAYMAN & KIRSTIE ROWSON

Published by Virgin Books 2010

First published with the title *The Alternative Guide to Weddings* in 2004

2 4 6 8 10 9 7 5 3 1

Copyright © Genna Hayman and Kirstie Rowson 2004, 2010

Kirstie Rowson and Genna Hayman have asserted their right under the Copyright, Designs and Patents Act 1988 to be identified as the authors of this work

Design: www.carrstudio.co.uk

First published in Great Britain in 2010 by
Virgin Books
Random House, 20 Vauxhall Bridge Road,
London SW1V 2SA

www.virginbooks.com
www.rbooks.co.uk

Addresses for companies within The Random House Group Limited can be found at:
www.randomhouse.co.uk/offices.htm

The Random House Group Limited Reg. No. 954009

A CIP catalogue record for this book
is available from the British Library

ISBN 9780753522448

CONTENTS

ACKNOWLEDGEMENTS

A big thanks to everyone that shared their stories with us. Your names are in print within!

David, Ginny, James, Susanna, David Steele, Chris Aked, Ailish O'Reilly, Ceri Davies, Lottie Loveridge, Bianca Rhodes, Kate Foster, Kim Parker and Sasha Brown. Sorry we couldn't include your words of wisdom – word counts rule we're afraid.

Not forgetting our support team; Elliot, Kim (you're a star), Jo, Emma, Elisabeth, Marilyn and Neil. Lots of love.

We're also really grateful to Kirstie, Mark, Helen and Jamie. And all the people at the various tourist boards, venues, register offices and embassies who helped us nail down the practical details, especially those who worked with us to put the chapter on **Getting Married in the UK** together and ensure its accuracy.

Many thanks to:
Bishop Jonathan Blake, SICM and Open Episcopal Church

Sue Burridge, Policy Adviser on Marriage and Family for the Archbishop's Council

Terry Prendergast, Chief Executive, Catholic Marriage Care
Chief Superintendent Registrar, Wandsworth Register Office

THE
COMPLETE
WEDDING
HANDBOOK

INTRODUCTION

Congratulations! You are officially a bride- or groom-to-be. So, just what are you meant to do now?

Most importantly, enjoy being engaged. Planning a wedding can be challenging, but be determined to enjoy that too, come rain or shine, mother-in-law or mother.

This guide is designed to spark your imagination and inspire you to create a wedding just for you. It will help you realise that you can have fun planning your big day and don't need to get stressed about living up to 'by the book' standards reinforced by your friends' or familys' weddings. Breaking away from the norm doesn't mean that you have to have something completely different or ridiculous, unless you want to. But it does mean that you can use alternative ideas to get creative and make your wedding special and unique.

Whether you're getting married on a shoestring or have cash to blow, this book will give you plenty of food for thought for every kind of wedding. Content is organised under all the chapter headings you would expect, the difference being that you will find all sorts of other options that you might not have considered. Pick and choose from the *traditional options* (marked by a top hat) and alternative ideas to create your perfect day and remember that the most memorable occasions are not necessarily the most expensive.

Contrary to what the wedding industry would have you believe, you don't need a huge budget if you are willing to tame tradition. So if you'd rather use your money for a deposit on a house, or perhaps you just don't have access to vast sums of cash without taking on a millstone of a loan, then check out our budget pointers.

We spoke to a lot of couples about their weddings and the gems of advice they wish they'd known in advance are included as quotes. These are attributed to the age people were at the time of the wedding they were involved in.

And last, but by no means least, have a fabulous day whatever you decide.

BACK TO BASICS

Getting married will be one of the most exciting things that will ever happen to you.

Planning your wedding will be fun and exhilarating but for some it should also come with a government notice: 'WARNING. You are about to enter the crazed world of weddings. This may damage your wallet, your relationship with loved ones and your sanity. A military approach to operations is advisable.'

At this early stage, before you get wrapped up in the details, you should commit the following to memory. The only legal requirements for a British resident to get married in the UK are that you:

✓ Are both over 16 (if you live in England or Wales and either party is under 18 you must have written consent from your parents or legal guardian)

✓ Are both consenting to the marriage or civil partnership

✓ Can both prove who you are

✓ Are both eligible (i.e. not married already and not an immediate family member)

✓ Have two witnesses

✓ Are married by a registered registrar or celebrant in a licensed venue

✓ Give a minimum of 15 days clear notice in England for a civil service (religious ceremonies may require a longer notice period)

Everything else is pure commercialism and old wives' tales. Banish all preconceptions from your mind. You don't have to wear anything specific, have any particular photos, transport, food or entertainment, or even have a reception or honeymoon at all. If you really wanted to, you could get married at a register office in your normal clothes and then start your married life with the adrenaline rush of a bungy or parachute jump rather than a reception. Always keep this in mind, especially if at any time you feel that your wedding is spiralling out of control. Legally, it is very straightforward. Socially, it can be a nightmare.

Between now and the big day, most couples will experience excitement, apprehension, nerves and some stress. The crucial thing is to agree what the two of you want first. With this in mind, anticipate what reactions you are likely to get from the people you care about and how you will handle these issues as they arise.

Sounds simple? It might. But the last hurdles you may not be bargaining on are the siren-like wiles of the wedding industry. You have to be strong to resist tradition wholeheartedly and may not even want to. But always be aware that everything you opt for above and beyond the seven legal requirements is down to your personal taste.

Good luck. May the planning commence.

ENGAGEMENT

So, one of you has asked and the other one has said yes.

And you may have already been bombarded with questions about setting the date and who your bridesmaids will be. But you don't need to rush headlong into the planning. This is an occasion in itself and should be savoured.

RINGS

Contrary to popular belief, you do not need to exchange rings as part of a wedding ceremony and in fact, you do not need to have rings at all – it is just how society recognises at a glance that you are married. This is another

Engagement rings and wedding rings symbolise an eternal circle of love, which some think originated thousands of years ago when cavemen would put a circle of rushes around their mates' hands and feet to bind them until they were sure that she wouldn't stray!

And in medieval times only one ring was given as opposed to separate ones for engagement and marriage.

The practice of the ring being worn on the third finger of the left hand started for one of two reasons:

- *The Ancient Greeks and Egyptians believed that the vein from this finger ran straight to the heart ... this has since been proven not to be so but the tradition remains*
- *A priest in medieval times would touch a finger in turn while reciting the Trinity – 'Father, Son and Holy Ghost' – starting with the index finger, so the final finger would be today's ring finger*

tradition that we have embraced as if it is law, but it is actually your choice whether or not to give a token of affection and whether that will or will not be a ring. If you decide not to give rings that section of the ceremony will simply be omitted.

WHAT WOMEN WANT

Today's women know what they want. And once they are ready to get married, they tend to start giving some thought to the kind of rings they like. Furtive glances and casual strolls past jewellery shops are not always as innocent as they may seem. Girls, don't feel bad if you would like a say in the ring that you will hopefully wear for the rest of your lives together. And guys, a few pointers might be just what you need. Trends are changing so that men often leave buying the official ring until after the proposal and either don't buy a ring at all, buy a decorative 'placeholder', or put a deposit to 'borrow' a ring from a jeweller so that you can go back and choose another one if you like.

If your man has surprised you with the actual ring he wants you to wear and you really don't like it, handle the situation with care. Remember to be sensitive about it when you're discussing it with him but also bear in mind that he will want you to have a ring that you love. Ideally you will both agree on your engagement ring because even if your fiancé is buying it for you, you are the one that will be wearing it.

PRACTICALITIES

When you are choosing your engagement ring, think about the kind of wedding ring you will want. How will they fit together? And if you're feeling lucky, plan for an eternity ring too!

If you both like different wedding rings, it's not the end of the world if they don't match. It's a marketing gimmick that they're sold as pairs. If you can't find matching rings that suit the two of you, don't worry, it doesn't mean that your union is fated. It just means you suit different kinds of jewellery.

> *We had my engagement ring and our wedding rings custom made in Birmingham's jewellery quarter. It meant that I could have exactly the ring I wanted at a fairly reasonable cost. And I had my wedding ring indented on one edge to make room for the diamond in my engagement ring so that they sit flush up against each other. I can't wear the wedding ring separately but then, I never intended to.*
>
> CLAIRE, 26

HOW MUCH?

Do you really want to spend a lot of money on an engagement ring? You might prefer to have no rings at all, a better wedding ring or an eternity ring on your first anniversary or on the birth of your first child.

The groom-to-be customarily spends one month's salary on the engagement ring, which is bought in advance for the proposal.

> *I really wanted something unique for my engagement ring and most of my friends had gone for incredibly expensive diamond solitaires. In the end we saw a gorgeous silver ring with an amazing turquoise stone when we were travelling in Mexico. I just fell in love with it and now I have also got amazing memories associated with it too. The other bonus is that I can wear it all the time and not have to worry about the financial implications in case I lose it or it gets stolen.*
>
> LISA, 28

Alternatively, you could hark back to days of old and have just one ring. This obviously saves you money but is also becoming an increasingly popular choice as fashions change.

Another issue could be if you both want to contribute to the ring so that you can afford to push the boat out. Or perhaps you could combine the cost with a birthday or Christmas present to make it more affordable.

WHICH STONE?

You are going to be wearing this ring for the rest of your life, so which is the right gemstone for you?

Diamonds

The word diamond comes from the Greek word 'adamas' meaning unconquerable and has been adopted as a symbol of eternal love. If you do decide to go for a diamond you are about to realise a whole new layer of complexity about them that you probably had no idea existed. Generally speaking, jewellers talk about diamonds in terms of the four C's: clarity, carats, colour and cut.

If you would like to be fully clued up before buying your diamond your jeweller will have information for you or visit www.debeers.com or www.buyadiamond.net for online guides.

Other gemstones

It is interesting to note that, even though diamonds have always been popular, the idea that they were the only gem to have in an engagement ring actually originated because of an advertising campaign in 1939. It certainly worked! The campaign was initiated by the son of the founder of De Beers LV, which was then, and still is, one of the biggest diamond mining companies in the world. A masterpiece of marketing genius that you should feel free to ignore.

Once you get away from the mainstream, there is a stunning selection of gems in a variety of colours on offer.

Over time, different gemstones have also come to symbolise different things. If you believe in the associated symbolisms or like the romanticism of it, you can choose the stone that means the most to you. Or maybe you would like to choose one of your birthstones.

Birthstones and their meanings

MONTH	STONE	MEANING	COLOUR
January	Garnet	Constancy, protection	Normally deep red but also in a range of other colours (except blue)
February	Amethyst	Sincerity, sobriety	Pale violet to deep purple
March	Aquamarine	Happy marriage	Sky blue to royal blue
	Bloodstone	Medicinal and aphrodisiac properties	Dark green speckled with red
April	Diamond	Purity, enduring love	Clear white, plus a range of other pastels and colours
May	Emerald	Harmony, eternal love	Green
June	Pearl	Pure, balancing	Opaque white
	Alexandrite	Empowering, a good omen	Green in daylight to red in artificial light
July	Ruby	Passion, unbridled love	Red
August	Peridot	Wards off evil spirits	Lime to olive green
September	Sapphire	Loyalty, faithfulness	Most commonly blue but also a whole range of other colours (except red)
October	Opal	Clarifying, spontaneity	A variety – and changes colour too
November	Topaz	Protects the faithful against harm	Pink, deep red, maroon, amber, peach, yellow and blue
	Citrine	Uplifting, happiness	Lemon yellow, amber and orange
December	Turquoise	Forget-me-not, protection, prosperity	Turquoise

You could also consider **tanzanite** if you really want to stand out from the crowd. Tiffany's first made this stone popular in the late 1960s after its discovery in Tanzania. It has an extremely striking blue colour and is a very elegant option.

Tourmaline is another possibility. Otherwise known as the rainbow gemstone, it tends to encapsulate at least two or three colours and has been attributed with magical powers for reinforcing friendship and love.

For more information about coloured gemstones, check out the US-based International Colored Gemstone Association (www.gemstone.org).

WHICH METAL?

Another consideration is which metal you would prefer to show off your gemstone. If you are going to go for something different from what you'd usually wear, buy a dress ring of the same colour and make sure that you're happy with it against your skin and alongside the rest of your jewellery. It'll be there for a long time after all.

Platinum. More pure, rare and expensive than gold but with the colour of silver. Platinum is considered the finest metal for jewellery because it is durable, will not tarnish and is also hypoallergenic.

Gold. Popular through the ages for its malleability yet durability. Diamond and gemstone rings are typically made using 18-carat gold (18 out of 24 parts, so 75 per cent pure), whereas wedding rings will often be 22 carat. White and yellow gold have similar properties but a different composition of metals (white gold looks like silver or platinum) and in 18-carat red gold the remaining 25 per cent is copper giving it a more coppery colour. Watch out for your gold being plated with a richer-toned gold – it is standard practice but may wear away, so make sure you are paying a fair price.

Palladium. A lighter, cheaper member of the platinum family. It is usually only used for gemstone or diamond settings. Some jewellers are now using it alongside silver in ring settings for added durability.

Silver. It may be cheaper but silver is a softer metal than gold or platinum and many jewellers advise that it will not withstand a lifetime's wear. Sterling silver is 925 parts silver, 75 parts copper, which gives it strength. If you still prefer silver, or cannot afford the more expensive metals, then you could opt for this but you may have to think about replacing your ring further down the line.

WHERE TO BUY YOUR RINGS

Although you have the option of many high-street stores throughout the UK you may want to look for something a bit more unusual. Here are some starting points:

Jewellery quarters. Find out where your nearest jewellery quarter is. Main cities like London, Bournemouth and Birmingham have areas of the city that are famous for their independent jewellers offering a different selection from the high-street chains and at very competitive prices.

Independent jewellers. For those jewellers located outside big cities, their overheads are not as great and so there is an opportunity for budget saving here too. Word of mouth recommendations are best, or look in the phone directories or bridal magazines for their adverts.

> *All I knew when we were choosing my ring, was that I didn't think I suited a diamond solitaire. I feel like I'm a bit too gregarious for that! Eventually we found the most beautiful and intricate antique ruby and gold ring. It wasn't exactly cheap but for what we got it was certainly a bargain. And it's so much more me than anything I could find in any of the high-street jewellers.*
>
> MARIE, 29

Antique shops. If you can cope with the idea that a ring has had a previous owner – you may even be intrigued by that – you can pick up some beautiful ornate and unique rings for good prices in antique jewellery shops. They also have the added bonus of having a better selection of gemstones other than just diamonds.

Jewellery workshops. A lot of independent jewellers will offer the chance to design your own ring. Some offer different packages for designing and creating your ring according to how many of your rings you want made with them, the type of metal used and the quality or type of gemstone.

Art, design and jewellery colleges. If you fancy a ring from an up-and-coming designer, you can commission a student to make one for you. You may have to purchase the raw materials, especially the gemstones, and then they can create the ring of your dreams for trainee wages.

ALTERNATIVE SCENARIOS

If you are not part of the conventional scenario of 'boy asks girl with ring in his pocket', one of the following might help you out:

You proposed to him. This is a tricky one. There is the possibility that he has not proposed to you before now because he can't afford a ring that he thinks you deserve. If you ask him, you cannot presume that he will buy you a ring. You might have to find a compromise where you share the costs, wait until he can afford the ring he wants to buy you, have no engagement ring at all, or give something else instead.

You want to buy him something. Seeing as your man has been so kind as to buy your engagement ring you might like to buy him a gift to mark the occasion.

Presents instead of rings. For whatever reason, you don't want to go down the rings route at all. A keepsake like jewellery, a pen or a hipflask may be your first thought, or you could give each other an 'experience' to remember such as a weekend away, parachute jump, drive round a racetrack or wine-tasting trip. See www.virginexperiencedays.co.uk or www.redletterdays.co.uk for ideas or contact venues directly, which can often save you money.

Keep it in the family. You might have a ring that's a family heirloom that would mean more to you than shelling out for a new one.

SHOUTING IT FROM THE ROOFTOPS!

Who do you tell first? This can be a problematic area because people can rate their importance to you in terms of how far down the list they were in being told. Just don't forget either set of parents in your excitement.

Announcing your engagement in a local or national paper is a traditional way to let the masses know about your news but, if you do this, make sure that all the important people know before they see your notice. You don't want your mum knocking your door down waving a paper aggressively in your face.

Close family members will probably appreciate hearing it from you rather than second-hand. You know better than anyone else who is most important in your life and how you want to handle it. If in doubt, try putting yourself in their position.

While parents and siblings are very important, another change in society is that many people getting married already have children together or from previous relationships. If they are from different relationships, they might be very sensitive about losing their parent to a new partner. Again, this is common sense – you know the relationship you and your ex-partners both have with your children. Anticipate any concerns they might have, keep them as involved as possible and give them lots of respect and love. You're the parents: you know the score.

Whatever you decide, if you ask your parents or friends to let other people know, tell them to make it clear that you want a small wedding, unless you know for sure that you are happy to accommodate everyone.

Back in the days before women's rights, a prospective suitor had to ask a lady's father for permission to have her hand in marriage, as he effectively 'owned' his daughter. Over the years this has become more of a courtesy extended by the groom to his future father-in-law to gain his blessing to pop the question rather than it being a make-or-break scenario. It's all very sweet, although not essential, but it never hurts to keep in with the future in-laws.

That way, people will feel honoured if they make it on to your final guest list and will hopefully be a bit more understanding if they don't. Upsizing is easy to explain; downsizing is something else altogether. If in doubt, remind yourself it's all about damage limitation and setting the right expectations before problems arise.

CELEBRATING IN STYLE – YOUR STYLE

Some couples still opt to have a party to celebrate their engagement but if they do it tends to be more low key and presents aren't necessarily the norm. You could mark the occasion with any kind of get-together you like, big or small, glitzy or laid back, cocktails, picnic or dinner party with friends, family or just on your own.

Historically the engagement party was the first public outing for the couple and an opportunity for their extended families to meet for the first time.

The mother of the bride would have distributed invitations and the bride's father would officially announce the engagement at the gathering. The groom then had a chance to propose a toast and thank everyone for coming and for their presents.

FIRST THINGS FIRST

Before you get immersed in the detail around your wedding you've both got some key initial decisions to make.

This chapter covers the main things to sort out before you involve too many other people because they are often the most contentious issues. If you can be sure exactly what you want in each of these instances and why, then you will be a lot more convincing and authoritative when you present it as a done deal to your friends and family.

You should start with the decision that you are most certain about. If you definitely want a small wedding party then start with 'Who do you need to invite?' and then you can look for venues that will suit your number of guests and budget. If you are only willing to get married in one particular venue then start there and that way your numbers and dates will be dictated for you. Alternatively, if you are intent on being a summer or winter bride, or want to get married on a date special to you both, you will be limited to venues that are available and affordable at your chosen time of year.

Take this opportunity to be absolutely clear about what you both want because if you are planning anything unconventional you may have a bit of a battle on your hands. We strongly recommend writing down your vision and reasoning for your ideal wedding before you discuss it with other people so that you can refer back to it if things get a bit crazy for you both and you can't remember what it was you wanted in the first place. This description could also double as a bargaining tool if you are sharing the costs with your family.

You might think you are not particularly adamant about anything but it is actually very useful if you can muster an opinion on at least one of the initial decisions as it will really help to narrow down your search. Otherwise, it can be quite a formidable task!

BEING HAPPY WITH YOUR DECISION TO GET MARRIED

Those of you that make it the whole way through your engagement without having any doubts at all should feel amazingly smug. Most people have niggling thoughts at some point or other and reportedly up to three out of five people even have doubts at the altar.

Don't worry if you've had a touch of the jitters – this is completely normal as you realise the enormity of what you have agreed to do. You are about to make a commitment to be someone's best friend, monogamous lover and companion for the rest of your lives together. We defy anyone not to be at least a little apprehensive. After all, only a couple of decades ago you were falling out with people and making friends with others on a daily basis over a game of hide-and-seek at school. Have things really changed so much? And when did it all get so complicated?

So, what about the upside of marriage? If you have found your soul mate, the person who helps you to grow, learn more about yourself and love yourself, who laughs with you and helps you to laugh at yourself, then you are amazingly lucky. You know there will be ups and downs and hard work along the way. And it will all be worth it as long as you want it to be.

If you've still got 'chilly' feet, then take some time to consider the following:

Think about your motivations. Nearly everyone has doubts to some degree – it's 'normal'. Ultimately, you need to want to be committed to making this relationship work and have faith in its longevity.

There's no shame in wanting to be sure before you commit. Professional relationship counsellors are not just for couples having 'problems', they can also help you to understand your motivations and your relationship in the context of your impending marriage. Longer term, if you both understand the basis for your marriage it can really help you tackle obstacles that crop up along the way.

Talk through your expectations, concerns or feelings with someone in confidence. You can get advice from your religious centre (many of which run marriage preparation courses) or from Relate (www.relate.org.uk), who call themselves 'the UK's largest and most experienced relationship counselling organisation'.

Once you're happy that your specific doubts are par for the course you can think about your wedding plans and enjoy gearing up to celebrating the start of your married life together.

WHO DO YOU NEED TO INVITE?

This is one of the most pivotal factors in planning your wedding. Early on you must have a good idea about the number of guests so that you can book your venue and confirm your budget, which then dictates the limits of everything else.

If you know you want a huge wedding to accommodate everyone and can afford it, then this is not a major problem. At worst, your main concern will be whether you have to invite the black sheep of the family/wannabe friend/dreaded partner of friend, or not. Of course you don't have to but it's worth remembering that you are highly unlikely to get around to talking to everyone anyway, and so shouldn't have a problem avoiding anyone you don't particularly want to spend time with. In the end, it comes down to whether you are willing to pay for the additional head and possibly catch eyes with them every once in a while in order to keep other people happy.

For those of you who want a small wedding, this is possibly the hardest question you will have to tackle during your wedding planning. A variety of factors can affect your answer but, most importantly, don't lose sight of your personal preferences. To keep yourself from getting stressed unnecessarily, assess in advance how important the 'who will come' question and its repercussions are to you and dig your heels in accordingly. Do remember, though, that this one point can end up dictating your requirements for a lot of the rest of your wedding planning.

On a practical level, on separate bits of paper write the names of absolutely everyone you know you want to invite and, if they are contributing, everyone your parents would like you to invite. Then put the bits of paper into four piles:

✓ Must come, for example, your immediate family and best friends – the availability of these people will decide your date

✓ Definitely invited – their attendance is not make or break but they are guaranteed an invite

✓ Wish list/evening only – for guests who you would ideally like to share your special day with but can't because you are limited by numbers or budget (if you are not having an evening reception, take the opportunity to invite these people to a future gathering, or maybe even a party the next day)

✓ Not invited

This can seem like a very callous process but really helps you get clear on who you can realistically invite before you tell anyone your plans about the size of your wedding or potential invitees. Beware: family members have a tendency to think that they have an automatic invitation, so be cautious if you are not intending to invite them all.

Whatever you decide, stick to it and watch out for being talked into having a wedding twice (or half) the size you want. You don't have to have the wedding everyone else wants you to have, but you must be 100 per cent clear about this from the outset. If you waver, you'll encourage false hope and possibly false invitations.

ETIQUETTE SCHMETIQUETTE

Etiquette around invitations was all well and good when everyone got married at 20 with no children, ex-partners, history of living together and had regular contact with all members of their extended family. But that's all a bit outdated now. By contrast, you may have been to university, lived all around the world, be friends with ex-partners, have children of your own, divorced parents, no contact with parents or live in a

> *Careful planning of your guest list is crucial. Think long and hard about which friends should be invited and what level of family, i.e. immediate, extended, etc. At the end of the day it comes down to a financial and practical logistics decision on where to draw the line.*
>
> ANDREW, 30

commune. Any which way, you are highly likely to have been exposed to a lot of different circles of friends, made some best mates who you hope you will know for life and, as for your family, you may not even see them any more.

Whoever you invite, make sure that you are clear about your reasons for your decisions and aim to avoid hurting people unnecessarily – it won't make you feel any better in the long run.

Invitation etiquette can make these choices very tricky. You might feel pressurised to bust your budget and invite practically everyone. But before you agree to anything consider the following.

Couples and 'plus-ones'. Forget about it being compulsory to invite 'plus 1s' that you have never met. You need to be aware that some people are still very sensitive about this but that if you are inviting someone as part of, say, a group of work colleagues, you do not need to invite their partner. It is a bit more difficult if you have met the partner a couple of times and your guest doesn't know anyone else. But then, in theory, you could also argue that your single friends who don't know anyone should be able to bring someone too. If possible, it's always a good compromise to invite 'plus 1s' to join you when numbers become less restricted, for example, at the evening reception. What's important is to be clear on the invitations exactly who you're inviting to avoid confusion and possible embarrassment on the day. It's also a nice touch to let couples know that you would love to invite them both but are restricted by numbers and so really appreciate their understanding. And be prepared that if your judgement is off base, neither may come.

Children. People can be very defensive about their brood and, while they might just be able to understand your reasons for not inviting any children at all, they will probably take it as a personal blow if they find that this rule isn't unanimous. It can also be tricky for people to leave very young children. If you're going to have one rule for some people and another rule for others you need to be very clear about why you are doing it, because you will undoubtedly be called upon to justify your decision. Be sensitive when you explain your rationale, thank people for their understanding and maybe even have a peace offering (something like a party bag that parents can take home to their kids or a follow-up kiddie-friendly party).

Cancellations. It is possible that you will have some last-minute cancellations but this cannot be guaranteed, so don't rely on a certain number of people dropping out unless you have a guest list of hundreds. When you book with the venue check their policy regarding cancellations. It's a long shot but see if you can negotiate terms to allow for a small percentage of no-shows on the day. Your other alternative is to ask someone in place of those that have dropped out – they will know they are second choice so make it clear you would love them to come.

Extras. It's usually a good idea to have a couple of provisional places put aside in case of last-minute additions to your list. Remember that when you start planning your wedding, you might not know your sister's boyfriend very well, but in 12–18 months' time when you get married they might be engaged too.

Celebrant or registrar. Because the person who married you may have been very involved in the arrangements for your ceremony, you are generally expected to invite them to your reception. A lot of people extend the invitation to their partner too, if they have one. Who knows if they will accept or how long they will stay. If you think you are going to a lot of weddings at the moment, imagine what it must be like for them!

Be selective. Think about the last time you saw or heard from the person you are considering. It's true that weddings can act as reunions, but if you have not been in touch with someone for two years and they only live half an hour away, is it likely that your friendship will continue? Or would a smaller reunion after your wedding suffice?

What you want. Are you still flitting between a huge celebration and a small intimate party? If you want to keep numbers down and are not having any joy with curtailing your families' enthusiasm for inviting their neighbours' babysitter's parents, then how about running away from it all and heading overseas with immediate friends and family instead? It can be a quicker and cheaper solution. Then you can have one big party when you get back, or one for your friends and one for your family and their friends.

WHEN TO GET MARRIED?

Summer is undoubtedly the most popular time of year for weddings but before you get set on a June date, also give some thought to these factors:

Planning. How much time do you need to plan? The likelihood is that more time you have, the more money you will manage to spend and the longer you will have to get stressed about details that you currently have no idea you care about. What is the right balance for you both?

Finance. How much time do you need to save money? If you are prepared to cut your coat (or wedding dress) according to your cloth then set the date first and set your budget in line with how long you have to save. If you definitely want a 'do' that you will have to save up for, then work out how much you can save each month and then set a date when you will be able to afford your dream wedding.

Seasons. Every season in the UK has some pros and cons:

✓ Spring. Easter holidays and skiing holidays could reduce your numbers of guests and April showers may affect your outdoor photo opportunities. But venues are still not at premium rate, a clear spring day is a breath of fresh air at the end of winter and delicate spring flowers are cheaply available. You also have the chance to get married before everyone gets a dose of wedding weariness in the summer

✓ Summer. The wedding season brings with it high prices, hay fever, holidays, other weddings and searing temperatures to make you sweat (elegantly, naturally) through your finery. On the plus side, you have a better chance of clear weather for photos, your guests can mill around outside as well as inside and the lack of snow, rain and ice makes travelling much easier

✓ Autumn. Although blustery days will wreak havoc with your hair and darker, colder evenings will give you less time for outdoor socialising, in autumn everyone is preparing themselves for winter – a great party is just what they need to bolster their spirits. Prices are cheaper and the wonderful rich colours of autumn can be the perfect backdrop for photos. Plus, if you are lucky and get an Indian summer you get all the benefits of summer without the huge price tag and competition for dates

✓ Winter. If you have guests coming a long way they might have problems with adverse weather conditions, which could also affect whether you can have photos taken outside or not. And December can be expensive because a lot of venues will be booked out with Christmas parties. December weekends tend to book up early for people for the same reason, so this is not a practical option for a last-minute wedding with a lot of guests. Having said that, winter weddings can be a lot cheaper, especially in the quieter months of January and February. Fewer people are on holiday and a room lit by candles and fairy lights and decked with evergreen plants can create a cosier, more magical atmosphere than a summer equivalent

✓ Overseas seasons. Remember to check the seasonal variations for your destination. Not only are the seasons reversed in the different hemispheres but the rainy and hurricane seasons can fall at very different times of year in the various regions. Prices will tend to reflect a combination of the local conditions and the holiday season in the UK, so make sure you understand what's what before you book

Event and holiday considerations. On the whole, there are very few anniversaries or events in the UK that will affect a wedding other than major sporting events, bank holidays, religious holidays, school holidays and possibly the Queen's official birthday if you want to book a public building. Before you book any date, double check that there are no clashes and especially that there are no major events being held in the vicinity of your wedding, otherwise accommodation could prove a logistical nightmare. The **Appendix** gives you a rundown of the timings of notable dates.

CELEBRITY SPOTLIGHT

Rachel Griffiths, of *Six Feet Under* fame, married her fiancé, artist Andrew Taylor, in a candlelit ceremony in Melbourne, Australia. The wedding took place on New Year's Eve so the newly-weds rolled two celebrations into one and followed their midsummer service (New Year is summer in Australia) with a party at the famous Palais Theatre on the beachfront in St Kilda.

Another couple drawn by the romance and party atmosphere of New Year were Sharon Osbourne and her rocker husband Ozzy. When Sharon read her own vows at a ceremony to renew their marriage vows, Ozzy got quite choked up.

Time of day. In England and Wales your ceremony can take place any time between 8 a.m. and 6 p.m. subject to availability and opening hours of the specific venue. But if you had your hopes pinned on a midnight wedding, help is near at hand – in Scotland anything goes. The timing is only subject to you finding a willing officiant.

A late wedding allows people to travel to the venue on the same day so they don't have to take more time off work or spend more on hotels, plus it's cheaper for you because you only have to feed and water your guests once. If you want to have a wedding early on in the day but also need to keep the cost down, you have two choices:

✓ Make it clear on the invitations that your guests are invited to the ceremony from e.g. 10 a.m.–11 a.m. and then the reception from 6 p.m. until late. In this case, be considerate in your choice of location so that your guests have options of things they might like to do in the interim.

✓ Keep the ceremony and daytime celebrations small and invite the majority of the guests to the evening only. You could also arrange for a blessing or the speeches to be later so that guests feel included in the wedding aspect of the occasion.

Day of the week. You can get married any day you like but if you go for anything other than a Friday or Saturday, people will probably leave before the wee hours if they have to be at work and school the next day. Even on a Friday, taking a day off work or school might deter some people from joining you until the evening, if at all. This is why Saturdays are booked up by venues way in advance and often priced at a premium. It's up to you to prioritise whether having everyone there, or getting married quickly and for less money is more important. You can always test the water with those that are most important to you before you confirm your dates. Alternatively, a weekday wedding might work to your advantage if your aim is actually to keep numbers and the presence of children low without offending anyone.

CELEBRITY SPOTLIGHT

Romance was at the forefront of Julia Roberts' mind when she married cameraman Daniel Moder in a stunning secret midnight ceremony at her home in New Mexico. Invitations simply asked guests to a barbeque and to wear white linen. Only on arrival did they discover the real reason for the Independence Day party. Marry by candlelight, fairylight, moonlight or follow Julia's lead and light up the midnight sky with fireworks.

Special dates. For a joint celebration, set the date for a significant day to both of you. For example, the anniversary of when you first met or got engaged, or one of your birthdays.

ALTERNATIVE RECEPTIONS – TO PARTY OR BUNGY?

Regardless of where or when you get married, you are probably assuming that you need to have a reception. Well, you don't. Or alternatively, you can have two or three to cater for the different groups of people that are important to you.

Lots of people still love the idea of a celebration but, as it is only convention that says you have to have one, you really do have free rein on what you feel suits you best. If the idea of a huge reception in a grand venue really isn't your thing, how about:

✓ A tandem bungy or parachute jump to kick off your marriage with an adrenaline buzz

✓ A day at the races on your own or with your guests, sipping champagne and nibbling on ripe strawberries as the fillies and colourful silks fly past you

✓ Hiring a whole cinema for just the two of you to watch your favourite movie

✓ A trip for all your guests to the theatre

✓ Go-karting for everyone – men versus women

✓ A family head-to-head sports day – have a crack at football, golf, baseball, basketball, French cricket, rounders or even the old three-legged and egg-and-spoon favourites

✓ A quiz game with general knowledge and questions about your family, friends and wedding

✓ A romantic hot-air balloon ride for up to sixteen guests

✓ Going straight on your honeymoon from the wedding ceremony

✓ Taking a small group of friends to an exclusive restaurant or jazz club

✓ Going on a circus skills training day

✓ Set up your own casino for the day or splash out and take a select few guests to Monte Carlo for the night

✓ An action-packed afternoon clay-pigeon shooting, 4x4 driving or paintballing

✓ Hiring a crewed yacht and sailing across the Solent for a leisurely lunch on the Isle of Wight and back again with the sunset, sipping champagne on deck

✓ Chartering a riverboat for a larger party, or a canal boat for a more intimate reception, and cruising the rivers and canals of Britain

✓ If you are getting married in the summer, find out if there are any outdoor concerts planned near where you want to get married. Big-band music, giant picnics and fireworks. And you wouldn't be out of place if you decided to wear black tie, haul along tables, linen tablecloths and all your best silver – honestly! These concerts are often set in the grounds of big old houses or castles as well, so you would have the perfect backdrop for your photos

A reception has customarily been the celebratory feast to mark the start of a couple's marriage. It is where they were given gifts to start their new life together and the bride's father hosted a lavish party to display his status to his new in-laws.

In short, there is nothing wrong with having a conventional reception and party but if it's really not what you both want to do you shouldn't feel restricted by tradition. If you are up to explaining your 'madness' to people about a hundred times over, go for the zaniest thing you can think of!

WHAT ABOUT A PRENUPTIAL?

A prenuptial is, in effect, an account of both of your assets before you enter your marriage and the way you agree to divide them should your marriage end, depending on the specific conditions that bring it to an end. So, is this heartless or practical?

We are used to hearing the idea of prenuptials bandied about in the context of Hollywood and celebrity weddings but with the divorce rate at two out of every five marriages, many other people are also considering them.

It seems a shame to taint the sanctity of eternal love and marriage (not to mention romance and passion) with the reality of a legal agreement should you split up. But for some people it is seen as a very real need, either to get family consent to go ahead with the marriage or to protect one or both partners' significant inherited or earned wealth. It can also be relevant if either of you have children from previous relationships – legally, a spouse has more right to assets than children have, unless there is a legal document of intent such as a will or prenuptial agreement to declare otherwise.

However, in England and Wales the law still does not recognise prenuptials in the same way that US law does. Instead of being followed to the letter, prenuptials do not prevent either spouse from challenging any division of assets and taking the matter to court for resolution. It is at the court's discretion as to whether they take the prenuptial into consideration. It can be a very useful document if the marriage ends within a couple of years, before the status of either partner changes dramatically. But the court will also consider whether the prenuptial was fair in the first place, whether any unforeseen circumstances or accrued assets have arisen or been lost, whether or not the couple have had children or if one partner has given up their career for the benefit of both parties.

If you want more advice on prenuptials you should speak to your solicitor. They will be able to advise you on the best course of action for you. Or there is a disturbingly named site called www.divorce-online.co.uk that has ready-made prenuptial packs ready to buy.

But enough of all that. You've got a wedding to get excited about!

WEDDING SUPPLIERS

The Internet really is a fantastic resource for finding unusual suppliers and those based outside your area. It is very easy to use, so if you are not currently *au fait* with it, it is worth getting someone to show you the basics.

Take care when appointing any of your wedding suppliers. This is a lucrative market and while there are many professionals and reputable companies, there are a number of sharks and questionable traders too. Always ensure that a supplier has:

✓ A contract to confirm the booking that is not simply a get-out clause for them but also protects your rights

✓ Recommendations and references that you can check

✓ Given you a final figure for your exact specification – be prepared that if this specification changes at all the costs will too, so make it as accurate as possible and ask about any variations you anticipate

✓ Any relevant insurance and a clear policy should they fail or be unable to meet their obligation to deliver their service or product to you

✓ Provided you with their contact details other than just an email address

If you are getting married where you live, you have the added bonuses of possibly being able to get local recommendations from people you trust and being near to your suppliers for updates and situation management in person.

Are you wondering whether to hire a wedding planner? If money rather than hands-on control is an issue, work out if it is realistic for you to tackle planning a wedding with your job, how much money you make an hour or day and if anyone else is going to help you. If organising a wedding is your basic nightmare then the cost of having someone to do it for you could be justified by you working overtime instead of spending those hours on the wedding.

Please note that all suppliers in this book are just indicated as a starting point for you to make your own enquiries and you should still follow the process above with all of them.

THINKING ABOUT INSURANCE

Another practicality that you should consider is wedding insurance. This can cover you against many possibilities – a family bereavement, one of you being injured in some way, being stranded and not able to travel to the wedding on time, the wedding photos not coming out, losing your rings, damaging your outfits, or being let down by your caterer or venue.

Don't dwell on any of these things – they could happen and there is nothing you can do about that apart from to be prepared. If you are happy that you can have an adequate backup without involving insurance, then fine. But if you are planning on spending a big budget, it is at least worth considering taking out insurance if only for peace of mind.

You might be surprised at how reasonable the costs are too – for the average £15,000 wedding budget cover starts at around £80–£150. Adding a marquee into the equation will add a hefty whack on top of this that usually more than doubles the quote.

All reputable insurance companies and even companies like Marks & Spencer and Debenhams offer wedding packages, so you should definitely shop around to find out the best terms and conditions, excess, period of cover and other details. You will get a wide variety of quotes back – this can be due to the quality of cover or you might just strike gold and get a really good value-for-money insurer. But make sure you read the small print before you sign. If you have any issues or complaints about your insurer you should contact the Financial Ombudsman (0845 080 1800, www.financial-ombudsman.org.uk).

> *One of the best bits of advice I got when I started planning our wedding was to remember that our guests were there because they wanted to share the day with us and not because they wanted to assess the flowers, the cake or the food, etc. If you can keep this thought in mind when planning it stops you from going over the top because the wedding is really about having fun, sharing your day with the people you care about and nothing else (well, except the vows, obviously!).*
>
> MARIE, 29

KEEPING THINGS IN PERSPECTIVE AND HAVING FUN WHILE PLANNING

Hopefully you are not feeling completely swamped with all this knowledge – there is a lot to organise but this can be such an exciting and fun time for you provided you've got the right support and a resilient and positive attitude. It is so important to remember that ultimately your friends and family just want to see you happily married (although they might need reminding of this from time to time too).

Your wedding is going to be at the forefront of your mind for a lot of your engagement, so take care not to become a wedding bore, for your own sake. If all you or anyone around you seem to talk about is the wedding, then ban the subject for days at a time. Or have organisational meetings once a fortnight to delegate tasks and get feedback, and only talk about urgent decisions outside those meetings. Make an event of them – wine, nibbles and wedding chat mixes particularly well.

Also, make sure that just because you are on a budget you don't stop going out. You should still go to prevent yourselves from going crazy – just tone down how much you blow in one evening. If you drive, you'll not only be popular with your mates but you can also make it a condition that they buy you your soft drinks for the evening instead of shelling out on a taxi.

Alternatively, seek out the free and cheapo events publicised in regional press. For those of you that are thinking that these are only horrifically cheesy evenings, think again. Street theatre, comedy nights, meal deals, guided walking tours, happy hours and special offers mean that you can go out and explore new things on a budget. Or invite friends over for dinner and get them to bring a dish each. They'll understand – you're getting married!

If you want to keep everyone involved motivated, you can get them all a gimmicky present like a countdown calendar. They're probably happy anyway but they'll be doubly chuffed if they feel appreciated as part of the team.

And don't forget each other or let the engagement whirlwind stress you out any more than is necessary. See the **Stress Relief** chapter for ideas on how to cope.

BUDGET, BLOWOUT OR BUST?

It would be lovely to think that you could just enjoy the whole wedding planning without having to think about money (and some are lucky enough to do so) but it's important to consider your budget straight away rather than bury your head in the sand about it.

Money might well come top of the list for causing stress, but it doesn't have to be that way if you just make sure you plan ahead and use a little common sense.

The average wedding in 2009 cost in the region of £15,000 but, before you call off the engagement, remember you really don't have to spend that amount to have an amazing and unique day. In fact all you really have to spend are the legal wedding fees that can be as low as £60–£100. You may also think that if you have £15,000 you would rather spend it on a house deposit or the holiday of a lifetime, either of which is perfectly acceptable, so don't worry about following your heart. Your wedding doesn't have to leave you with a debt hangover that lasts well into your marriage as long as you are committed to staying within your budget.

Realistically everyone's circumstances are different. Some couples are fortunate enough to have some assistance from family, but if you are marrying in your late twenties or thirties you may feel a bit awkward about asking your folks for money. And then there are the natural planners and savers who have been putting money aside for a while towards their big day. Or maybe you, like many others, are starting from scratch. Whichever way, everyone needs to have a budget, however large or small, and so we'd recommend you read this chapter and go into your planning with your eyes wide open.

Traditionally the bride's family have been responsible for a large part of the wedding costs, which were supplemented in part by the groom's family. The typical breakdown is:

Bride's family	Groom's family
Press announcements	*Engagement and wedding rings*
Wedding stationery and postage	*Church and licence fees*
Bride's and bridesmaids' outfits and accessories	*Groom, best man's and ushers' outfits*
Make-up and hairdressing	*Bouquets and buttonholes*
Church and reception flowers	*Transport to get best man and groom to the venue*
Reception – venue hire, entertainment and catering	*Transport for the bride and groom after the wedding – the 'going away' car*
Wedding cake	*Bridesmaids' and best man's gifts*
Wedding favours	*'Going away' outfits*
Bridal car to the wedding	*First-night accommodation and honeymoon*
Photography/videoing	

A modern addition to this is the added expense of hen and stag parties.

SETTING YOUR BUDGET AND STICKING TO IT

Before you go any further, are your family likely to offer you financial assistance? If so, try to bring up their contribution at an early stage in the planning process. This will help you to understand your limitations from the outset. But remember that if your parents are helping you out they may expect to have a say in the style and guest list for your wedding, so lay out your ground rules early and openly discuss what you would like to do for your day and who you would like to be there before they commit their cash.

Out of all the brides and grooms we spoke to, no one stuck completely to their original budget because it is so difficult to anticipate all of the charges that can crop up. To be as accurate as possible, you need to set up a record detailing all the expenses you could incur, preferably on a computer so that it's easy to change all the sums involved and their knock-on effects. Make sure that you tailor the budget plan to your particular wedding requirements and don't feel restricted by any templates that you see, especially if you are not having a traditional wedding.

PRACTICAL BUDGET BUILDING

One way of thinking about how to set the budget is to think about how much you are willing to pay for the wedding itself (not forgetting the rings and honeymoon) and add on how much you are willing to pay per head. This will help you to be realistic about the costs involved and give you a budget to stick to for each area of the wedding.

Next, get three comparative estimates for all major or bulk items on your wish list. Then in each instance decide which out of the three suppliers most closely matches what you want on all counts including price, apparent efficiency and responsiveness, location and standards. Sometimes the difference in price is so slight that the supplier you opt for might be the most expensive because they meet all your other criteria. On other occasions, you might opt to accept slightly lower standards because the price difference is so vast.

When searching for quotes, some costs can be highly inflated whenever the 'w' word is mentioned. You might want to try your luck and book suppliers without mentioning that it is a wedding. If you feel like taking a chance, and it works out more cheaply, then book as if you are an 'event' but always have money put aside in case there is something to catch you out in the small print in your contracts. That way, anything you can get away with is a bonus rather than critical to the budget.

> The wedding industry is incredible. We found that as soon as we told caterers and other suppliers we were having a wedding, the prices shot up and economies of scale went out of the window. I would say avoid the traditional wedding suppliers. Everyone wants their wedding to be fantastic and perfect and the costs are easier to justify as 'you will only do it once'. Then they can spiral out of control. Save money where you can and bring yourself back down to earth every once in a while to keep things in perspective.
>
> SHILPA, 27

Once you're happy with your list, flag each item as either:

✓ Must have

✓ Would like to have if budget allows

✓ Not justifiable

Take the overall budget that you have in mind and take off 10 per cent as a contingency buffer. For example, if you've allowed £10,000 for your wedding, take off £1,000, which leaves you with £9,000. In this instance, you need to set your initial budget strictly to £9,000. Go through your list of 'must haves' and subtract them from your total budget. Then prioritise your 'would like to haves' and subtract these and so on until you use your whole £9,000 budget. Do not be tempted to delve into the £1,000 buffer at this stage because it is very likely you will need it at a later date.

Instead, either re-evaluate the money you will need for your ideal wedding, or re-evaluate your list and see if any of the items are a lower priority than you first thought. This will help you to clarify what is really important to you. Do your best not to get bogged down in the whole question of finances, although they are obviously important. If you find yourself getting panicky, stop and check you are not budgeting for things that are expected of you, only what you want.

The wedding company Confetti has a great example of an online budget planner that you can personalise at www.confetti.co.uk. Or simply use it as a guide for creating your own.

CONSIDERATIONS

It is all about balance. If you think you are going to have to save all the money yourselves, be sensible. It is totally up to you how strict you want to be on budget but bear in mind that the more you push yourselves, the less you will be able to go out and enjoy your engagement. It may also mean you will be taking a larger debt into the start of your married life together.

Saving, avoiding debt and compromising. Divide the total sum by the number of months until your wedding, plus a maximum of three to six months of your married life. That's how much money you will need to save every month to avoid being in debt for a long time after you get married. If it doesn't seem realistic, don't put yourselves under too much pressure – financial stress is a big reason for relationship breakdowns and you don't want to expose yourselves to that! Instead, either downsize and cut your costs or consider pushing back the date of the wedding to when you can afford it.

> From the start I think it helps to sit down with your man and work out what your priorities are because the money is not endless. For Andy it was really important that we could invite as many friends and family as possible and that we would pay for the bar. For me it was important that as many people as possible could come, that the venue looked great (in terms of decoration), that the atmosphere was good and that we'd give people a really entertaining evening, because I hate it when weddings fall flat at about 8 p.m. That immediately helped us to prioritise what we would spend money on and gave me a budget to identify a theme of sorts.
>
> MARIE, 29

Open a wedding bank account. This is the best way of really keeping a track on what you are spending.

A wedding for your wedding list. If having a huge blowout day is all-important to you, you could make your wedding-present list up as elements of your wedding. In some parts of Asia, guests even buy their 'ticket' to the wedding to help ease the financial burden.

Advice. For those who have a lot of debt already, look into speaking to a financial adviser. By moving all your debt into one consolidated pot, you may be able to get more competitive rates of interest. A good starting point for free advice is the Citizen's Advice Bureau at www.adviceguide.org.uk, or visit your local bureau.

Keeping it real. If you feel you need to get your plans back in perspective, pretend it's a landmark birthday party rather than a wedding. This may be a once-in-a-lifetime day, but it is only *one day* and you should think about the consequences before you push yourselves too far.

Everyday savings. In the lead-up to your wedding you may need to be a bit frugal with your cash, so think about your opportunities to cut corners to put a few extra pounds in the pot.

Don't buy every wedding magazine available. The advice features are pretty much the same from month to month. But the photos of real-life weddings, bridal attire advertisements and ideas for receptions are usually excellent and can be great for sparking your inspiration. Flick through an issue in the shop and see if there is anything that grabs your attention and means you must buy that particular edition. Otherwise, wait until the following month and save your money.

☆ CELEBRITY SPOTLIGHT

There is no shame in keeping your wedding low budget and low key if that's what you want. Charles Saatchi and Nigella Lawson opted for a very low-key wedding reception at their London home. There were no flowers, only a handful of guests including the couple's three children from previous marriages, Nigella wore a black floor-length dress, Charles followed a smart-casual dress code and the food was reportedly prepared by Nigella herself.

OBVIOUS BUDGET SAVERS

Pay in cash. If you are a bit of a bargain hunter and don't mind bartering, then try to get a discount for your venue, flowers or transport by offering to pay in cash rather than by credit card. The vendor may be grateful of the immediate income and will also save money on transaction charges. Make sure you get confirmation of bookings in writing.

Reception. On average this accounts for 36 per cent of the overall cost of a wedding, so is a major area where you can cut corners. Number of guests, type of food, venue and decorations can all have a huge bearing on budget, as can the traditional trimmings. Keep costs under control by only having what you both really want.

When you get married. As discussed in **First Things First** marry out of season or later in the day.

Where you get married. Prices vary in different parts of the UK with the south-east of England topping the bill, so you could think about decamping for your wedding day. Weddings abroad can also cut a lot of costs – see the **Getting Married Abroad** chapter.

Helping hands. Rope in friends and family to do jobs instead of a supplier.

Useful contacts. Ask around for anyone with contacts for caterers, photographers or entertainment, as they may be able to help you with a discount.

Have a double wedding. A slightly unconventional spin if you don't mind sharing the spotlight and it can cut your costs almost in half.

Get creative. You can save money by making your own outfits, cake, invitations, menu cards, decorations or favours. You don't have to be a home-craft goddess and don't worry that your efforts will end up looking like something from *Blue Peter* as many effective designs and ideas are very basic. Enlist (un)willing volunteers to help you.

For more budget savers for flowers, cake, photography, getting married overseas, decorations and finishing touches, see the individual chapters for ideas.

HANDLING FRIENDS AND FAMILIES

Along with budgeting this can be one of the trickiest aspects of wedding planning.

Your family might be 100 per cent into a traditional big white wedding that wouldn't be complete without the entire extended family and all their friends, not to mention sugared almonds and other claptrap. But what if you want to personalise the occasion with unique touches or even strike out for something very different? How do you keep everyone happy while making sure that you and your partner get the wedding you want?

 Weddings are traditionally a family affair, often with mothers and future mothers-in-law ruling the roost. The stereotypical nightmare finds the bride and groom melting into the background as family feuds are ignited and suddenly your wedding is full of unwanted guests that you've been forced to invite just to keep the peace.

AWKWARD FAMILY SITUATIONS

Family life can be very complicated these days, what with divorced parents, stepfamilies, feuding siblings and future in-laws to consider. But have no fear; with a bit of courage, tact, good communication and some give and take you will be able to find your way through the maze of issues that arise. See **First Things First** for pointers for getting clear about what you both want and who you want to invite before you go public. This is where that clarity comes to the fore.

> We were bombarded as soon as we flew home from Florence where we got engaged. My family knew it was on the cards because Simon had asked for their blessing. In retrospect I wish we had put our foot down at the outset and pushed back on them to give us the space to think about what we wanted. But they were completely excited and wrapped up in it from the beginning and we found ourselves bogged down with so much detail, it was much more stressful than we imagined. I wish we had insisted on more time for the two of us to enjoy our post-engagement glow, completely devoid of any wedding planning at all. And because we got swept away with other people's plans and ideas so early on without understanding what was really happening, it became much harder to manage things to get them the way we wanted later on. I would say, set ground rules immediately – tell everyone to calm down and understand that you won't do anything until you are ready because it is ultimately about what you both want.
>
> SHILPA AND SIMON, 27 AND 30

Over-eager mother or mother-in-law. Some mothers do have a tendency to take over and you can suddenly find that it is more their wedding than your own. If you can see this behaviour emerging and it is unwanted, one or both of you should sit her down and gently explain your side of things. Tell her how fantastic it is to have her support but that you need to do things your way. She may not have even realised that she has been overbearing, so don't get aggressive or defensive unnecessarily. It may also help to give both mums (and dads) some select jobs to do so that they don't feel left out.

Although your mum and mother-in-law might be driving you batty by the time of your wedding, they will both probably be as excited as you. Each of them is likely to be most interested in fussing over their own offspring for your last few hours of freedom. As the bride, a really great gesture is to get your mum (and maybe your mum-in-law to be) involved in the getting-ready ritual with you and your bridesmaids. As the groom, just give your mum peace of mind that you will be well turned out and sober and she will be equally delighted.

Feuding relatives. If you suddenly find yourself in a situation where one relative is refusing to attend your wedding if another one is coming then try your best to rise above the situation. Invite them both and explain that you'd love them both to come but then leave it to them to decide what to do. It is their choice and it is more important for you to concentrate on enjoying your day. Alternatively, if it's you that's engaged in the feud or if it is just easier for you and your partner, you could simply not invite them. And perhaps if you explain why, this will help them to put their differences aside.

Parents who want to invite their entire circle of friends. As discussed, this can be tricky, especially if parents are contributing and also because they are proud of you. It is totally understandable not to want the world and his wife at your special day, but try to reach a compromise. You could agree to a few of them coming along but seat them at the back or just invite them to the evening do. Or if you are having a gathering the day after your wedding such as a garden party or big brunch, how about inviting them along to that so that your parents can show you off without taking over your day? You could even wear your wedding outfits again if necessary.

> We were so lucky that my parents took on the traditional 'parents of the bride' role in paying for the wedding and also Jonnie's parents offered a contribution. It became awkward because my in-laws then wanted to invite loads of their friends, therefore making the numbers go up and making it more expensive. It was very hard to keep it as our day and have our say on who came and who didn't when we weren't paying for it all, but we all talked things through and in the end everyone was happy.
>
> VICKI, 31

Stepchildren. Be sensitive to stepfamilies – insecurities can result in some seemingly unreasonable behaviour. Children can worry that they are losing their parent to a new family where they will love other children instead of them. Reassurance and an unshakeable positive mental attitude will help you to break through in the end. Support each other but also be aware that, if circumstances change, you might not always be each other's husband and wife, but you will always be your child's father or mother. Involving them as much as possible in the planning and the ceremony can avoid family conflicts and give you peace of mind to take a honeymoon with just the two of you if that is what you want. If you feel apprehensive about how to address this situation, take the time to visit a relationship counsellor, such as Relate (www.relate.org.uk), for some objective advice and perspective rather than just taking the advice of people who have a personal opinion about the situation.

Who doesn't sit next to who. See **Reception Logistics** for more about table plans, but if you are having trouble with feuding relatives who want to come along but will cause problems if they are put too close together, make sure you seat them well away from each other. Go to the lengths of organising a strategic seating plan for your ceremony if that's what it takes! Alternatively if the table plan is proving to be a headache because you have too many people who need to sit next to others then scrap it altogether and let them all sort themselves out.

> *When my cousin got married last year, he was faced with juggling the various family feuds. He and his wife found it so tricky to anticipate what could possibly happen, they took the law into their own hands and choreographed the whole day for the guests, from labelling their seats in church, to arranging car groups between the church and venue, to seating plans at the venue. It all went off without a hitch much to everyone's amazement!*
>
> HENRI, 32

GETTING AWAY FROM TRADITION

Your wedding is your day, your occasion, but one of the most difficult things to do is sticking to your guns about your plans when you feel like

> If there's one thing I've learned it's that the people you know best can still surprise you when it comes to your wedding. Family members who appear to be liberal and understanding on the surface turn into the worst kind of traditionalists imaginable. The upsets begin because 'you're not doing it properly'. The mistake we made was to then try and appease everyone and go from our ideal of a lovely quiet overseas wedding to having a reception for my husband's family in Adelaide and then a church blessing for my family in the UK. Tradition was banging on my door all along the way: 'Are you having a cake? You must have a cake' – 'What, no bridesmaids?' And even for Darren: 'Why aren't you having a stag night?' (Instead he had several parties with different mates, managed to keep his clothes on throughout them all and nearly needed his liver removed anyway.) This is not to mention the invitations ... the battle over a couple of words. We had no idea things would escalate to that degree!
>
> Don't get me wrong, our families were absolutely delighted that we had eventually decided to get hitched. But the demand on any parent is hard. The emotions that we all went through turned the most reasonable of people into irrational nutcases. It is really hard to keep your focus while everyone around you is turning into psychopaths and threatening bodily harm if you don't agree to have orders of service and flowers in the aisle.
>
> In retrospect, we would definitely handle our families differently from the outset. We would be completely clear about how we wanted to get married and not give in because we thought it might make things less hassle in the end. Stick to your guns if you know what you want!
>
> VANESSA AND DARREN, 29 AND 31

everyone's criticising them. If you are not going the traditional whole nine yards, there will always be someone who will question your choices. Naturally you need to be sensitive to your families' and friends' feelings but you should also explain to them why you would like to do things in your own style. You only have one chance to do this your way!

Another tip is to thank your nearest and dearest regularly for their understanding in giving you some space and respecting your decisions – especially before they have time to give any negative feedback. The theory is that this can reassure them that they are important to you and help to convince them to keeping their opinions at least a little more under control.

CONSIDERING YOUR FRIENDS

Smug married. Now that you are officially leaving your life as a singleton you are at serious risk of being labelled a smug married through no fault of your own. Suddenly you will be invited to everything as a couple, you won't be included on nights out on the pull and everyone will assume you are spending all weekend with your fiancé. If you aren't happy with this, put a stop to it straight away. Your friends won't be able to help themselves assuming you have entered the realms of coupledom, never to return. Let them know that you are still your own person and can hold a decent conversation without needing your man (or your woman) by your side to finish your sentences.

Don't become a wedding bore. Your wedding is going to be one of the most exciting and demanding things ever to happen in your life and you should feel free to get as wrapped up as you like in the moment. However, do remember that your friends' lives go on too, so make sure you are keeping up to date with them and listening to their news and highs and lows. Of course they will be excited for you but that doesn't mean they don't want to talk about anything else in the year of preparations.

Be sensitive. It is very common for friends to feel jealous of their newly engaged mate even if they don't realise it themselves. If your friends start acting strangely or becoming more distant as soon as you show off your engagement ring, consider that they may be feeling left out or that your happy news may be highlighting their own situation to them. If you think this might be the case and feel it is appropriate, tentatively raise the issue with them. Bringing things out into the open often dissolves problems before they start. If the situation is too far down the line and you feel you have been as sensitive and open as you can be, then this is unfortunately your friend's issue – it is up to them to sort it out. But don't burn any bridges; people will often come round in their own time.

ROLES AND RESPONSIBILITIES

Is a chief bridesmaid really expected to hold up the bride's dress while she's on the loo?

And what if the best man is 100 per cent guaranteed to lose the rings if he has to hold them? More importantly than that, what if your best man is a woman, your chief bridesmaid is a man and the mother of the bride is giving her away? Just how far can you push the boundaries of wedding etiquette?

The conventional roles of each member of the wedding party tend to be as ingrained as all other wedding traditions but what happens if you want to break away from the mould? Remember that these customs are only there as a guide. If they do not make sense to you then completely ignore them and redistribute any relevant roles – either to whoever you know will handle it best, or who it will mean the most to. Nothing is set in stone. If you don't want to have bridesmaids and a best man, or you want your sister to give you away then go ahead. Making up your own rules will free you to do things the way that means the most to you both.

When it comes to distributing responsibilities it will very much depend on your own personality and the type of wedding you are planning. If you are having a small gathering or you are a control freak it is your prerogative to do everything yourself if you want to. If, on the other hand, you are planning a massive 'do', conventional or otherwise, then you may want to hire a wedding planner or become a full-on events manager yourself, delegating tasks left, right and centre. Ideally you will have total say-so over who does what, but if you are relying on other people volunteering to help out, then you need to take their preferences into consideration too.

In planning a big wedding, one of the best ways to keep your sanity intact is to delegate. This is quite a skill in itself but it is worth the effort if you can master it. Make a list of everything that needs to be done, big and small, and think about the jobs that you and your partner will be able to cover or want to control directly. You are bound to find some tasks that you simply don't have time to do or that you feel someone else might be better at or like to help you out with. Think about who you trust to do jobs so that you don't end up with twice as much to do if they don't come through.

Most importantly, once you have delegated, trust that decision so that you don't spend as much time chasing people and worrying as you would have spent organising it yourself anyway.

REMEMBERING YOUR PARTNER

In the flurry of excitement the bride-to-be often becomes centre of attention and the groom-to-be gets relegated to the wings. Many men are happy to sit back, keep their effort and involvement to a minimum and let things take their course – this can either be a source of frustration or relief for brides. Other men will want to have more of a say in the details. There are no hard-and-fast rules. Relationships are all about give and take, so make sure you both work on balancing your ideas for your perfect day and support each other to create it.

Salient points to help you in your planning include:

Investing in your relationship. While you are planning your wedding you might find that you seem to have less and less quality time with each other and that when you do, you don't have any money to do anything. Rather than get to the day with unfounded doubts, make it your jobs to spoil each other and yourselves every once in a while. Massage each other, take a pampering day, a joint trip to the gym, long summery strolls or wintry walks to blow the cobwebs away, candlelit baths filled with bubbles, or nights curled up under a blanket in front of a movie with a carpet picnic. Most importantly, do not let your wedding planning get in the way of your relationship for all the obvious reasons.

Family damage limitation. You will always be your parents' children but once you are married, your ultimate commitment is to each other. While you might be trying to keep everyone happy, things could go awry unless you bite the bullet and take a stand on issues that are important to either or both of you. Also, keep any disagreements between you both over the wedding to yourselves and present a united front to parents – this will help to avoid any unnecessary clashes, resentment or doubts amongst the in-laws.

Time management and organisation. Now is the time to hone your project management skills. There are two of you, so you have the opportunity to play to your strengths and work on your complementary qualities. Be structured and clear in your planning, keep records and update each other on progress regularly. It really is a lot less panicky and stressful if you don't leave everything until the last minute.

YOUR ROLES AS THE BRIDE AND GROOM

Bizarrely there are no traditional responsibilities for a bride in the wedding. And yet the groom has a list of jobs as long as your arm.

The reality is that unless you agree that one of you will head up your wedding planning, or one of you surprises the other, you will both end up fulfilling this main role together and maybe a few others besides. Organising a wedding can be too much for any one person to take on.

Work out the budget. This is the key to keeping your perspective in your wedding planning.

Set a wedding date and draft the guest list. All sorts of external factors may influence setting your date but ultimately it must be one that you are both happy with. Initially try to keep the drawing up of the guest list between the two of you to ensure that you end up with the wedding you want (see also **First Things First**).

Choose your bridesmaids. If you're struggling to work out who to have as your bridesmaids or your chief bridesmaid, remember that you do not have to have either. Or alternatively you can have as many as you like. Be sensitive to those you don't ask who might be disappointed. You can invite them to be ushers, witnesses, dress and make-up advisers or hen-night organisers instead.

Choose your best man and ushers. Unless you have a clear contender, this is every man's nightmare. Will your mates be offended if you relegate them to being ushers while your brother is your best man? Or worse still, what if you have to choose between your mates? Other than the usual oldest friend/closest friend/pecking order considerations, also think about who will be best at the speeches, who will give you the stag night you want (or don't want) and who is likely to be the most helpful in the planning stages? The answer is simple – have as many best men as you want.

And anyway who says your best man has to be a man? If the groom's best friend is a girl then there are no rules that say she can't fill this role.

> At the end of my husband's groom speech, he surprised everyone when he said: 'And now for the best man, who is actually my best person and best friend ... my wife Tania.'
>
> TANIA, 31

Choose your witnesses. You might not be having bridesmaids or a best man, or you may just want the opportunity to involve someone else.

Select your poems and readings. Think about who you will ask to deliver these and also if you want to involve your guests in putting together the music for your ceremony. See **Choosing Your Ceremony Frills** for further ideas.

Buy the rings. You may already have an engagement ring and, regardless of who pays for the wedding rings, it can be a momentous occasion to shop for them together. If you are not having rings then you might choose to surprise each other with alternative presents – see **First Things First**.

Choose outfits for yourselves, groomsmen and bridesmaids. Traditionally the groom shouldn't see the bride's outfit before the big day, but if you want to shop for your outfits together then go ahead.

Book the honeymoon and first-night accommodation. Although this can be a joint decision, if one of you feels confident that you know what the other will like this is your opportunity to pull out all the stops and surprise them.

Organise your wedding day transport. This is another opportunity for one of you to surprise the other, this time with a classy exit or maybe an outlandish getaway. If you make this decision together this is a good one to delegate.

Write your speech. For the groom this is customarily your moment to say your thank yous and to tell your assembled guests how much your bride means to you, but there's no reason why a bride shouldn't have her say too.

Help choose gifts for your best man, ushers and bridesmaids. It is a lovely gesture to buy mementoes of the day that show your gratitude for the part that your attendants have played. It's also a nice touch to give parents gifts too, especially if they've helped out financially or otherwise. For ideas see the **Gifts** chapter.

Make sure all bills are settled on the day. Decide in advance how all bills will be handled and agree this with your suppliers. Be prepared with spare cash just in case. Or you could delegate this responsibility to your best man, chief bridesmaid or parents so that you don't need to think about finances on your day.

REVIEWING TRADITIONAL ROLES

The rest of the bridal party also have traditional roles and responsibilities. We have detailed these in the table over the page to give you the chance to see if they are relevant to you at all or to delegate them to somebody completely different. Some of the tasks, e.g. organising the reception, could be broken down – venue, seating plan, entertainment – and delegated to several people. To make your life easier, delegate, delegate, delegate.

> *If you trust your best man and chief bridesmaid (or maid of honour), I would really recommend delegating to them as much as possible. Give them roles or responsibilities and get them involved in planning the wedding. This also means that they are the ones that have to worry about the details at the wedding itself. I've got my best man to manage the day and where people are going to be from start to finish – he's taking care of the photographer's logistics, table decorations and plans, music and anything else we think of!*
>
> JIM, 28

Before you hand out tasks willy-nilly give some consideration as to whether you are being realistic. Will your four-year-old bridesmaid be as excited as you anticipate when you crush her as you hand her your weighty bouquet?

You might notice that there are no traditional roles for the groom's parents. If it is appropriate, don't forget them in your planning.

Task	Traditionally delegated to:	You will delegate to:
Before the wedding		
Help to choose wedding and bridesmaid dresses	Chief bridesmaid	
Help to choose the groom's and groomsmen's outfits	Best man	
Help to choose the stationery	Chief bridesmaid	
Confirm guest list	Mother of the bride	
Keep a record of acceptances and refusals	Mother of the bride	
Oversee wedding gift list	Mother of the bride	
Organise hen night	Chief bridesmaid	
Organise stag night	Best man	
Help to organise reception	Mother of the bride	
On the day		
Help bride get ready	Chief bridesmaid	
Help groom get ready	Best man	
Brief ushers	Best man	
Distribute buttonholes	Ushers	
Control parking	Ushers	
Hand out orders of service and hymn books	Ushers	
Arrange bride's veil and train	Chief bridesmaid	
Organise young attendants at venue	Chief bridesmaid	
Give the bride away	Father of the bride	
Hold bride's bouquet during service	Chief bridesmaid	
Baby-sit wedding ring	Best man	
Organise photo calls	Ushers	
Ensure all guests have transport to reception venue	Ushers	
Direct guests to reception venue	Ushers	
Make a speech	Father of the bride; groom; best man	
Toastmaster	Master of ceremonies; best man	
Read out messages	Best man	
Announce cutting of cake	Master of ceremonies; best man	

OTHER JOBS TO DELEGATE

With so much to do you may be happy to hand as much of it as you can over to friends and family. And if you want to make it a real group affair, involve as many people as possible.

> *One of the best things about my wedding was the fact that my close family and friends all added something to it and got involved in the planning – I can look at pictures from the day and identify all of their contributions. Basically, different family members offered to help arrange certain things. So one sister went to France on a booze cruise for our champagne, another came with us to plan the groomsmen/pageboy outfits, another came on the bridesmaid dress trip with me, another did the flowers, another the cake and then they all helped to decorate the hall. The wonders of having a big family! My friends gave me greenery from their gardens, which we used in all the flower displays and on the beams of the barn. It worked really well because it meant that all my family had a role in helping with the planning (and also helped in financing the day for which I am eternally grateful!) but I still had overall control of what was happening.*
>
> MARIE, 29

Here are some less obvious ideas for jobs that you can share out:

Helping to spread the word. Rope parents in to telling the world but make sure they know not to invite everyone they talk to!

Researching venues and entertainment options. Brainstorm with your creative mates to come up with ideas for a unique celebration.

Researching wedding insurance quotes. If you have a mate who is frugal and good at comparing deals then ask them to have a look at this area for you. It may not be the most exciting task but it is an important one.

Helping to make stationery. Hand-making cards and invitations can be a lot more time-consuming than you think, so enlist a production line of helpers and crack open a bottle of wine to have fun while you work.

Drawing up a seating plan. Someone close to you can help with this task and may be able to make suggestions about how to overcome any logistical issues that arise.

Home-made favours. Whether this is making cookies or sweets or just the containers for them, you will find a few hands on deck will be invaluable. This is another task that can take a lot longer than you think. Weigh up cost versus effort when you are deciding on which favours to have, if any at all.

Home-made cake. For that personal touch.

Decorating the venue. Doing this the night before or on the day itself is not a task you will want to undertake on your own.

Pampering the groom on the day. Everyone accepts that the bride has a swarm of people fussing around her on the morning of the wedding, but what about the groom? Instead of sinking a few beers down the pub before the ceremony, give someone the task of booking him in for a massage, male manicure or luxury shave so that he can enjoy the morning with a glass of champagne in hand, relax and look great too.

Picking up flowers on the day. If your florist does not provide this service nominate someone to make sure all the bouquets and buttonholes are in the right places at the right time. There is no point you having Auntie Betty's corsage in your hand when she is five miles across town.

Kids' entertainment. If you've got children who are likely to be very demanding if they are not being entertained, then give someone the task of arranging things for them to do.

Venue checks. Delegate someone to ensure that everything is squared with the venue. You may feel more comfortable doing this yourself, but if you are happy to hand it over then go ahead. They can make sure times are fixed, welcome drinks are ordered, the DJ and/or band are happy with arrangements and food orders are confirmed.

Photo collages for the reception. Give someone the task of putting together the photo collages and Polaroid memories as detailed in **Decorations and Finishing Touches**.

Keepsake book. Ask a sociable friend to mill around your reception asking guests to write messages in a visitor book for you to have as a memento of the occasion. Alternatively, if you are giving your guests loose pages to write in advance, ask someone to compile the guest book for you.

Bar. If you are running your own bar, delegate a 'bar manager' to organise a rota, float, bar 'staff' shifts, supplies, glasses, bottle openers and overall budget.

Catering. For self-catered weddings, it is imperative that someone is appointed to run the show. They need to co-ordinate the food, additional supplies such as cutlery, linen, tables and chairs, glasses, crockery, ice, storage space (chilled or dry), waiting staff, clearing up and budget control.

Keeping your belongings safe. If you are not planning on going home before you go on your honeymoon, then someone will need to ensure your cases are secure and waiting for you and they should also be able to store your wedding outfits until you are able to pick them up. Nominate someone to keep an eye on your house while you are away, to water plants and turn lights on and off.

Wedding presents. If you receive presents on your wedding day but have no time to open them and take them home before you jet-set off, ask someone to keep an eye on them until you return.

Tourist-tastic. Delegate a well-organised person to research and prepare packs for the venue detailing local tourist information and events so that your guests have the option to make a short break of their trip.

Games. For one of the more outgoing members of your wedding team. They will be put in charge of organising games on the day and the day after the wedding.

Next-day party. You will have your hands full with the day. So if you are planning to prolong your celebrations either rope in a like-minded friend or enlist the help of someone who may otherwise feel hard done by to run the show.

More photos. Ask someone to round up as many photos as they can from the wedding, including collecting the disposable cameras or asking people for a duplicate set of their pictures. That way you will be able to build a complete picture of what happened during your day.

SURPRISE WEDDINGS

Imagine not having to spend months discussing and rehashing every detail of your wedding with your family and friends, stressing over opinions and clashing over guest lists, fending off phone calls while you are at work, explaining your various decisions to people and trying not to care but wanting approval all the same.

What a relief!

Right now, you are probably wondering whether you could carry this off because the idea of a low-fuss wedding and the element of surprise has caught your interest.

On the other hand, if you have a completely surprise wedding you won't be able to voice your concerns or get advice without giving the game away. The anticipation and tickles of excitement will be private, not shared. You won't get treated to hen and stag weekends and if you are banking on a gift list to help you set up home you need to think again unless you are happy sending it out after the wedding.

If a surprise wedding still appeals, you are probably:

✓ A couple who like to surprise everyone at every given opportunity

✓ A couple who don't want to get sucked into the wedding circus and want to keep control over the where, when, who and hows without having to battle with everyone else's opinions

✓ A old romantic who, very confidently, wants to surprise their partner

✓ A second or third-time rounder and you and your parents have already experienced the wedding frenzy before – this time you have different priorities

✓ In a relationship where one or both of you have fallen out of favour with your future in-laws and so a surprise wedding gives them less chance to 'sabotage' it

All are popular reasons for surprise weddings, but if you fall into the last category give some thought to what your perfect wedding would be if your families were more compliant. Has your heart always been set on that dream? If so, think twice before you give it up. Also, consider whether this will make the family rift deeper – do you really want to begin your married life with even more bitterness? And what effect will it have on family birthdays and at Christmas or once you have children to think about? If you are in doubt, get in touch with relationship counsellors, such as Relate (www.relate.org.uk), and explore your options. It might even be worth swallowing your pride and apologising in order to diffuse the situation and rebuild some bridges to make your future lives together that much easier.

ABSOLUTELY STUNNED OR JUST MILDLY SURPRISED?

To what extent do you want your wedding to be a surprise? Because so many people are involved in the traditional wedding planning scenario, you obviously have a lot of choices about how many people you tell.

The most extreme surprise weddings involve either the bride or groom not being told. Now that's risky! Here are some thoughts on a few variations to help you work out what is right for you.

Everyone except the bride or groom knows. A huge surprise. And amazingly, we've been told about quite a few of these. Responses have varied dramatically. One groom-to-be told his unsuspecting girlfriend (not even fiancée) that he was treating her to a pampering, hair and make-up day in advance of a posh night out (presumably so that she did not go to town and get a facial peel or other sunburn-like treatment). When she came home her best friend was there to break the news to her that she was going to be married that evening. Her boyfriend had taken care of everything – he had bought her dress, shoes, underwear, flowers, arranged the cake, photographer, guests and venues. When they got to the church and she walked down the aisle, he dropped down onto one knee and proposed. She was ecstatic (evident by her muffled sobs).

On the other hand, women do have a tendency to make mental notes about their ideal wedding once they are getting close to being ready to get married. By springing it on them as a surprise they might feel cheated that they did not get to plan their dream wedding. And men or women might feel miffed that you were so presumptuous as to assume they would say yes without question.

What about their outfit? Do you know his or her taste in wedding attire? Do you know their tailored size? This is hard because it's so personal. Suits for men might look very similar on the peg but will have completely different fits according to a man's frame. And wedding dresses are renowned for looking terrible on the hanger and fantastic on, or vice versa. If you have to think hard about this question, also think about how withdrawn you could become while you have to handle all the other decisions around the wedding – your relationship could actually suffer because of your good intentions.

Plus, what will you do if they say no? If that is a doubt in your mind, you need to ask yourself if you are springing a surprise wedding to pressurise your partner into something that they might not agree to otherwise.

And finally, don't forget that if a bride is denied the opportunity to organise her own wedding, you may be playing a big part in creating a wedding monster for a future daughter or daughter-in-law of tomorrow. Can you live with that?

No one except the bride and groom know. This is a good compromise because you can be sure that both of you want to get married and can create the wedding you want without having to run it by everyone else on the

CELEBRITY SPOTLIGHT

Star Trek's Vulcan Subcommander T'pol, AKA Jolene Blalock, was an alternative bride. Not one to wait like a wallflower to be proposed to, she took the situation into her own hands and arranged a surprise wedding to her then boyfriend. She planned their romantic ceremony to coincide with their holiday to Jamaica and only proposed to him 24 hours before they were due to walk down the aisle. Everyone was in on the surprise except him. Thankfully he said yes.

'wedding panel' first. It can also be really exciting to have a secret proposal and such a big surprise that only the two of you know about.

This option means that hen weekends, stag weekends and gift lists are not on the agenda and it is also reliant on you covering all the costs yourselves and not just hedging your bets on whether your family will contribute afterwards. Budgets may be reduced overall because you are pleasing fewer people, but the things you do opt for can work out more expensive because you will have to use suppliers for things that family and friends could otherwise have helped out with.

You need to come up with a convincing and compelling ruse to ensure that your guests will come – an engagement, landmark birthday, moving-in or ticket-only party are good ideas – but still bear in mind that if someone is invited to another wedding on the same day, you will have been trumped because your guests don't know the truth and so you risk them not turning up.

Another major consideration has to be your parents. Will they be thrilled that you have eventually got around to getting hitched or will they be hurt that they couldn't be involved at all or get excited about the day? What effect will it have on your relationships longer term – will they get over it? To sidestep this issue you could just let your parents in on your secret a couple of days before so that they feel special to have been taken into your confidence.

Only the bride, groom and speech-makers know. With similar cons as only the bride and groom knowing, the pros are greater. Although the surprise will still be the same for most people, you will be able to have your best friends and possibly parents know in advance so that they can entertain everyone with prepared speeches and anecdotes about you on the day. And if you choose to tell these people a couple of months rather than weeks in advance you will also have them to support you to sort out the details and confide in. You might even get small hen and stag nights.

Only a small group of 'must be there for us to get married' people know. This means that you can ensure that everyone you feel must be there will know why it is so important for them to make the effort. Those nearest and dearest to you will feel honoured to be included in the inner sanctum, you will have plenty of support and even be able to have a limited gift list if you so choose.

Again, you don't have to let your select few know from the outset. Give yourselves time to choose the date (you do need to tell everyone to book this well in advance for whatever compelling reason you think appropriate), book the venues and arrange the guest list and logistics. Then tell your 'must be theres' the real reason for the get-together between one week and two months before the day. This gives them the chance to be prepared and get excited but, because it is a surprise, they can't go inviting whoever they choose. You can also argue that if your dad's second cousin wouldn't be

> *Before I proposed, I talked to Alex's parents and a small number of friends who were all worried that she would want to organise her own wedding and may not react as I hoped. But I felt that after six years together I knew exactly what she would want and doing it like this would be a more romantic gesture. This was also a way of letting us have our dream wedding without the pressure of what everyone else wanted.*
>
> NICK, 29

> *Nick took me for a walk in the park where we came across the picnic. Halfway through he handed me what I thought was a card but when I opened it up was an invite to my own wedding in three months' time. He then produced the ring and proposed. And he had even arranged for a friend to lay out the picnic and then hide in the bushes until we arrived. Nick had planned and organised the whole wedding – all I had to do was buy a dress and choose some flowers (and lose a stone, of course).*
>
> *The best thing about it? Everything – but I loved that it was a surprise. It was exactly the wedding I would have arranged but with far less stress. It was the perfect day.*
>
> ALEX, 30

on your guest list for your 'engagement' or 'birthday' party then they really shouldn't be on the list for the wedding.

MORE ALTERNATIVE OPTIONS

A surprise wedding is undeniably an alternative option, but if you want a bit more food for thought, read on:

Go European style. If you want your guests to come to a blessing instead of the civil or religious ceremony, get the legalities out of the way at the register office a couple of days beforehand rather than dragging everyone there with you if it doesn't really mean anything to you. You only need to go with two witnesses and the register office can usually supply you with them if they are given notice. Then you can have any type of blessing you want at the surprise event. The bonus of this is that a blessing does not have the legal restrictions of a wedding – in theory you can get blessed anywhere that the celebrant is willing to travel to. Alternatively you can choose to be blessed by a friend. Details are in the **Getting Married in the UK** section.

Fancy-dress theme. Even if you are pretending that you are having an engagement party, the two of you can dress as bride and groom and mingle with your guests as they joke about you getting married. Then once everyone is there you can start the proceedings. If this appeals then you need to check with the venue and officiant that this will fit in with any rules they have about dress codes.

New Year's Eve party. This is a tricky one if it is going to be a surprise because your guests are highly likely to receive more than one New Year's Eve party invitation. It can also be problematic if you are asking people to come without their partner or their children. But if you can carry it off, you have the perfect premise to host a black-tie party or masked ball so that everyone is in their finery ready for you to give them a New Year's Eve to remember.

On a group holiday. Volunteer to organise a group holiday for all your friends or family. If you are in charge of logistics, you have the perfect chance to add a couple of extra events to the schedule without anyone suspecting a thing. The only problem with this option is that unless your friends and family mix on a regular basis, you might have to choose between whether you do this with one group or the other. Either way, you can have secondary celebrations on your return.

CELEBRITY SPOTLIGHT

Celebrities will go to all sorts of lengths to keep their weddings secret and private. Kate Winslet and Sam Mendes got married in the West Indies (aged 27 and 37) with just three witnesses and Kate's daughter, Mia. Even their parents weren't told. Once they returned from their paradise wedding, the couple had intimate celebrations with the friends and family that had not been able to share their special day with them. It was Kate's second marriage.

A riverboat party. Choose the surprise combination that suits you best but have the reassurance that if people know, or think, that they are going on a riverboat party they also know to be at the jetty at a certain time or miss the celebrations altogether.

Ticketed picnic ruse. A fantastic budget option is to invite your family and friends to some kind of outdoor event that you need advance tickets for, such as an open-air concert. Let everyone know that you've arranged a coach but instead of taking them to the concert (unless this is also part of your plan) whisk them off to where you are going to get married and then have your reception picnic at a favourite spot. The bonus is that everyone will have brought their own seating, blankets and food so you can spend your budget on the extras instead. Get the date in people's diaries three to six months in advance to be sure they can make it.

PLANNING TIPS

Once you have decided to go ahead:

- ✓ Make sure everyone knows they are getting to the venue for a specific time. Telling people that there is going to be a meal, speech, transportation or a presentation at a set time helps to ensure that they will be there with at least a few minutes to spare

- ✓ If you don't want everyone to attend your actual wedding, invite your close family and friends to a surprise ceremony followed by an intimate meal and speeches. Then have everyone else turn up for a party in the evening, which they then discover is actually your reception

- ✓ Think in advance about dress code. If you would like to have a theme or make sure that everyone is dressed smartly then you need to pick a pretend event that is consistent with your choice and convey this from the outset

GETTING MARRIED IN THE UK

To make your wedding unique to you the only factors that you are tied by are the legalities of marriage

CHOOSING YOUR CEREMONY

Besides the legal considerations, you can build your day to suit you and the marriage ceremony can be as major or minor part of the day as you like. Opt for a civil or religious ceremony depending on your preferences and background, but bear in mind that most faiths believe a church or temple wedding should be respected as a religious decision. If your church charges fees, these will cover the use of the church and the services of the minister. There may also be fees for bell-ringing, the organist and the choir, which will vary according to the parish church council and should be discussed with the local minister.

CIVIL CEREMONIES IN ENGLAND AND WALES

This is a nonreligious ceremony performed by a registrar in a register office or at a location that has been licensed for civil marriage. Civil ceremonies are becoming increasingly popular as more house, hotel and unusual venues become licensed. The General Register Office will be able to provide you with a full list of venues in your area. At the time of going to press the civil ceremonies laws were under review and in a couple of years it may be the registrar who will be licensed as opposed to the venue, so there could be even more freedom of choice in where you can be married.

Once you have decided where you would like to have the ceremony and confirmed availability with the venue, the first legal step is to visit your local register office in person to inform the superintendent registrar of your intention to marry. To do this, you must have been living in the district where you are applying for a minimum of seven days.

The registrar requires some form of identification, so you will need to provide your passport or other official identification documents to confirm your name, address, date of birth and nationality. If you have previously been married they will also ask to see your decree absolute. Widowers or widows will need to provide the death certificate. All documents you produce should be originals (photocopies are not acceptable) and if they are not in English a translation by an authorised third party should be provided. You will also be asked to pay a fee at this stage. You should check with your local registrar for up-to-date costs.

A notice of your intention to marry will need to be displayed to the public for fifteen days to allow anyone the chance to object before your ceremony takes place, after which time you will each be issued with a certificate of authority for the marriage.

These certificates should be delivered to the registrar conducting the ceremony in advance of your big day. Your ceremony must take place within twelve months of your initial statement of intention to marry; otherwise you will have to give notice and pay the fee again.

You will need to arrange for a registrar to perform your marriage ceremony, whether this is in the register office or at a licensed venue that you have chosen. If you are marrying away from your home town you will probably be stating your intention to marry to one register office and arranging your ceremony with another one – just make sure you have all the relevant paperwork wherever you need it to be!

If you are not from the UK but are arranging your wedding in England or Wales you will need to allow a period of at least 24 days. This is so that you satisfy the seven-day residency requirement, give notice of your intention to marry, wait for the required 15 clear days for the public notice period, then have your certificates issued so that the ceremony can take place.

For more information contact the following:

General Register Office Certificate Services Section
PO Box 2
Southport PR8 2JD
(0845 603 7788, www.direct.gov.uk)

Or if you are interested in finding out about the legal variations for the Channel Islands contact:

General Register for Guernsey (01481 725277)
The Greffe
Royal Court House
St Peter Port
Guernsey GY1 2PB

General Register for Jersey (01534 441335)
10 Royal Square
St Helier
Jersey JE2 4WA

CHURCH OF ENGLAND OR CHURCH IN WALES CEREMONY

If you are opting for a Church of England or Church in Wales wedding you have the right to get married in the parish church where you live or where you worship (provided you are getting married for the first time).

Once you have decided that you would like a church wedding find out where your parish church is and arrange to visit the minister to see whether your chosen date is available. It is likely that he or she will be keen to meet you face to face to discuss your plans but you do not have to be a regular churchgoer or to have been baptised to get married in the Church of England or the Church in Wales. However, because of the commitment of both churches to lifelong marriage, it will be up to the minister to decide whether they will conduct your wedding if you have been married before. As with a civil ceremony, you will be expected to make your intention to marry public. This is done in the form of banns, which are read in church for three consecutive Sundays during the three months before your wedding. Banns must be read in the church in which you intend to be married and in your local parish church if these are different. After your banns have been read you will be issued with certificates of banns. But if for any reason you do not get married within three months you must have your banns read again.

If banns cannot be read, or if one or both partners live abroad, the marriage can be performed by Common Licence. Partners who live abroad and want to get married in the UK but cannot satisfy the 15-day residence requirement can apply for a Special Licence permitted by the Archbishop of Canterbury. But they will have to show a demonstrable connection to the church where they wish to marry.

For more information and for details about special circumstances contact the following:

Church of England (020 7898 1000, www.cofe.anglican.org)
Church House
Great Smith Street
London SW1P 3AZ

Church in Wales (02920 348200, www.churchinwales.org.uk)
39 Cathedral Road
Cardiff CF11 9XF

GETTING MARRIED IN SCOTLAND

In Scotland the clergy can marry you outside if they wish but this is very much dependent on the particular church's or minister's standpoint, so you should check in each instance to see whether this is possible. The laws have been relaxed so that civil marriages can take place in a wide variety of licensed venues throughout the country including outdoor and more unusual locations. If you have a particular spot in mind ask your registrar to consider it and apply for a licence for temporary approval, although you should allow extra time for this. You do not have to be Scottish or to live in Scotland to take advantage of this possibility.

You will each need to fill in a Marriage Notice form (available from any registrar in Scotland or from the General Registrar website) and return it to the registrar in the district in which you intend to wed. They will also need to see your birth certificates and any other documents you need to prove your status and eligibility for marriage. Your information will then be verified and you will be issued with a Marriage Schedule. Ideally you should submit your paperwork four to six weeks in advance but in some cases this process can take a minimum of 15 days.

As churches in Scotland do not give notice by banns you will need to pick your Schedule up in person from your registrar (no more than seven days in advance of your wedding) and deliver it to the celebrant who will marry you. For civil weddings, your registrar will keep hold of the Schedule in preparation for your marriage.

General Register Office for Scotland
(0131 314 4447, www.gro-scotland.gov.uk)
New Register House
3 West Register Street
Edinburgh EH1 3YT

Church of Scotland (0131 225 5722, www.churchofscotland.org.uk)
121 George Street
Edinburgh EH2 4YN

GETTING MARRIED IN NORTHERN IRELAND

The laws have recently been changed in Northern Ireland so that civil marriages that were previously limited to register offices can now take place in licensed venues throughout the country. In line with Scottish rules, notice for all marriages should be given to a registrar, so contact the office in the district you would like to get married in for more information. The clergy can also marry you outside if they wish but once again this is at the discretion of the particular church or minister.

General Register for Northern Ireland (02890 252000, www.groni.gov.uk)
Oxford House
49–55 Chichester Street
Belfast BT1 4HL

ROMAN CATHOLIC CEREMONY

To be married in the Roman Catholic Church you must obtain a certificate from your superintendent registrar before the wedding to satisfy your legal obligations, as you would for a civil ceremony. If you are an active worshipper you will be able to get married in a church within your or your partner's parish. If you want to get married in another parish where neither of you live, you will need to seek the permission of the local priest.

Arrange to see your priest at least six months before the wedding and take your baptism and, if available, confirmation certificates with you. There are three requirements for marrying in the Catholic Church: at least one of you must be a baptised Catholic; you need to have a formal preparation for your marriage; and both of you must be free to marry (in addition for the Catholic Church you must not have been married before and divorced). There are no exceptions for divorcees unless one or both of you have had an annulment of a previous marriage.

If only one of you is a baptised Catholic you will need to apply for special dispensation for the non-practising partner to be accepted into the church. The priest will usually apply for this by gaining permission for the marriage from the bishop.

A Catholic ceremony may or may not include Mass, depending on your situation. It is more usual for a Nuptial Mass to be conducted as a part of the marriage ceremony when both partners are Catholic as it offers communion to the bride and groom and to Catholic members of the congregation. Alternatively you can have a full ceremony but without Mass and Holy Communion.

For more information contact **Catholic Marriage Care** (020 7371 1341, www.marriagecare.org.uk).

CIVIL PARTNERSHIPS

Civil partnerships were legalised in the United Kingdom in 2005, giving same sex couples the same legal rights and responsibilities as a couple entering into marriage. This includes equal treatment financially, for example with regard to pensions, inheritance, life assurance and maintenance for children. Civil partnership also gives same sex couples next of kin rights.

The main difference between civil partnership and marriage is that currently civil parnership can only be performed by a registrar therefore it is not possible to form a civil partnership in church. It is also the signature of the second partner that denotes the partnership as legal rather than the exchange of spoken words as with heterosexual couples. This means that if desired the union can be entirely private as the second signature need not take place at the same time as the first.

In the same way as a civil ceremony you must give notice of intention to enter into the partnership and a record of the partnership will be kept as a public document by the General Registrar. Although this all sounds rather mechanical, you can of course make yours a memorable and unique occasion by adding personal or cultural touches to your ceremony. For more information contact your local register office.

HUMANIST CEREMONY

Humanist weddings are gaining in popularity and are an option for those who want a completely nonreligious ceremony. You should bear in mind that a humanist marriage is not legally binding so you will also need to have a civil ceremony, however brief, to make your marriage valid in the eyes of UK law. Your wedding can take place anywhere that the celebrant agrees to and it can take any form that you agree on. No two humanist ceremonies are the same as they are wholly reflective of the couple getting married. Take a look at the website for the British Humanist Association at www.humanism.org.uk to find out more.

SOCIETY FOR INDEPENDENT CHRISTIAN MINISTRY CEREMONY

Another option for your ceremony is the Society for Independent Christian Ministry (SICM) that was founded in 2000. Its philosophy allows you to have a religious or secular ceremony somewhere other than a church or licensed venue. Bishop Jonathan Blake, founder, believes that the marriage ceremony should be a celebration of the love of the couple rather than a legal contract. As with the humanist option, a SICM ceremony is not legally binding so you will also need to have a civil ceremony. You can arrange to combine the two or have each on a separate day. It is entirely up to you. The ministers of the SICM are all church ministers so if you would like a religious element to your day without being in a church they will be able to provide this compromise. This is also a good option for inter-faith couples who want to design a ceremony that takes into account both of their backgrounds. A source book is provided

> *Dreams I have helped come true include: a couple who bumped into one another under water on holiday and who also wanted their marriage to be sub aqua; another couple who trekked their family up the Brecon Hills to be married around an ancient stone circle; another couple who spoke their marriage vows on a yacht off Monte Carlo with their five bridesmaid children being baptised straight after; another pair who married in the clouds borne aloft on a Cessna; and another couple who wanted to be married over the Internet as their courtship had been.*
>
> *Other couples have chosen orchards, forests, settings abroad from Crete to Marrakech, Saxon villages, football pitches, beaches, abbey ruins, zoos, parks and gardens. Couples coming from different backgrounds have been able to weave together their cultures: Christian, Jewish, Hindu, Muslim, Pagan, American, Thai, Spanish, French, Filipino, Indian, African. A kaleidoscopic array in which I have used various religious texts, languages and attire to accommodate the couples' needs.*
>
> BISHOP JONATHAN BLAKE

with religious and nonreligious texts for inspiration on their website at www.sicm.co.uk. However, the emphasis is on an entirely personal and tailored experience for the individual couple.

OTHER RELIGIONS

Every religion and denomination will have its own regulations for marriage ceremonies, so ensure that you talk to the celebrant at your chosen place of worship well in advance of your wedding to make sure you understand all that is involved. You will also be required to give notice of your intention to marry to your Superintendent Registrar as you would with a civil ceremony.

Contacts for other religions include:

The Buddhist Society UK
(020 7834 5858, www.thebuddhistsociety.org.uk)
58 Eccleston Square
London SW1V 1PH

Greek Orthodox Archdiocese of Thyateira and Great Britain
(020 7723 4787, www.thyateira.org.uk)
5 Craven Hill
London W2 3EN

Jewish Marriage Council (020 8203 6311, www.jmc-uk.org)
23 Ravenshurst Avenue
London NW4 4EE

Methodist Church (020 7486 5502, www.methodist.org.uk)
Methodist Church House
25 Marylebone Road
London NW1 5JR

Muslim
There is no central advisory body for the Islamic faith but www.confetti.co.uk is a good starting point for information.

Scientology (www.scientology.org.uk)

Seventh Day Adventist (01923 672251, www.adventist.org.uk)
Stanborough Park
Watford WD25 9JZ

United Reformed Church (020 7916 2020, www.urc.org.uk)
Church House
86 Tavistock Place
London WC1H 9RT

BLESSINGS

If you feel that neither the church nor civil options complete your dream wedding scenario, a blessing for your marriage could be just what you are looking for to put the finishing touches to your commitment to each other.

You might want a blessing if:

✓ You get married abroad and want to allow friends and family who were not there to see your marriage blessed as part of your celebrations once you get home

✓ You are an inter-faith couple who want to get married in the tradition of one faith but also want to respect the other faith

✓ You are Catholic and have been married before. Talk to your local parish priest about receiving a blessing as they will be able to advise you whether this will be possible in your local church

✓ You want to get married in a particular church that is too small to hold all of your guests. As long as your reception venue is nearby you can ask the same celebrant if they are willing to bless you in front of all your guests. And it does not even have to be on the same day

✓ You have somewhere that means a lot to both of you, for example where you first met. If that was outdoors, you may not be able to get a licence to marry at that spot but you can have a blessing

✓ You do not feel strongly about having a church or a civil wedding. The blessing is more important to you as you can tailor it to your own requirements once you have the legal bit out of the way

✓ You would like a friend or family member to conduct a blessing for you. As blessings are not legally binding the person performing it does not have to be official

✓ You have something more alternative in mind

Most religious blessings take place in church but your celebrant may be flexible if you propose a different location that is respectful of your religion (although this is not commonplace). A nonreligious blessing can take place pretty much anywhere that everyone will agree to.

> We actually had two weddings, as we got married in a register office in the morning with just close family and then had another ceremony later in the day for 70 or so friends and family. We had exactly the wedding we wanted doing it this way. As we were already married, we made up our own ceremony with a good friend acting as registrar. And we had the blessing outside which is what we had always wanted. It was relaxed, fun and a real reflection of our relationship. It did rain a bit – so we delayed the wedding a little – but the sun came out (and a rainbow) and my dad walked me down a lavender-lined path in a beautiful garden, as the guests sang 'Going to the Chapel' as my wedding march.
>
> ALEX, 30

MIXED CULTURE WEDDINGS

If you are both from different cultures, then see if you can incorporate an element of both your backgrounds into your wedding, from the ceremony to the rituals, outfits, music and food. Or even go for two different celebrations during your wedding day or weekend.

> We had two ceremonies on the same day because I'm Indian and Simon is English. In the morning we had a Hindu ceremony where I wore a red and gold sari and Simon wore a sherwani (Nehru suit). In the afternoon I wore a white dress and Simon wore a morning suit. We loved that all of our families and friends were there to experience both weddings. And it was something really different for our guests. Having the two ceremonies in one day was a really special, magical day (if a little hectic!). We took the best things from both cultures to create our own wedding and loved it.
>
> SHILPA, 27

WEDDING REHEARSAL

It may well be traditional, but it is also practical. Where possible, have a full wedding rehearsal before the wedding. It makes sure that everyone knows where they need to be and what they need to be saying, when. This is also an opportunity for your photographer or videographer to check with the officiant where they are allowed to take pictures.

VENUES

When it comes to deciding on the location for your special day, as well as the traditional church option, it is well known that you now have an abundance of licensed venues to consider if you choose a civil ceremony. And, of course, you can have your reception wherever you like.

For listings of beautiful stately homes, classic country house and city hotels and a lot more besides, there are several very comprehensive online directories including:

✓ www.weddingvenues.com

✓ www.confetti.co.uk/venues

✓ www.forbetterforworse.co.uk

As mentioned previously, you can also contact the General Register Office for a complete list of licensed venues. Or have a look at publications such as:

✓ *Wedding Venues and Services* (www.weddingvenues.co.uk)

✓ *Nobles Wedding Venues Guide* (www.noblesvenues.com)

✓ *Wedding Directory UK* (www.theweddingdirectory.co.uk)

ALTERNATIVE VENUES

If you are looking for that unique something for your ceremony, reception or both, we've put together a tantalising selection of what's on offer to whet your appetite.

Art galleries. If you have a passion for the arts you may feel inspired by the idea of being surrounded by beautiful paintings, sculptures and stunning architecture. Think along the lines of the Royal Society of Arts in London (www.thersa.org/house) or the Pump House Gallery in Battersea Park (www.pumphousegallery.org.uk).

Barns. Whether you fancy a beautifully refurbished Tudor, medieval or more modern barn, there are loads to choose from. The wedding venue guides have comprehensive listings for around the UK, or keep your eyes peeled for a rustic heap of sticks in the country.

Castles. Where better than a fairy-tale castle to get married, a truly dramatic setting for your wedding day? The Castles of Britain website is a good place to start your search and will show you just what's on offer (www.castles-of-britain.com/castletd.htm). There are many to choose from but amongst those that stand out for sheer 'wow!' factor are Belvoir Castle in rural Leicestershire (www.belvoircastle.com), Highclere Castle in Newbury (www.highclerecastle.co.uk) and Leeds Castle in Kent, which has its very own moat and maze (www.leeds-castle.com). Or head for Aberdeenshire for the fifteenth-century medieval splendour of Lickleyhead Castle complete with bagpipe serenade (www.upperdonside.org.uk).

Film studios. The ultimate wedding for a media junkie or true film buff. Both Heatherden Hall at Pinewood and Littleton Park House at Shepperton Studios have opened their function room doors to allow civil weddings to take place (www.pinewoodshepperton.com). At Pinewood you can get married in the room where *The Great Gatsby* was filmed for some authentic 1920s class. If you like the idea of an air of celebrity, the British Academy of Film and Television Arts (www.bafta.org) is another option for afternoon receptions (they are not licensed for ceremonies). The rooms are for corporate hire but some have film stills and BAFTA logos to add to your experience. Or choose beautiful Houghton Lodge in Stockbridge (www.houghtonlodge.co.uk), which was used in the filming of *Wilde* with Stephen Fry and Jude Law amongst other high-profile projects.

Football clubs. Which avid footie fan wouldn't jump at the chance at getting married at their beloved club? Contact your club directly to see if they are licensed to hold your ceremony or enquire as to whether they have conference facilities where you can have your reception. If you're lucky you might even be able to have your pictures taken on the pitch.

Gardens. Due to licensing requirements, the closest you can get to marrying outside in a civil ceremony (apart from in Scotland where you can marry anywhere) is in a temple, pagoda or other 'walled' structure within gardens.

For sheer romance it's hard to beat Stowe Landscape Gardens (www.nationaltrust.org.uk/main/w-stowegardens) in Buckinghamshire, where two temples are licensed. Bicton Park Botanical Gardens (www.bictongardens.co.uk) in Devon offers ceremonies in its 1830s glass-panelled Palm House. And Mount Stewart House, Garden and Temple of the Winds in Newtownards, Northern Ireland, is another stunning choice, where you can get married overlooking Strangford Lough with beautiful gardens as the backdrop for your photographs.

London Eye. Unique and also increasingly popular, you can be married in your very own capsule decorated with flowers. Be pronounced man and wife as you reach the top of the wheel with a panoramic view of the capital city and then sip champagne as you descend (www.londoneye.com).

Museums. Many types of museum are now licensed for marriages. These can make for a distinct alternative as a place to exchange your vows or to entertain your guests once your ceremony is complete. The foyer of the Natural History Museum in London will make a striking backdrop for your reception (www.nhm.ac.uk/business-centre/exclusive-events/weddings), or switch church bells for a steam whistle and get married alongside Queen Victoria's carriage at the National Railway Museum in York (www.nrm-event.org.uk/weddings.htm). For those with a flair for aviation choose the Officers' Mess at the Imperial War Museum in Cambridgeshire (www.iwm.org.uk/duxford) or if you have a penchant for vintage and classic cars choose the Sussex-based Bentley Wildfowl & Motor Museum (www.bentley.org.uk). Alternatively, if you have a strange desire to get married underground look no further than the Big Pit Mining Museum in Torfaen, pit ponies and all (01495 790311).

Racecourses. You will find that the majority of racecourses are licensed so that you can marry in function rooms within their grounds. These include Chester (www.chester-races.co.uk), Ascot (www.ascot.co.uk), Kempton Park (www.kempton.co.uk), Doncaster (www.doncaster-racecourse.co.uk), Cheltenham (www.cheltenham.co.uk), Brighton (www.brighton-racecourse.co.uk), Musselburgh (www.musselburgh-racecourse.co.uk) and Haydock Park (www.haydock-park.co.uk) for starters. Conduct your ceremony with a panoramic view of the racecourse so you and your guests can all have a flutter once you are wed. Most courses will have dining facilities for a full sit-down dinner or finger buffet.

Ships and submarines. You can even get married on the ocean wave (albeit tied to the dock) – to become a licensed venue for ceremonies a boat must be secured and not free to sail. Several restored warships are options, including HMS *Warrior* in Portsmouth (www.hmswarrior.org) and HMS *Trincomalee* in Hartlepool (www.hms-trincomalee.co.uk). You can even get married on a submarine if you so desire – check out HMS *Alliance* at the Royal Navy Submarine museum in Gosport (www.rnsubmus.co.uk).

Theatres. If you've always harboured an aspiration to be an actor and have a desire to tread the boards, getting married in a theatre will be a dream come true. Exchange your vows in the stunning Georgian auditorium of the Bristol Old Vic (www.bristololdvic.org.uk). Or create your very own production and get married on the stage at the Landmark Theatre in Devon (www.northdevontheatres.org.uk) or within the crimson, cream and gold surroundings of the Richmond Theatre auditorium (www.richmond theatre.net).

Zoos. If you have a Doctor Dolittle side to your personality and want to share your wedding with the animals, get married in a zoo. No, unfortunately this does not mean you can have your ceremony in an animal enclosure (well, not yet anyway) but usually in the more sophisticated surroundings of the zoo's conference facilities. However, Chester Zoo (www.chesterzoo.org) can arrange an evening safari for you and your guests, and at Whipsnade Wild Animal Park (www.whipsnade.org) you can have your photos taken with the animals (by prior arrangement).

HOME

If you have no desire to look for a venue at all, or are on a tight budget, you could opt to hold the celebrations at home. Unless you are fortunate enough to live in a mansion of sorts a home reception will probably be more suitable for a relatively small number of guests. It will obviously save you costs on

> Our wedding was pretty much homemade and that's what I liked best about it. It was very relaxed and intimate. Everybody contributed something – Mum made the cake, my sister iced it, my sister-in-law did the flowers and we all helped make the picnic. We had a day in the kitchen where everyone pitched in so it felt like a real family effort. Everyone went back to our house for the party, which was great as again it was very relaxed, informal and especially sentimental to be in our home.
>
> Jo, 25

hiring a venue and can give the whole thing a very relaxed atmosphere. You could even arrange a blessing in your own back garden. Enlist a handful of helpers and decorate your home the day before your wedding, or perhaps

> When we organised Vicki and Jonnie's wedding at our home we tended to go for smaller firms, particularly for catering. An outfit that only does one wedding on a particular day will give you undivided attention but, of course, must be reserved early. We started by making a list of everything that needed to be fixed from hiring toilets to levelling a piece of field for the marquee site. Then when each item was decided I made a detailed calendar of what was due to happen when. I had time and event experience and I found that I needed plenty of both!
>
> JIM, FATHER OF THE BRIDE

your friends and families would like to decorate it for you so that it is a surprise when you walk through the door. In the summertime you can deck your garden out with fairy lights and candles and let your guests spill outdoors and in the winter hire outdoor heaters to make the most of all the space that is available. If you are having a home reception on a larger scale you might consider hiring a marquee to put in your garden.

MARQUEES

A marquee can be a great idea if you are catering for a large number of guests when you don't have indoor space or even simply for providing shelter for a buffet. You can use a marquee as additional space at a hired venue, or if you have a garden or patio big enough this can be the perfect setting for your wedding at home. Companies that hire marquees will often be able to advise you about the practicalities, such as positioning, lighting, heating, seating, electricity, hiring a bar, the dance floor, toilet facilities and space for your caterers. And marquees now come in a variety of shapes and sizes, including Bedouin tents, with all sorts of interiors from coloured silks to a ceiling full of starlike lights. Find a specialist company that is willing to visit your location and discuss with you exactly what you need. But remember that a marquee is not necessarily a cheap option when you start to add on all the extras and insurance, so work out final costings before you set your heart on it. Check out www.marquee celebrations.co.uk and www.oasistents.co.uk for starters. And contact the Raj Tent Club (www.rajtentclub.com) for tents with an Indian or Bedouin flavour.

BUDGET VENUE OPTIONS

If location isn't a done deal for you, think about the north of England, Scotland or Wales. In terms of normal hotel venues and suppliers you will find that your money goes a lot further than in the south of England. The exceptions are the alternative and unique venues, which can still charge a premium.

But unique venues and celebrations don't have to be expensive. We know of a couple who hired a riverside warehouse for their reception. While backpacking on a motorbike around Asia, they had got married in India in a very simple ceremony. When they returned to the UK they decked out the warehouse in old parachute silks and deep red roses and, when all the guests had arrived, they rode into the reception on their motorbike wearing the summery wedding outfits that they had been married in a couple of months before. Their friends took turns to man the makeshift bar and gave some 'donations' to help out with the booze-cruise haul that they'd brought back from France.

If you still can't stretch to a unique venue or conference hotel, or do not have the right setup at home, you could opt to have your reception in restaurants, clubs, pubs, or school or community halls. A lot of village halls have had makeovers thanks to lottery grants, so don't dismiss them out of hand.

CONSIDERATIONS

Considerations to bear in mind when you are looking for your perfect venue or venues are:

One venue for all? Do you want to have your ceremony and your reception in the same venue? This could save you money on extras such as flowers and transport and it saves your guests from decamping from one venue to another.

Convenience. Is your ideal reception venue easy for your guests to get to? Not only that, if your guests are staying off-site, is it in close proximity to other hotels in the area and also to where you will have your ceremony if it's on the same day?

Size matters. Can the place where you are intending to have your ceremony hold the number of guests that you would like to invite? Some licensed venues only hold a small number due to health and safety regulations, so bear this in mind if you want everyone to be able to hear you say your vows.

We want to be alone. Do you have sole use of the venue for the day? Some venues will host more than one function at a time while others will only hire their facilities out to one wedding on one particular day, so you can make your choice based on this fact if it is important to you.

Whatever the weather. Is it going to be warm/cool/dry enough? If not, will any provisions to combat this cost extra? Unfortunately the Great British weather will come into play in your planning. It may seem obvious but make sure you are being practical with your choices, i.e. don't book a garden-party reception with no cover, however beautiful the gardens are, as your guests won't thank you when it tips with rain.

Overall effect. When you are spending time and money piecing together your dream wedding, will this venue provide the perfect backdrop for the tone, theme and colour scheme that you have in mind?

Is it secure? Your guests may leave bags unattended. Some will also bring your presents to the reception. So make sure you provide somewhere secure to leave them.

Seating plans. What layouts are possible in the venue? Make sure you have the capacity to accommodate your number of guests comfortably if they are sitting down for a meal.

Support. Some wedding venues have wedding co-ordinators to help you plan your event. This could be especially useful if you are not based close by.

Extra costs. Venues might offer you a wedding package, but you should always enquire as to any possible additional costs to understand the true impact on your budget from the outset.

Decorations. If you are organising the decorations, table settings and finishing touches yourselves then you will need to gain access to the venue prior to the big day to set up (and maybe even afterwards to tidy up) so make sure this is possible. If the venue supplies all of the decoration and settings make sure you are happy with what they have to offer.

Party poopers. Are there any noise restrictions if you are planning on playing music or being generally rowdy until the wee hours? You should also check if there is a curfew.

Smoking. Is there an area where your guests can smoke and, if not, is this an issue for you or your guests?

BYO. Does the venue operate a 'bring your own' policy? Beware of hidden charges for corkage as these can soon spiral out of control.

Changing facilities. If you are leaving for your honeymoon direct from your reception you probably don't want to be crammed into a toilet cubicle trying to get changed!

Photos. If you are having photos taken at the venue think about where you would like these taken and the practicalities of the photographer being able to set up.

Tidying up. It might be a condition of your contract that you need to vacate the venue by a certain time for the next people using it. And, shock, horror, you may be expected to tidy it up before you leave or face a fine.

If your venue is not usually used for events, you also need to consider:

Access. What kind of access do you have for your guests and suppliers? Think about how your guests are going to arrive, where they can park and how practical your venue is. Also consider caterers and other suppliers and the various items that you may want to move in and out.

Facilities. Are there adequate cooking, clearing up and toilet facilities for the number of guests that you have?

Utilities. You might have to arrange for a power, gas or water supply to be connected to the venue. Or you may even have to temporarily provide generators, gas cylinders and water tanks yourselves.

Once you have thought about all the practical considerations make a shortlist of a couple of your favourite venues. And at the risk of sounding like a broken record, choose the venue that really suits the two of you rather than one that you think others will expect of you.

GETTING MARRIED OVERSEAS

The modern-day version of eloping is a lot less shocking and potentially more glamorous than it used to be.

If you are willing to travel, the world really is your oyster in terms of where to get married and you might even choose to invite your family and friends to go with you. From beaches to mountain tops, lakesides to movie sets, cities to underwater, trapeze wires to skydives, anything is possible. What's more, it can end up costing you a fraction of a big blowout wedding back home in the UK. Marvellous.

This chapter covers the basic legalities and some inspirational ideas for getting married abroad. And you have the choice of organising it yourself or sitting back and letting a holiday company provide the whole hassle-free package for you.

MAINSTREAM DESTINATIONS

Many reliable and experienced companies provide full packages for getting married abroad, try the following for a variety of mainstream destinations:

First Choice (www.firstchoice.co.uk)
Kuoni (www.kuoni.co.uk)
Sandals (www.sandals.co.uk)
Thomson (www.thomson.co.uk)
Virgin (www.virginholidays.co.uk)

LEGALITIES

With all these destinations you usually need to provide the following in English (copies certified by a notary or solicitor are sometimes accepted in place of original documents – you will need to check with your destination for confirmation):

✓ Valid ten-year passports (with a minimum of six months left to run after your return date to the UK)

✓ Original birth certificates

✓ A statutory declaration or affidavit to declare single status (if never previously married)

✓ Decree absolute (if divorced)

✓ Spouse's death certificate and previous marriage certificate (if widowed)

✓ Proof of adoption (where relevant)

✓ Proof of name change by deed poll (where relevant) – this may also apply to divorcees if they have reverted to their maiden name

✓ Parental consent for under-18s in the form of an affidavit or statutory declaration signed by a notary (some destinations require that you are as old as 23 to get married without consent, so check before you book)

✓ For religious ceremonies, confirmation from your church or temple at home that they give their consent to you getting married overseas

In addition, although it is not compulsory in a lot of countries, it can save significantly on explanation time and confusion if you both provide your own personal, signed letters of intent to marry (or preferably official statutory declarations) on arrival that state:

✓ Proof of your personal details, including name, address, nationality, occupation, employer's address and religion for the official documentation

✓ Intended marriage location and date

✓ Full names, addresses and signatures of both sets of parents to indicate their consent to your marriage

Some countries, such as Australia, ask that you get an official Certificate of Intent to Marry before you travel.

It is also advisable to make at least two photocopies of each original document that you are taking with you – one to leave at home and one in case it is needed while you are away.

Statutory declarations or affidavits can be obtained from a Commissioner of Oaths, who are listed under 'Solicitors' in business directories. Because your statutory declaration is personal to you, the bride and groom should have one each. To ensure details are current, you should also make sure your authenticated statutory declarations are dated within three months of the wedding date. Charges can vary, so shop around to get the best rate.

Another important factor is the minimum residency requirement for these countries. The majority require between one and seven days, but you need to be absolutely clear about the current laws for the country you are visiting. If in doubt, have a couple of extra days on your own beforehand to familiarise yourself with the area – that will also give you a chance to find local finishing touches or tourist highlights before your guests arrive.

Finally, if you are using a reputable holiday company, double-check all the details with them when you book and before you leave to ensure you are still up to date on requirements. If you are in any doubt at all then check for yourselves with the authorities for that country for peace of mind. For the sake of a few enquiries you could save yourself a lot of anxiety in the long run.

PRACTICALITIES

Before you get excited about booking your dream location, there are some practicalities to think about:

Climate. What are the typical weather conditions in your chosen resort during your wedding month? Remember that seasons are reversed between the northern and southern hemispheres and also that the seasons do not necessarily equate to what we are used to – in some countries, summer is the wettest, stormiest season. Rainfall, sunshine hours, temperature, humidity and any extreme weather conditions are all things to look up.

Safety. Check with the Foreign and Commonwealth Office (0845 850 2829, www.fco.gov.uk) to ensure they do not have a current warning about your destination. If they do, this may nullify any insurance you take and could jeopardise not only your wedding but your safety too.

Vaccinations. Do you require any vaccinations or malaria tablets before you travel? Or are there any restrictions on where you can travel because you have recently had a vaccination or been somewhere that is blacklisted by your destination? If you are getting married relatively soon, is there enough time to have all the vaccinations? You should also check that the guests you are sure you want with you are all happy to have the required medication.

Visas. These vary from country to country and are usually relatively easy to obtain from the embassy of that country in the UK. The main warning here is not to leave things to the last minute – while the process is usually relatively straightforward, sometimes complications arise and a sense of urgency is often lacking. Before any of your party send off applications, clarify with the authorities exactly what documentation they require with your application and if in doubt, send them more rather than less (but do not send original documents unless absolutely necessary). It is also a good idea to enclose a covering letter stating the dates you need your documentation back by (ideally a month before the wedding for peace of mind), even if it feels like months away.

Legal clarification. Always check with the authorities for a country to ensure that the laws have not changed during the course of your wedding planning. You can obtain a list of the UK-based foreign embassies, consulates and high commissions that will be able to help you from www.fco.gov.uk, which also provides useful links to a range of services from automobile associations to immigration and customs authorities.

Public holidays. Planning your wedding or honeymoon abroad over national holiday dates for that country can create problems in getting affordable, available accommodation for your wedding party and may also affect transport links and services.

Culture and religion. Think about the culture where you are going. If you are booking through a tour operator then they will be able to advise you of any dress codes or alcohol restrictions and often the hotels they use will be 'westernised' so this may be less of a concern. But if you are organising your wedding yourself look into any restrictions that could be imposed. Many cultures find it offensive if a woman shows too much flesh e.g. her legs, shoulders, upper arms or back, and alcohol is restricted in some Muslim countries. Does this fit in with your wedding plans?

Logistics. If you are planning on honeymooning in the same place that you marry, do you want your other guests to be in the same resort as you all the time? If not, you can arrange a two-centre holiday for either them or yourselves. Or maybe you would like to have two or three days to yourselves after the wedding but want to come back and join the rest of your group before you fly home.

Timescales. Package 'weddingmoon' tour companies usually ask you to provide all documentation three months before departure.

Details. The great thing about an overseas wedding is that it is easier to distance yourself from organising the details than if you were at home. That is, if you want to take that approach. But it is still worth giving some consideration to each query that your venue or tour operator asks you and not taking anything for granted. You might think that you don't care about the flowers because you would love some local flowers from your tropical island paradise, but knowing that you are British might prompt your venue to fly in British flowers to try to please you. If you are inclined to say 'whatever you usually do' to any questions, then ask 'what do you usually do?' instead. It keeps the hassle factor low and also clarifies any areas you might want to change or personalise.

Photos and follow-up. Getting married overseas means that once you fly home, it can be a lot harder to chase suppliers for your photos, additional negatives or even your marriage licence. Where possible, be safe rather than sorry and keep as much original material as you can at the time.

> I'm not sure how other people get their photos but our proofs were in strips of small colour photos. The best bit was that when we got back from the beach the day after the wedding, they had been pushed under the door. We selected the ones we wanted and they were ready a few days later before we flew home. From what we gather from other people, the whole process was much quicker (but possibly more rough and ready) than in the UK. You don't get them presented in a big padded album or anything, but for me that was a bonus, as I would rather choose my own way of displaying them. The good thing was that when we arrived back in this country, we already had photos of the big day to show everybody.
>
> Something to be wary of is that sometimes when you are abroad they only give you the negatives of the photos that you choose to have printed. Luckily we negotiated having all of the negatives, so that we had the option to have more printed over here if we wanted.
>
> CLAIRE AND ADRIAN, 26 AND 27

Additional costs. Find out what comes as part of the wedding package you are looking at and what the additional extras are, even if the package is termed 'all inclusive'. Some resorts will give you your ceremony for free as part of the total holiday cost. If there are a lot of things you would like that fall outside the package, shop around over the Internet and you are likely to be able to get more competitive rates. The downside is you may not have the peace of mind of using a supplier recommended by your tour operator. Also consider the currency exchange rates and how much you can expect to get for your money – although flights to some destinations will be a lot more expensive than others, how affordable everything is once you get there can make a huge difference to your budget.

Support. Depending on how specific you want to be with the details of your wedding, the degree of support that your venue offers you may be pivotal to your choice. Alternatively you can hire a local wedding co-ordinator in your destination, but you should make sure that you have comparative quotes, are not pressured into making decisions before you are ready and actually speak to the consultant before you retain them. Or you could just decide not to get bogged down in the small stuff.

Travel. It might be your dream destination but after an expensive and arduous journey will you and your guests still be up for a dream wedding? Make sure you get the balance right.

ENSURING YOUR MARRIAGE IS LEGAL IN THE UK

A concern for a lot of couples is whether your marriage will be legal in the UK. To avoid a Jerry Hall–Mick Jagger style mix-up, check with the British authorities for that country or a UK register office to nail down any requirements. A tour operator will be able to advise you but there is no substitute for checking the details yourself.

A legal overseas marriage will always remain registered in the country in which it was conducted rather than the UK, because the Foreign Marriage Order of 1970 states that 'a marriage solemnised in accordance with the local law of a foreign country cannot be registered in this country'. Your overseas marriage certificate is proof enough of your status, so consider ensuring you have an authenticated English language version, as you will need it to update all your legally recognised documentation on your return. To avoid problems with needing to apply for copies of your marriage certificate from overseas sources, if you are a British citizen, you can apply to have your official documents transferred back to the UK and held at the General Register Office. Contact the ONS General Register Office on 0151 471 4801 for further information.

ALTERNATIVE IDEAS

Here are a few taster ideas to get you thinking about civil ceremonies overseas. If any of them appeal, contact the embassy for that country to check the latest legislation and requirements. If you would like a religious wedding the process can be a lot more complicated and so you should speak to your local religious centre and the appropriate embassy for advice.

With regards to Europe, it is worth noting that Belgium, Denmark, France, the Netherlands, Norway, Portugal, Spain and Switzerland all have a fair amount of red tape to work through for nonresidents. But where there's a will there's a way.

DO-IT-YOURSELF

The hassle-free option is to get a tour operator to organise your holiday for you, but there is no reason why you cannot organise it yourself. If you are going to do this you should start researching as soon as possible and do not steadfastly build your timescales around the approximate times you are given – the wheels of bureaucracy can move very slowly in government offices and hold-ups are common.

The embassies or consulates in the UK for each country are an excellent source of information. Again, find their contact details from www.fco.gov.uk and allow up to a couple of weeks to hear back from them. Some of them, like those for the Cayman Islands and Thailand, have DIY wedding packs they can send out to you to get you started.

By contacting the individual country tourist boards, you might also be able to arrange a more personal venue and even save some money too. Or another option is to ask the tourist board to recommend a local wedding planner – just make sure they speak English or any other language you are competent in and remember that local interpretation might be different to what you have in mind, so be explicitly clear in your communications at all times.

In theory, you can achieve anything you want to, but to avoid even more stress than if you were organising your wedding at home, it is easier if you scale down your plans accordingly. You should also bear in mind that in traditional service economies such as the United States, standards are much easier to anticipate than if you pick a local venue in a less developed country. This is part of the charm of going off the beaten track, but if you have doubts you either need to stick to the internationally recognised chains or five-star rated resorts, or risk being disappointed.

ALASKA

One word: breathtaking. With snowcapped mountain ranges and ancient glaciers looming over tranquil icy fjords and lush green hills, this spectacular place is sure to blow you away. You can combine your visit with river rafting, a more sedate river kayak trip or a wildlife tour to spot brown bears fishing for salmon. In summer you will experience the famous midnight sun and at other times of year you can see the night sky dance with the colours of the northern lights. And the best thing about Alaska is that it is an easy destination to marry in. You can avoid the three-day residency period with a postal application and you can get married anywhere on land by any Alaskan resident who is registered as a marriage commissioner. The downside is that none of the major tour operators, other than Princess Cruises, go there so, before you book, check all the current requirements with the American Embassy in London (0207 499 9000, www.usembassy.org.uk), or the consulates in Belfast, Edinburgh and Cardiff. You can get advice from the state tourist office (www.travelalaska.com).

AUSTRALIA

It might be a package wedding destination but it does not do Australia justice to dismiss it that glibly. The country is enormous and the climate and terrain incredibly varied. From kangaroos, wallabies, koalas and platypuses, to thorny devils, fairy penguins and dolphins, Australia is an animal lover's paradise. Scuba dive on the Great Barrier Reef, watch the sun rise at Cape Tribulation, see the sun set on Ayers Rock, go wine tasting in the Barossa, dance around the Pinnacles, bake on Bondi and climb Sydney Harbour Bridge for a view of the opera house and city. Whatever time you've got probably won't be enough. And in theory, civil celebrants can marry you anywhere the minute you step off the plane. You can find a list of them under 'Celebrants' on the Australian Yellow Pages site (www.yellowpages.com.au). At least six weeks before you intend to marry, you must get an authenticated Notice of Intent to Marry from the Australian High Commission (020 7379 4334, www.australia.org.uk), which must then be forwarded to your celebrant to reach them between one month plus one day and six months before the wedding for it to be valid.

By arranging your wedding yourself you can choose from some more unusual venues than the wedding package operators provide. They tend to stick to Sydney Harbour side, Ayers Rock and other well-known tourist spots. But what about going underground in Coober Pedy or a tree house in the rainforest?

BALLOON WEDDINGS

For those of you who want to exchange vows or have your reception in a hot-air balloon, Blast Valve is a great resource to find ballooning clubs throughout the world (www.blastvalve.com).

CANADA

Like Australia, this is a mainstream destination but there is so much to it you could explore it for yourself and find plenty of gems that you might not see on an organised trip. And again, because English is the first language (apart from in Quebec), you should easily be able to arrange the wedding yourselves. The minimum residency period is three days in some parts of the country. Don't feel restricted to the packages that are on offer – design your own dream wedding. Canada touches two major oceans on its east and west coasts – the Atlantic and the Pacific. The Pacific coast runs from Seattle up to Alaska and it has the attractions of Vancouver, Vancouver Island, Orca whales and the picturesque Rockies with Lake Louise in all its glory. And in the winter, it all turns into a skier's and snowboarder's paradise. For those who want to experience the Canadian interior, the vast expanse between the coasts is all yours! In the eastern provinces, the influence of Quebec gives the cities more of a Francophile flavour and the scenery here is less mountainous, but the white wooden homes of Prince Edward Island, the Great Lakes and Niagara Falls don't make this any less striking in its own way. Plus the cities of Toronto, Ottawa and Montreal are within a day's drive of each other. Contact the Canadian High Commission general enquiries centre (020 7258 6600, www.canadainternational.gc.ca) for further information.

CAYMAN ISLANDS

A mainstream wedding destination with a twist. In Grand Cayman the chance to bless your wedding with 'aqua vows' is growing hugely in popularity. And the trio of tropical island paradises boast exactly the kind of sun-soaked white-sand beaches you may have dreamed about. Relax with a game of golf, watch the iguanas or parrots that live on the island, explore the wrecks and colourful reef under the aquamarine sea or swim with the stingrays and turtles. We found that the tourist office was incredibly helpful and totally geared up to helping you to organise your own wedding. There is no minimum residency requirement but you are asked to confirm all your arrangements in advance of your trip to expedite paperwork. Contact the Government Information Services in Grand Cayman on +345 949 8092 for further information on the practicalities. And the Department of Tourism in the Cayman Islands (www.caymanislands.ky) or in the UK (www.caymanislands.co.uk) can help you with finding the right accommodation, schedule and marriage officer or provide you with a list of local wedding planners.

CZECH REPUBLIC

With beautiful bridges, old castle buildings, golden church domes, classical music and charming squares, Prague is a city of romance and fun. And the surrounding countryside boasts beautiful scenery and picturesque villages. To treat yourselves to a luxury wedding package completely organised for you, contact the Four Seasons in Prague (+420 2 2142 7000 or freephone on +800 6488 6488, www.fourseasons.com/prague).

You can also contact the Czech Embassy in London (020 7243 1115, www.czech.embassyhomepage.com), or the British Embassy in Prague (+420 257 402 111, www.britain.cz).

DISNEY

Whether you fancy California or Florida, Disney can make all your fairy-tale dreams come true. You can choose from an 'Intimate Wedding' package for up to eight guests or custom design your wedding with Cinderella's castle as your ceremony backdrop. Unfortunately, as yet Disneyland Paris does not offer a wedding service. For more information see www.disneyweddings.com.

ICE HOTELS

For something really different for a small wedding party, get married in the Ice Chapel of the Ice Hotel in Sweden (www.icehotel.com). Situated in Jukkasjärvi, which means 'meeting place', the Ice Hotel books up at least a year in advance. Once you can bear to leave the cosiness of the furs in your room, venture out for a sauna followed by a lesson in ice sculpture, snowmobile tour of the last wilderness in Europe and a drink at the Absolut Ice Bar.

Another Ice Hotel is based in Quebec, Canada (+1 418 875 4522, www.icehotel-canada.com), and the latest, very impressive, Ice Museum in Alaska (+1 907 451 8104, www.chenahotsprings.com) where you can marry and then stay in the comfort of their lodge. At the time of going to press, some of these do not have chapels, but as the hotels are rebuilt every year that could well change so check with the venues for details. Or you always have the option of a civil ceremony.

IRELAND

Although not supported by the main package companies, Ireland is nevertheless a popular wedding destination and has hit the headlines with celebrity couples attracted by the beautiful countryside, castles and infamous hospitality of the Irish.

CELEBRITY SPOTLIGHT

Victoria Adams and footballing god David Beckham exchanged their vows in a flurry of publicity at Luttrellstown Castle in Ireland. Other celebrities who have followed suit include Pierce Brosnan and Keely Shaye Smith, who celebrated at Ashford Castle.

Marriage by civil ceremony in Ireland must take place in the Office of a Registrar of Civil Marriage and there is only one of these offices per county. The minimum age for marriage is 18 and you need to send your intention to marry by post to the Registrar of Marriage for the relevant district to arrive at least three months before the wedding.

Residency requirements for civil marriages are fairly complicated at the moment, so it is best to check directly with the General Register Office (+353 1 635 4000, www.groireland.ie) which has a comprehensive website covering the requirements for marriage in Ireland, including the Notification of Intention to Marry form and contact details for the civil registrars.

Religious marriages are, from a legalities point of view anyway, much easier. You just need to comply with the three-month notification requirements. Most (but not all) religious marriages are recognised by the Irish State as civil marriages, there are no residency requirements and there are a lot more churches than there are registrar's offices. You need to make your own arrangements for the wedding with an appropriate clergyman and satisfy the religious requirements of the church in question.

ITALY

Home of the canals of Venice, the cobbled streets of Romeo and Juliet's Verona, Rome's Trevi fountain, the countryside of Tuscany, the beautiful peninsula of Sirmione in Lake Garda and the Amalfi coast. With more reliable weather than the UK and only a couple of hours' flight away (with the bonus that many cities are served by the budget airlines), the romance of Italy is certainly alluring. Organising a wedding yourself can be daunting because the process is very bureaucratic and paperwork needs to be in Italian, whether by translation or as an original document. You must obtain a Certificate of No Impediment from your local register office in the UK, which must then be certified by the British Embassy in the Italian city where you want to marry. The embassy will issue you with your *certificato di nulla osta* then, depending on the register office in question, two to four days before your wedding you may also need to give a 'Certificate of Intent to Marry' to the registrar. The British Embassy in Italy hosts an excellent website that clarifies the legalities and processes involved (www.britain.it). You can also contact the Italian consulate in the UK (020 7235 9371, www.conslondra.esteri.it) and Italian Tourist Board (020 7408 1254, www.enit.it).

If your ideal is the Italian dream, then don't be deterred; with perseverance and a minimum of three to four months, anything is possible. Or simply employ the services of a wedding consultant to reduce the headache. Use this list as a starting place or search the Internet for more:

✓ Weddings Italy (www.weddingsitaly.com)

✓ Florence Weddings (www.florence-weddings.com)

✓ Venice Weddings (www.venice-weddings.com)

✓ Venice Events (+39 041 523 9979, www.veniceevents.com)

LAS VEGAS, USA

It's a cliché. But if you can imagine it, you can probably find it or arrange it in Vegas. As you would expect in the desert, summers are phenomenally hot, so plan to get married from October to April as it is slightly cooler. Alternatively, think about an evening wedding. One word of caution: avoid Valentine's Day and New Year's Eve if possible because they are crazily busy with long queues of bridal couples waiting for their turn.

Just a few of the weird and wonderful ideas from this city include: drive-thru chapel weddings where you don't even have to get out of your car; being married by 'Elvis'; naked weddings; *Treasure Island* pirate-ship weddings; and now you can even get married and have your reception Trekkie style on a replica of the *Enterprise* set in the Las Vegas Hilton. See www.vegas.com for more details. This site also gives information on the legalities of getting married in Vegas and links to the Clark County Marriage Bureau to apply for a marriage licence.

CELEBRITY SPOTLIGHT

Chris Evans and Billie Piper decided to avoid the media circus and tied the knot in a low-key wedding at the Little Church of the West in Las Vegas. Several other celebrity couples have previously married at the same church, including Noel Gallagher and Meg Mathews, Richard Gere and Cindy Crawford, and Bob Geldof and Paula Yates.

Both Chris and Billie headed down the aisle in casual dress – she wore a simple pink sarong and white cotton blouse while he wore stripy trousers and a green shirt. The £200 ceremony included the service, music played by the church organist and a set of glossy photos.

Other stars who married in various venues in Vegas include Frank Sinatra and Mia Farrow, Michael Jordan, Jon Bon Jovi, Elvis and Priscilla Presley, Judy Garland, Jane Fonda, Paul Newman and Joanne Woodward (who bucked the trend and, remained married until he passed away in 2008) and Dennis Rodman and Carmen Electra.

But don't relegate Vegas purely to the Mecca of the mad, mafia and gamblers: you can also watch amazing desert sunsets, check out the Hoover Dam and raft the Colorado River, take a helicopter flight to experience the vastness and timelessness of the amazing Grand Canyon, or visit Route 66 and Death Valley close by. And don't underestimate the lure of the lights – to arrive in Vegas after dark and, from miles away, see the beams of light in the black sky of the desert night is incredible, even for the disapprovers. A town of contrasts, its hotels are luxurious and opulent with amazing shows and acts to attract you through their doors.

The American Embassy (020 7499 9000, www.usembassy.org.uk) has offices in London and consulates in Belfast, Edinburgh and Cardiff.

NEPAL

Trek the Annapurna Ranges or prepare to tackle Everest and squeeze in a wedding beforehand. To relax after the climb and all that crisp, clean mountain air, head south to the jungle and the Royal Chitwan National Park to embark upon an elephant-back safari to track down rhinos and maybe even catch a glimpse of the elusive Bengal tigers. Contact the British Embassy in Nepal for further information (www.ukinnepal.fco.gov.uk/en). Can you feel an extended wedding-cum-honeymoon coming on?

NEW YORK – THE NUTTIEST WEDDINGS ON EARTH?

If you haven't already been won over by Carrie's adulation of the Big Apple in *Sex and the City*, New York has so many alternative options that one is bound to appeal.

After Cary Grant waited for Deborah Kerr on the Observatory Deck in *An Affair to Remember* and Tom Hanks met Meg Ryan in *Sleepless in Seattle*, who could doubt the romance of the Empire State Building? So it is no surprise that it is also a popular marriage spot. Weddings are possible all year but there is a special event on Valentine's Day for a select number of couples. To be eligible, you must have an application in by 30 November the year before. For more information about all wedding options, see www.esbnyc.com/tourism.

Other ideas include a ceremony under the Statue of Liberty on Liberty Island followed by a helicopter flight over Manhattan, a lighthouse (+1 845 247 0656, www.saugertieslighthouse.com) or even the Yankee Stadium, Brooklyn Bridge or the New York Aquarium.

To marry in New York State you must apply in person for a marriage licence from the town or city clerk. For more details have a look at www.cityclerk.nyc.gov. You must get your licence from the borough where your venue is located. Contact them to clarify all details.

NEW ZEALAND

For some reason very few main wedding package operators offer services for New Zealand, despite the country being absolutely breathtaking and perfect for a romantic wedding, as well as possibly attracting a few die-hard *Lord of the Rings* fans for their nuptials.

If you are a British citizen, you can marry in New Zealand once you have made a statutory declaration in person stating that there is no lawful impediment to your marriage. You can do this at the New Zealand High Commission (020 7930 8422, www.nzembassy.com) or at the registrar's office in Auckland, Wellington or Christchurch. They will give you a marriage licence that is valid for three months only.

There is a fantastic variety of venues including:

✓ Slipper Island, a picturesque private isle just off the Coromandel on the North Island (+64 21 776 977, www.slipper.co.nz)

✓ A harbour cruise wedding in Auckland

✓ A hot-air balloon wedding celebration (+64 3 302 8172, www.nzballooning.co.nz)

✓ A chapel at the foot of waterfalls on King Arthur's Pass

✓ Bungy from the Kawarau Bridge near Queenstown (www.ajhackett.com)

✓ The Church of the Good Shepherd at Lake Tekapo

The last is our personal favourite. Photos cannot do the scenery justice – the minerals at the bottom of the lake give the water a mystical blue colour and it sits in full view of Mount Cook. The chapel itself is right on the edge of the lake. It is a small, intimate venue with an uninterrupted window along the side meeting the water. The views are breathtaking. The only drawback is that this is a popular tourist spot because of its natural beauty and so you should book your wedding service for early morning, before the crowds arrive en masse but ideally after the mist lifts from the mountains.

New Zealand is well established for helping foreign nationals plan their weddings. You will find a selection of New Zealand-based consultancy services on the Internet if you decide to recruit someone to help you.

If you would prefer to buy a package, a specialist wedding and honeymoon company for New Zealand (in addition to those listed at the start of this chapter) is The Wedding Company (www.thewedding company.co.nz).

SOUTH AFRICA

Virgin Weddings are one of the only mainstream companies to offer packages to South Africa, although it is also quite easy in principle to organise the wedding yourself if you would prefer. As long as all the necessary documentation is in order you can get married as soon as you arrive. A list of marriage officers is available online on sites such as www.celebration.co.za you need to contact a marriage officer directly as they will advise you of the final legalities and paperwork at that time.

As in England, you are restricted to getting married in a permanent structure but amongst the many and varied locations available are an elephant park, private game reserves, the infamous Mount Nelson Hotel in Cape Town and small chapels in the winelands of Stellenbosch or Paarl.

With all South Africa has to offer, you will have lots of amazing opportunities for your perfect honeymoon too. Safaris in Kruger National Park, whale and dolphin watching, wine tasting, Robben Island, the Drakensburg Mountains, sunset cruises and beach days all offer relaxed but unique distractions. For the more extreme, you also have the options of the world's highest bungy jump, shark cagediving, black water tubing or abseiling down Table Mountain.

For further information on legalities, a useful pack is available from the South African High Commission in London (020 7451 7299, www.southafricahouse. com).

SPAIN

Although not a popular destination for weddings because of the weighty bureaucracy, you can get married in Spain. And you have the option of a religious or civil ceremony, provided you have official permission from your parents and your priest. The residency requirement and/or Spanish citizenship of at least one of you is at the discretion of the locale where you would like to marry. You need to contact the Civil Registry in Madrid (+34 91 397 3700), or for places outside the capital the District Court for your chosen area, to apply for a civil marriage licence. Allow three–six months for the lengthy paperwork to be completed and do not book anything until you are completely clear that you are eligible to marry, because the process can be much more complicated for nonresidents. After the wedding, you can apply to have your Spanish marriage certificate certified with an apostil by the Secretaria de Gobierno, Tribunal Superior de Justicia in Madrid. For further information, contact the British Embassy in Spain (+34 91 714 6300, www.ukinspain.com/english) and the Spanish Tourist Office in the UK (www.spain.info).

If planning your wedding in Spain is just too daunting, then Gibraltar can offer a much simpler alternative and has the bonus of the ceremony and documentation being in English. You need to finalise all paperwork in person at the Marriage Registry between three months before and 10.30 a.m. of the day before the wedding. The ceremony must take place in a church, at the Register Office or in one of these approved venues:

✓ The Dell at the Alameda Gardens

✓ The Mount

✓ The Caleta Hotel, Eliott Hotel or Rock Hotel

The official government site is www.gibraltar.gov.uk/gettingmarried.php and it details legal requirements and a list of wedding suppliers.

CELEBRITY SPOTLIGHT

When you marry on the Rock, you are in good company. Those that have gone before you include John Lennon and Yoko Ono, Sean Connery (twice) and Frederick Forsyth.

SRI LANKA

Yes, Sri Lanka is a mainstream wedding destination but worth a mention because this beautiful and diverse island in the Indian Ocean is a microcosm of what Asia has to offer. From herds of wild elephants to tea plantations in the lush hill country, paradise beaches, turtle watching, festivals, impressive ancient ruins, waterfalls and spice gardens, you can always find something to occupy you. And you can get married on a beach at sunset.

Just as a precaution before you book, check with the Foreign and Commonwealth Office (www.fco.gov.uk), because Sri Lanka has also experienced a lot of political turmoil in its recent history and some parts of the island are unsafe for travel.

For more information, check out the brochures of the reputable wedding package operators and contact the British High Commission for Sri Lanka (www.britishhighcommission.gov.uk/srilanka), the Sri Lankan High Commission (www.slhclondon.org) and the Sri Lanka Tourist Board (www.srilankatourism.org). If you decide to organise your wedding yourself, ensure you take direction from the High Commissions because it can be tricky to work out what information you can and can't believe from other sources.

SWITZERLAND

If you want crisp air, lakes and snowcapped mountains in Europe rather than Canada or New Zealand, take a look at Switzerland as your dream destination. Swiss legislation does mean that you have to have a civil ceremony in the town hall, although you can arrange a religious blessing afterwards. You will need to file your 'application for the preparation for marriage' with the register office you intend to use and will also need to authorise a 'declaration for the conditions of the marriage' at the Swiss Embassy in person (although you can apply for exemption from appearing in person). Finally, the solicitor's signature that witnesses this must be legalised by the Foreign and Commonwealth Office. Luckily, the Swiss officials are some of the more efficient when it comes to paperwork, so the process is fairly straightforward. Contact the Swiss Embassy in the UK for further details on procedures, documentation and fees (020 7616 6000 or search on 'marriage' at www.swissembassy.org.uk).

TREE HOUSES

Close to Mount Rainier, USA, the Cedar Creek Treehouse is an arboreal retreat with incredible views and ideal for a small wedding party. The two-storey tree house also boasts a glass-enclosed observation deck, ideal for stargazing or just contemplating the mountains over your morning coffee. And on your doorstep are trout fishing, swimming and bird watching. Not to forget that the owners are musicians, so your wedding music would be covered! For details ring +1 360 569 2991, or see www.cedar-creektreehouse.com.

For something a bit more tropical, opt for a tree house in the Australian rainforest. Situated between Cairns and Port Douglas, the luxurious Daintree Eco Lodge and Spa (+61 7 4098 6100, www.daintree-ecolodge.com.au) is a treat you will never forget and is also right at the northern gateway to the Great Barrier Reef. If the Daintree resort is too rich for your blood, a cheaper option is the Treehouse YHA at Mission Beach (www.yha.com.au/hostels, search on 'Mission'). It is very popular with backpackers because of its excellent facilities and stunning surrounds.

TROPICAL ISLAND BEACH PARADISES

There are many gorgeous beach destinations for weddings and some of them are still unusual, if only because they are not served by the mainstream tour companies. For a raft of ideas for beach weddings, check out www.islandbrides.com.

UNDERWATER NUPTIALS

The upside to an underwater wedding is that you don't have to consider spending a fortune on your outfits. Unless you are silly, of course.

Other than the aqua vows in Grand Cayman, there are a number of other options open to water lovers. In many countries underwater ceremonies are followed by a signing of the register on land to cover all the necessary legalities. By searching on the Internet you will find a range of suppliers for places like Australia, Fiji, the Philippines, Malaysia, Thailand and the Maldives. Before you book your ceremony, remember to check out your legal situation and requirements with the authorities for that country.

If you want an excuse to head to Florida then plan something a bit different for while you are there. The Jules' Underwater Lodge (named after Jules Verne) in Key Largo is 21 feet below the surface and you will need to scuba down to the entrance hatch and prepare before your public notary joins you to conduct the service. Or you can spend your wedding eve and first few nights of your honeymoon underwater too. How alternative is that! You need to apply for a marriage licence prior to the ceremony from the Monroe County Clerk's Office at the Plantation Key Government Center (+1 305 852 7145). The lodge site has information about how they conduct weddings (+1 305 451 2353, www.jul.com/weddings).

Also based in Key Largo is Captain Slate, who claims to be the originator of underwater weddings. Ceremonies are conducted underwater at the Christ of the Abyss statue, a 25-minute boat ride from the dock. And the great thing is that a glass-bottomed boat is used, so your guests can witness the proceedings. Contact Captain Slate for more information (+1 305 451 2353, www.captainslate.com).

VICTORIA FALLS

Because the Falls bridge Zambia and Zimbabwe, there are different legal considerations depending on which resort you choose. Marrying by the spectacular falls will be something that you and your guests will remember for ever. And as if that is not enough, you can take balloon or elephant rides, boat cruises and even a bungy jump.

Venues range from luxury African lodges to colonial-style hotels. And the views are magnificent.

> *One of the best weddings I ever went to was at Vic Falls. The couple married in the open air by a small lake in the grounds of a hotel and we ate in a candlelit marquee. A real bonus was that we all got there a week early, went on trips including safari and canoeing together and there were loads of little parties and get-togethers, so by the time it came to the wedding we knew everyone! It was simple, sophisticated and generally excellent.*
>
> ANDY, 30

MORE DESTINATIONS

These are just a sample of ideas to spark your imagination. If you have experience of another country or a burning desire to go somewhere specific then contact the embassy for that country and the British Embassy or Consulate in that country for advice. Alternatively, maybe you are intent on getting married in a lighthouse, windmill, castle or cave. If so, follow your dream!

For inspiration for more destinations, have a look in the **Honeymoon** chapter. The information is not wedding specific but if you get your heart set on your dream honeymoon, then you can look into whether or not you can get married there too.

For something a little wackier, you can have your civil wedding blessed online with the First Electronic Church of America (www.fecha.org/wed.htm).

Crazy but true. To understand more about getting married in America, check out www.usmarriagelaws.com/search/united_states.

MIX 'N' MATCH OPTIONS

If you are not bothered about doing everything in the same place, you can get married in the UK and then hold your reception (or one of your receptions) abroad or vice versa. Why not?

CELEBRITY SPOTLIGHT

If you fancy holding your wedding celebrations abroad but have no time to arrange the formalities, or you cannot meet residency requirements for the country of your choice, then find a way round it like Radio One presenter Sara Cox did when she married DJ Jon Carter. They legally tied the knot in a quiet ceremony in a London register office and then headed over to Ireland for the rest of the celebrations.

PROS AND CONS

Average costings. For overseas wedding packages these are £3,000–£5,000. This is clearly a big budget saver as the average UK wedding comes in at a frightening £14,000–£15,000 (although this does include rings, outfits and separate honeymoon that are not covered in the overseas wedding packages). In addition, if your plan is to have a celebratory party when you get home, include both sets of costs in any budget plans. Two of the main cost savings are:

✓ You are unlikely to have as many guests to cater for than if you stayed at home

✓ You are already on honeymoon

Letting go. If you are an amateur control freak, an overseas wedding could be a blessing as long as you are able to accept that decisions are taken out of your hands and there is nothing you can do about it. But if either of you are really extreme cases then you might find the lack of involvement with some of the detail hard to handle. Think about what role you want to play in organising your own wedding.

More control. Ironically, although you need to be willing to let go of some of the detail, because everyone else is also distanced from the organisation it is equally difficult for them to interfere. You can have your dream wedding and then come home and have one or more parties that will keep other people happy.

> *Going away can be very straightforward and romantic; we wrote our own vows and didn't have any religion to contend with. Our only advice in hindsight would be to make sure you have the wedding sooner rather than later during your stay so you can enjoy your honeymoon (we only had one day before we had to leave and start the marathon of family receptions so we could 'share the happy day' over the following five weeks).*
>
> VANESSA AND DARREN, 29 AND 31

Two's company. The whole of your wedding party with you on your honeymoon could be considered a crowd. Arrange to spend some time alone after your wedding ceremony but make sure you are clear with your guests about how much time you will and won't be spending with them.

Sort the wheat from the chaff. Guest lists can be a lot easier to manage with overseas weddings because, not only do people understand if you want to keep your bridal party small, on the whole only your closest friends are willing to make their annual holiday your 'weddingmoon' (isn't that word awful?) and fork out to fly halfway round the world.

> *We did not want our wedding to spiral out of our control and become something that wasn't us. So instead, we headed for the Isla Margarita just off the coast of Venezuela with our two closest friends as witnesses. It was a very low-key wedding with just the four of us at the ceremony on the white sand beach and at the reception meal immediately afterwards. And it was exactly what we wanted. When we got back to the UK, we had a reception, all wore our wedding outfits and gave speeches. There wasn't the pressure we would have had if we'd opted to do it all on one day, in one place, in front of all those people. It ended up reminding us again of our amazing memories and was a great party for everyone else.*
>
> CLAIRE, 26

Of course, this can also be a downside to getting married abroad. If your friends have children in school, no spare annual leave or are short of cash, then the likelihood of them coming is slim. Not to mention your 90-year-old granny who isn't up to a two-hour car journey let alone an eight-hour flight. To encourage as many people as possible to make it, opt for a destination that involves the least cost in terms of money, travel time and days off work.

Get generous. If your main motivation for going overseas is to keep the guest list and fuss down rather than save money, this means that you are in a position to contribute to costs for guests you definitely want to make it but who have financial limitations. Just keep any financial assistance for anyone other than immediate family quiet or face the very wedding hoo-ha you are so desperate to avoid.

CHOOSING YOUR CEREMONY 'FRILLS'

The 'frills' around your ceremony are your opportunity to top and tail the standard patter and tailor it to suit you both.

This is your chance for a touch of personal or artistic expression to let your characters really shine through.

Ironically, the parts of the ceremony that invite you to make your own choices often still end up being some of the most traditional. Many couples almost subliminally pick poems, music and readings that have been heard time and again just because that is what they associate with weddings. Select music and words that inspire and mean something to you as a couple to complete your ceremony. Failing that, just choose something you like.

MUSIC

Music is a perfect way to personalise your ceremony and will add to the atmosphere and emotion of your wedding. It is up to you how you incorporate it but it is usual to have music playing at the following times:

- ✓ As your guests enter the venue or while they are waiting for the ceremony to begin

- ✓ As you enter the church or venue and walk up the aisle or towards your officiant (in which case, think about the beat of the music – are you going to be able to walk calmly or are you likely to be sprinting up the aisle?)

- ✓ As part of the ceremony to sing along to

- ✓ While you sign the register

- ✓ When you leave the church or room where your ceremony takes place

✓ As your guests mingle after the ceremony while photos are taken or when they arrive at the reception venue

INCIDENTAL MUSIC

The traditional classical options are still popular or you could consider a contemporary alternative.

Classical	Contemporary
'The Bridal March' – Wagner ('Here Comes the Bride')	'Have I Told You Lately' – Van Morrison
'Grand March from *Aida*' – Verdi	'Kissing You' – Des'ree
'Pomp and Circumstance' – Elgar	'Moon River' – Henry Mancini
'Arrival of the Queen of Sheba' – Handel	'Unforgettable' – Nat King Cole
'Trumpet Tune and Air' – Purcell	'She Loves You' – The Beatles
'Ave Maria' – Schubert	'How Sweet It Is To Be Loved By You' – James Taylor
'Amazing Grace' – John Newton	'I Do, I Do, I Do, I Do, I Do' – Abba
'Wedding March' from *A Midsummer Night's Dream* – Mendelssohn	'I've Got You Under My Skin' – Frank Sinatra
'Wedding March' from *Marriage of Figaro* – Mozart	'It Had To Be You' – Frank Sinatra
'Toccata and Fugue in D minor' – Bach	'You and Me Song' – The Wannadies
'Canon' – Pachelbel	'Someone Like You' – Van Morrison
'Spring' from *Four Seasons* – Vivaldi	'Chapel of Love' – Elton John
	'Come Away With Me' – Norah Jones
	'My Baby Just Cares For Me' – Nina Simone
	Theme from *Titanic* – James Horner

HYMNS

Many people go for hymns they remember from their childhood, but be careful not to turn your church service into a flashback to school assemblies with everyone mumbling along giggling. Try to choose hymns that everyone will recognise, but also look at the lyrics and think about what the hymn is saying and the sentiment behind it. If possible make sure everyone has access to a hymnbook or order of service so that they have the words and can sing at the tops of their voices. Having said that, hymns are one of the most difficult types of music to sing.

Some popular choices are:

✓ 'All Things Bright And Beautiful'

✓ 'Morning Has Broken'

✓ 'Lord Of All Hopefulness'

✓ 'Give Me Joy In My Heart'

✓ 'Amazing Grace'

✓ 'Make Me A Channel Of Your Peace'

✓ 'As Man And Woman'

✓ 'Love Divine'

✓ 'Jerusalem'

✓ 'Lord Of The Dance'

✓ 'Praise My Soul The King Of Heaven'

✓ 'One More Step Along The World I Go'

> *Be REALLY careful with the hymns you choose. You may think that they sound fine but if no one knows the words or tune you'll have that awful half-singing in the background or if, like me, you choose a song with the highest, longest 'Gloria' on the face of the earth you just end up with your guests in hysterics ... If in doubt try and get the church choir in.*
>
> MARIE, 29

ALTERNATIVES

As long as your officiant agrees you can have whatever music you like, so it's best to talk to them first and find out where they draw the line. Remember that in churches they are keen to promote religious music but in a civil ceremony you are not actually allowed hymns.

> At my friend's wedding there was the typical murmured singing going on. The priest decided enough was enough and held a microphone right in the groom's face while he was knelt at the altar. It was hysterical and certainly a lesson to me never to choose a song that people just can't sing.
>
> ELLIOT, 29

For more inspiration:

✓ Listen to a collection of classical or chill-out CDs to pick out something a bit different from the old faithfuls

✓ Choose a jazz piece, love song or tune from a musical

✓ Look for lyrics or a musical style that complements your theme

✓ Ask a musical friend or relative for advice or see if they are willing to sing or play as part of your ceremony

✓ Look at your list of options for your first dance – if you can't choose between two you could play one of them during your ceremony (see **Reception Music** and **Entertainment** for ideas)

✓ Speak to your registrar or celebrant about music that they have heard at weddings in the past

✓ Have a rousing sing-along to something other than a hymn and perhaps even use this in place of your wedding march

✓ Hire a professional or band to serenade you and your guests, perhaps an opera soloist, a bagpipe player or even a past *X Factor* contestant (they're ten-a-penny these days) – failing that get a one-man band with cymbals strapped to his knees and suffer the consequences

CELEBRITY SPOTLIGHT

Charles and Di set the precedent at their royal wedding way back in the 80s. Kiri Te Kanawa's dulcet tones filled St Paul's Cathedral during the signing of the register.

POEMS AND READINGS

Again, you need to have your officiant's agreement to your choices and there are endless texts to choose from. Some popular options for ease of reference follow. You also need to give some thought to who you will ask to deliver them on the day.

NONRELIGIOUS READINGS

Shakespeare always provides a good starting point for old-fashioned inspiration:

- ✓ *Hamlet,* 2.2.123–6
- ✓ *Love's Labours Lost,* 4.3.327–55
- ✓ *Romeo and Juliet,* 2.2.139–41
- ✓ Sonnets 18, 29, 43, 88, 116
- ✓ *The Merchant of Venice,* 3.2.17–19
- ✓ *Twelfth Night,* 3.1.151–6
- ✓ *Venus and Adonis*

Other pieces include:

- ✓ 'The Blessing Of The Apaches' – Author Unknown
- ✓ 'How Do I Love Thee?' and 'If Thou Must Love Me' – Elizabeth Barrett Browning

✓ 'Love Seeketh Not Itself To Please' – William Blake

✓ 'She Bewitched Me' – Thomas Burbidge

✓ 'She Walks In Beauty' – Lord Byron

✓ 'Marriage' – Mary Coleridge

✓ 'Why Do I Love You, Sir?' – Emily Dickinson

✓ 'The Prophet' – Kahlil Gibran

✓ 'A Thing Of Beauty Is A Joy For Ever' – John Keats

✓ 'The Passionate Shepherd To His Love (Come Live With Me)' – Christopher Marlowe

✓ 'The Promise' – Eileen Rafter

✓ 'Sonnet' – Christina Rossetti

✓ 'Love's Philosophy' – Percy Shelley

✓ 'He Wishes For The Cloths Of Heaven' – W B Yeats

RELIGIOUS READINGS

Your celebrant is the best person to advise you here, or you may have some readings that you are particularly fond of. If you are finding it hard to know where to start, take a look at these:

✓ Colossians, Chapter 3, 12–17

✓ 1 Corinthians, Chapter 13, 4–13

✓ Ecclesiastes, Chapter 4, 9–12

✓ Ephesians, Chapter 3, 14–19

✓ Genesis, Chapter 2, 18–24

✓ Isaiah, Chapter 54, 10–14

✓ 1 John, Chapter 4, 7–8, 12

✓ John, Chapter 2, 1–12

✓ John, Chapter 15, 1–8, 9–17

✓ Mark, Chapter 10, 6–9

✓ Matthew 5, 1–10, 13–16

✓ Proverbs 31, 10–12, 25–31

✓ Psalms 67, 121, 127, 128, 136

✓ Romans, Chapter 12, 9–12

✓ Ruth, Chapter 1, 16–17

✓ Song of Songs, Chapter 2, 8–10, 14, 16

✓ Song of Songs, Chapter 8, 6–7

MORE IDEAS

If none of these suits you and you want to look for more inspiration, take some time out to:

✓ Make an event of deciding and settle in for an evening with a bottle of red wine and as many poetry books as you can both lay your hands on

✓ Buy a book of quotations and look up those referencing love and marriage, or dip into a specific book on wedding readings to see if any inspire you

✓ Listen to your favourite songs and see if any of the lyrics would be suitable for a reading

✓ Put pen to paper and write something yourselves

✓ Ask a creative friend to write a verse for you or employ a professional such as Ginny Walker (www.specialoccasionpoetry.co.uk)

✓ Choose a passage from a book that you think is a suitable reflection of your feelings

✓ Edit a favourite poem or reading to your liking

ALTERNATIVE FRILLS

If you have a liberal registrar or celebrant then you might have the opportunity to get more creative with personalising your ceremony content. Other than the obvious alternative, which is not to have any music, poems or readings at all, you could look into a:

✓ Dance performance, be it classical or modern

✓ Short play or scene, possibly an excerpt from a film

✓ Conjurer or illusionist to introduce special effects to reinforce the sentiment of your service

✓ Medieval minstrel to perform a meaningful ballad

✓ Fireworks as you kiss

✓ Releasing of white doves as you say your 'I do's

ORDERS OF SERVICE

Giving your guests an order of service allows them to follow your ceremony word for word. Printed in the style of your wedding stationery this could also make a nice keepsake for your assembled throng.

Orders of service are not compulsory and so an alternative option is to either simply hand out hymnbooks if you are in church, or use photocopies of your running order and song words. Alternatively abandon the idea altogether and allow everyone to soak up events as they unfold. Just don't expect them to sing or join in with responses if they don't know what to say.

VOWS

Go with the standard ceremony format that is offered to you if you are happy with the words you are saying and you feel they reflect your ideals (or if the ceremony is more of a formality for you). These vows are written to encapsulate the sentiment and legalities of marriage so may be exactly what you are looking for. Alternatively you can, of course, get creative and write your own. As with all parts of the ceremony, you will need to run these past your officiant to check they are happy to include them. You may be marrying for the second time or feel there is more that you want to say. Writing your own words may really complete things for you and will certainly give your day a very personal and unique feel.

TO BE GIVEN AWAY OR NOT TO BE GIVEN AWAY

This is all a bit outdated these days but many girls still choose to follow tradition and ask their father to walk them down the aisle. But what if your dad is not around or your mum means a lot more to you? Or maybe you just don't agree with the idea of being 'given away'? You are your own person, after all. There are other options so discuss with all concerned what you are happiest doing and go with your gut instinct.

As the bride you can:

- ✓ Meet your groom at the door and walk up the aisle with him

- ✓ Walk up the aisle by yourself

- ✓ Be given away by your mum, uncle, grandfather or other relative or friend

- ✓ Walk in ahead of your guests with your groom and stand at the front as they all seat themselves (this avoids being watched as you walk down the aisle)

- ✓ Follow Jewish tradition and ask both of your parents to walk you up the aisle

- ✓ Ask your own children to escort you to your waiting groom or all walk in together

- ✓ Wait at the altar and let the groom walk down the aisle to you – this might be particularly pertinent if you proposed to him

 Traditionally a bride was considered to be her father's property and was therefore granted permission to marry and given away by him.

WHAT TO WEAR

We all have an image in our minds of the conventional wedding party, but what will yours look like?

THE BEAUTIFUL BRIDE

Will it be white or red? Meringue or chic? Dress, suit or bikini? Whichever way you look at it, all eyes are on the bride, so do you have to blow four-figure sums (or more) to get the right outfit?

Searching for an outfit is one of the most exciting and indulgent parts of planning a wedding but can turn into an epic quest if you're not careful. And to make things even more complicated, you also have options other than the traditional image of the virginal blushing bride. These days you can get married in pretty much anything that you want to wear (provided you are in the right surroundings). Perhaps you prefer the idea of wearing a smart trouser suit, a floaty skirt and glamorous top, or even jeans and a T-shirt, or a bikini and sarong? It's your call (see 'Alternative Options').

Before you shop for your outfit, get in the right frame of mind – feel good about yourself and you are a lot more likely to find a dress that you are happy with. Treat yourself to some nice moisturiser, lose a couple of pounds or exercise the day before to avoid having a 'fat' day, get your hair done and wear pretty undies.

Factors that can affect your decision include:

Budget. This will be a major consideration. If you have an unlimited budget, the world is your oyster and you'll probably be quite overwhelmed at the choice. Whatever budget you have, you'll be tempted to push it further. You need to balance your love of an outfit with what else will need to be cut back if you overspend.

Before the wedding industry was born, brides married in their Sunday best, whatever the colour. The main exception to this rule was green, allegedly because the groom would assume the bride had been rolling around in the grass with another suitor and was wearing green to cover the grass stains. Slightly paranoid. At the same time white was also considered to be too impractical for 'commoners' to afford. Meanwhile, royal brides married in luxurious silver robes until Queen Victoria came along and broke the tradition by wearing white for her marriage to Prince Albert in 1840. This started a new trend and, as fabrics became more affordable, white became the most popular and accepted colour for brides to wear. It was also seen as a symbol of purity and was thought to discourage evil spirits.

Something old, something new, something borrowed, something blue, and a silver sixpence in your shoe – this well-known Victorian rhyme refers to age-old traditions that are said to bring luck and wealth to the bride. The 'something old' is often a garter given by a happily married woman so that her fortune is passed on; the 'something new' is often the dress and is symbolic of the happy couple's flourishing future; 'something borrowed' is given by the bride's family and must be returned to its rightful owner to ensure good luck; and 'something blue' originates from ancient Israel where blue was representative of fidelity.

Your surroundings. If you are getting married in church you will be expected to cover up accordingly, whereas civil weddings will be a lot more relaxed about dress code. Your celebrant or registrar can advise you on their guidelines.

What your fiancé is wearing. If he has a full morning suit in mind perhaps a casual summer dress isn't your best bet. Try to complement each other's outfits.

The once-in-a-lifetime factor. This is your big chance to wear what you have always dreamed of as you marry the man of your dreams, so try not to let others' opinions sway you. If you want to wear a big meringue, wear a big meringue. But think about the fact that you probably won't wear it again unless you've specifically bought a useable outfit. Not to mention the perils of food stains and children with sticky fingers who will all want to touch you as their princess for the day. Balance these facts when you buy and remember that whatever you decide to wear will look gorgeous.

Circumstances. If it is your second time around you might want to wear something very different to your first wedding. Or maybe other circumstances affect your choice, such as your culture or perhaps you are pregnant.

Fabric characteristics. Choose a breathable fabric and one that will not crease. That way you will look fresh all day.

Comfort. You may be spending all day in your chosen outfit, so ultimately go for something that is comfortable and allows you to move around freely without looking robotic or like you have a stiff neck.

What suits you. You have always dreamed of a sleek column dress but when you come to try one on find it clings in all the wrong places. If it just isn't right then surrender the fantasy and go for something that really flatters you. Try on as many dresses as possible because they will be very deceptive on a hanger. And definitely make sure you have a 360-degree view of yourself before you commit. Take along someone you trust to help with your choice – you'll know you've got the right dress when you see their lip start to tremble and tears in their eyes.

> *When I went to try on dresses, I was determined not to have a meringue but my sister managed to get me to try one on. I was amazed. And it was the dress for me.*
>
> HELEN, 29

One of the most famous old wives' tales is that it is considered bad luck if the groom sees the bride in her wedding outfit before the ceremony. Don't panic if he catches a glimpse by accident – it's only superstition.

Sizes. Larger or smaller sizes can be tricky to track down. You will find that a lot of sample dresses are limited to sizes 10–14, so you may need to arrange an individual fitting or go to a specialist outlet. Remember that having a dress made or fitted will take longer, so allow yourself plenty of time to avoid fretting about how it will look. Too many women will start worrying about their size and shape at times like this but try not to let this affect your excitement for finding the right dress because you *will* find one! And don't set yourself unrealistic targets and order a size 12 along with six months' supply of Slimfast if you are a size 18 now, as you will only give yourself more to worry about. If you are on the opposite end of the scale and feel too petite for any of the dresses you try, ask about having it altered so that it is perfect for you.

Colour co-ordinating. If you can't find the right shoes or bag in a colour to match your outfit, buy white or cream ones and dye them.

DESIGNERS, BRIDAL SHOPS AND INSPIRATION

The mountains of bridal magazines on the market are full to the brim of wedding dress adverts that will bombard you with hundreds of pictures of beautiful models in fairy-tale white dresses with impressive price tags to match. But they are not just limited to traditional options – there are some rather alternative ones featured too. A picture speaks a thousand words and these mags are a great starting point to get some ideas about what's out there and at what price.

Another forum to discover new designers and the latest wedding fashions are wedding shows. There is a huge cross section of what's on offer, both on the stands and headlining on the catwalks.

Alternatively head out to the shops, take a deep breath, grab your closest allies including at least one very honest one, and brace yourself.

There is all manner of choice out there on the wilds of the high street from bridal-shop chains such as Pronuptia (www.pronuptia2you.co.uk) and Berketex Bride (www.bbride.com) to smaller one-off boutique stores (you will find a list of these in the Yellow Pages and in bridal magazines). Budget permitting, you also have the choice of a whole host of designers vying for your business and continually bringing out beautiful collections of ever-more stunning dresses. A lot of bridal-wear designers and shops display their wares in online catalogues so you could even start your search from the comfort of your living room (or desk).

BUDGET OPTIONS

Phone around. Take a note of serial numbers and designers of dresses and although you might fall in love with a dress at first glance, don't be afraid to phone around a few suppliers – you can sometimes get a better price elsewhere.

Approach fashion colleges. You may find a budding designer who will create a unique outfit for you at a fraction of the price you would pay an established designer. You will get something cheap and original but there are no guarantees, so you should allow extra time for any issues that could arise.

Dressmaker. Cut costs by asking an individual rather than a wedding shop to tailor-make your wedding dress and shop around for good-value material to make this option worthwhile. Ask around for recommendations for a dressmaker in your area. You can supply them with patterns or if possible point out the wedding and bridesmaids' outfits you have seen and they may be able to recreate them for you.

Make your own. Clearly this could be a bit ambitious if the last thing you made was a pencil case at school, but if either you or someone close to you is a dab hand with a sewing machine this can save you a significant amount of cash.

Second-hand dresses. If you are comfortable with this option look out for classified ads or browse the Internet for possibilities. If you are lucky you can find just what you are looking for at a fraction of the price.

Hire your dress. Not everybody feels they need to keep their wedding dress for ever. If you're not going to get too emotionally attached to it, think about hiring as this could save you a lot of money. Alternatively you could just hire your veil or bridesmaids' dresses.

Sales and discount opportunities. These could be the deals offered at wedding shows or end-of-season sales in dress shops. And if a sample fits you perfectly, ask the shop if they will sell it to you at a discounted price. One bride told us how she bargained with a shop to do this, as the display dress she loved was the last one they had in stock – they even steam cleaned the dress and took up the hem for free.

Hit the high street. Debenhams carries an excellent range of high-street designer wear at high-street prices. Monsoon also produces some classic occasion-wear lines for adults and children and Adams has a good selection of kids' formalwear too. As their success grows, expect to see other quality high-street stores follow suit.

> *When I went to look at dresses I nearly fainted with shock! It's all very well and good being free with the cash if someone else is paying, but we were covering our own wedding costs and, while we didn't want to get hung up on money, we wanted to evaluate our options. In the end, I got my dress from Monsoon and felt fabulous in it. I didn't save the money either but bought some very lavish underwear that I know I'll wear again and a foxy dress for our honeymoon!*
>
> MEGAN, 33

ACCESSORIES

Accessories can make or break an outfit. But for your wedding, don't get carried away with all the beautiful options on offer and overdo it. Your outfit and the way it defines your figure should be the focus of the look. Too many accessories can just make it look cluttered, less effective and a lot cheaper than it really was.

Tiara. Delicate or dramatic, a tiara may be just what you're looking for to complete your princess look.

Shoes. Whatever you do, make sure your shoes are comfortable. Don't buy heels that you can't walk in, however glamorous they look! That rule goes for your bridesmaids too. Practise walking around in your shoes at home so that they are comfier for the day. And if you opt for open-toed shoes, treat yourself to a pedicure a couple of days before the wedding.

Gloves. Long and slinky for that Marilyn Monroe screen-goddess look, or short wrist-length gloves for more of a 50s girl-about-town vibe. Just remember gloves will make things a bit tricky when you come to exchange rings, so be prepared to take them off once you have made your initial impression. Or just reserve them for your bridesmaids.

Veil. The epitome of the traditional bridal outfit and very much optional.

Veils come in all manner of lengths and styles, plain or covered in glittering jewels, and you can wear them over your face, shoulders or as part of a train. An alternative to wearing a sheer veil is to choose a scarf or decorated mask. Just remember to let your hairdresser know in advance if you decide to wear one so that they don't have to completely redesign your hairdo on your wedding morning.

The idea of wearing a veil stems from the belief that it protects the bride from evil spirits on her wedding day. The veil is also symbolic of the bride's chastity and is thrown back when the couple are announced husband and wife to reveal her face. Ta-daa!

Lingerie. This is a perfect opportunity to get yourself properly measured and to treat yourself. Watch out for a VPL and consider a different kind of bra shape than you would usually go for if it sets your outfit alight. You can find gorgeous underwear to suit any budget to make you feel sexy and sultry under your virginal façade. For starters there's Marks & Spencer, Agent Provocateur and La Perla. It will also be a nice surprise for your new husband (if he's in a fit state to notice it) and an indulgent private reminder of your wedding day whenever you wear it in the future.

Bag. It is a bit tricky to carry around your usual Tardis of a handbag on your wedding day and realistically you're not going to need your diary, pen, old receipts, hair ties, packet of sweets, spare house keys, etc. so hone it down to a few bare essentials. Buy a small handbag that co-ordinates with your outfit, or perhaps with your mum's or bridesmaid's outfit if they will be the one carrying it. A few necessities are:

✓ Make-up and mirror – to do those little touch-ups

✓ Tissues – to mop up your tears of joy and stop your mascara streaking down your face as you exchange vows

✓ Spare tights or stockings – in case of ladder emergencies

✓ Painkillers – just in case a headache creeps up on you

✓ Mini hairbrush – you might need it if you are wearing your hair down, but if it's been carefully structured it's probably best left alone (but be prepared with a back-up option in case of collapse brought on by your enthusiastic diva-like dancing)

✓ Perfume – for a top-up; it's going to be a long day after all

✓ Something minty – a quick freshen-up never does any harm

Jewellery. Again, this is an opportunity to treat yourself or, even better, for someone else to treat you. Perhaps use it as one of your 'something old, something new ...' collection if you are adhering to tradition. Do you opt for a new matching set or wear jewellery that has sentimental value to you? Or maybe you want to hang on to your rebellious streak with toe, nose, eyebrow or tongue rings.

Flowers. To co-ordinate with your bouquet and colour scheme think about entwining fresh or artificial flowers in your hair. There are plenty more ideas in the **Flowers** chapter.

Co-ordinating umbrellas. Because you can never trust the weather!

ALTERNATIVE OPTIONS

Silver. It was good enough for royalty until the start of the twentieth century, so how about reviving the fashion?

Colours. Don't restrict yourself to white, cream or ivory. Try a Baileys colour or subtle pink or blue. Or forget the lighter options altogether and go for something striking and bright such as a burnt orange, deep red or purple.

Themes. Choosing a themed wedding may dictate your choice of outfit and allows you to be as creative as you like. See many more ideas in the **Themes** chapter.

Cultural influence. Look to other cultures for inspiration. Separates influenced by saris and the heavy gold embroidery can look stunning and similarly Oriental cheongsams can make a slimline figure look incredibly elegant.

No dress. Don't feel limited to a dress. And in Las Vegas and some naturist resorts, you can even get married in the nude. That's certainly one way to take away the 'what to wear' trauma – but then you'd just have a bigger hairdressing issue.

Star spotting. Look at the latest celebrity fashion trends – the perfect excuse to buy a trashy magazine all in the name of 'research'.

⭐ CELEBRITY SPOTLIGHT

When Dita Von Teese married Marilyn Manson she looked stunning in a dark violet Vivienne Westwood gown and when Bianca Jagger married Mick she ditched the gown altogether, sealing her place in fashion history by wearing an Yves Saint Laurent trouser suit.

Shop abroad. For a really alternative tailor, travel overseas to have your dress made. And this does not have to cost a bomb. If you head for Asia, especially countries like Thailand and Vietnam, you can combine a holiday to top up your tan with a shopping trip. Local tailors can replicate any look that you show them in photos at a fraction of the cost and in local fabrics like Vietnamese silk. The garments are not built to last but unless you are Miss Havisham, they don't need to.

Lengths. Even if you do go for a traditional wedding dress it needn't necessarily sweep down to the floor. See if different shapes suit you, such as ballerina-length dresses with a 50s-style flared skirt.

Fun with shoes. An athlete might want to wear trainers. An Elton John fan might go for some huge glittery boots. Or platform shoes for the vertically challenged. They don't have to feature in all the photos if you don't want and can add a quirky touch to the day for your guests to remember.

More than one. If you are having a register office marriage and a separate ceremony then you will get the chance to wear two outfits and you might even be able to justify a third as your going-away outfit. So if money is no object and you are having difficulty choosing between convention and contemporary, take advantage and have both.

Dress down, dress up. The idea of weddings tends to invoke thoughts of formalwear but celebrities are trailblazing the way for dress-down attire. Surely it's easy enough to find a middle ground with all that in mind!

CELEBRITY SPOTLIGHT

Multimillionaire pop star Nicky Byrne from Westlife thought he'd keep his register office marriage low-key and turned up in T-shirt, jeans and a baseball cap to marry Georgina Ahern. The couple did, however, dress up a little more for the official day in France four days later.

Other brides that have followed the dress-down trend for their register office weddings but dressed up for the official 'do' are Sara Cox, who wore a floral summer dress, and pal Zoë Ball, who wore a cowboy hat, ripped jeans and carried a bottle of Jack Daniel's.

When actor and comedian Johnny Vegas married after a whirlwind romance with Catherine Donnelly he opted for a gangster edge to his outfit and turned up in a 70s-style suit topped off with a trilby.

And last, but not least, one of the most extreme celeb examples of rejecting the traditional outfit has to be the ill-fated marriage of Pamela Anderson and Tommy Lee, who got married in skimpy beach wear.

BRIDESMAIDS

Half the fun of shopping for your wedding outfit is going along with your bridesmaids and choosing what they will wear. After making all the usual jokes about how you're going to truss them up like turkeys you can get down to the serious business of finding something that will not only complement your colour scheme but also the bridesmaids themselves. As with a lot of choices this will probably come down to budget, at least

Bridesmaids and groomsmen traditionally dressed to resemble the bride and groom to confuse evil spirits so that they wouldn't be able to curse the happy couple. Meanwhile, back in reality ...

in part. Bridesmaid dresses tend to start at fairly criminal prices (for something they will probably never wear again) but there's no reason why you need to buy a dedicated bridesmaid dress. In fact your bridesmaids will no doubt thank you for NOT doing so. Short sassy dresses look great for summer weddings and there are a whole host of evening dresses in the shops that could be just what you're looking for. This can end up costing you a lot less, which in turn will leave money for accessories, hairdos, makeovers and so on.

Remember to be considerate of your bridesmaids' different shapes and sizes and make sure their dresses are as flattering as possible to all of them. Alternatively, there is no reason why your bridesmaids need to be dressed identically. You will probably want to keep some semblance of a theme but some variety in the colour, cut or fabric can look very effective. We've even heard of a wedding where each bridesmaid wore a different colour of the rainbow and we are assured that this was to stunning effect.

But it is not necessarily all fun with your bridesmaids. An astonishing number of brides have horror stories to tell about their attendants chucking wobblies about what they are asked to wear and totally losing sight of the role they have been asked to play. Faced with this situation try to avoid confrontation but don't give up your dream. Do your best to talk the issue through; be reasonable but resolute in what you want to achieve. It is your wedding after all.

There is a school of thought that says that your bridesmaids should pay for their own dresses. That seems pretty unreasonable to us, especially since they probably won't wear the outfits again and they might not be to their taste. What is more acceptable is to ask them to buy their own shoes, provided that they are definitely something that they will wear again.

GEAR FOR THE GROOM AND GROOMSMEN (A NOTE FOR THE MEN)

As the groom it is up to you whether you want the bride to see your outfit before your wedding day and she may not want you to see hers. But if you have agreed to follow a theme, take any fabric samples or colour palettes along when you shop so that you can co-ordinate your outfits. Whatever you decide, take the time to have a proper fitting. You might find out that you can dress in a much more flattering manner than you do at the moment and learn something about trouser and sleeve lengths.

The ushers and best man generally wear the same as each other and often the same as the groom, although you don't have to stick to this format. One groom-to-be we spoke to was determined his groomsmen were all going to be dressed in white flared 70s suits on the day, while another dressed his in light linen suits complete with Cuban cigars for later in the evening. One note of caution: if you are going to hire suits then make sure you reserve them well in advance, particularly in the busy summer season.

 A morning suit is the traditional choice and easy to hire or buy from any specialist. Wedding etiquette dictates that morning suits should be black in the morning and grey in the afternoon (an expensive, unnecessary convention) and the bottom button of a waistcoat should be left undone. There is also the option of frock coats to consider if this is to your taste. But only the best man and groom should wear cravats. Everyone else is stuck with ties.

If you want further inspiration, then check out the bridal magazines – they have outfits for both brides and grooms. As well as the basics of their outfits guys should think about the extras too. Cufflinks, ties, jewellery, watches and maybe even a hipflask for steadying the nerves.

Guys always seem to be a lot easier to dress than girls. Put them in a morning suit and everyone's happy. But before you plump for the first thing that comes to mind, remember that you do have other options.

Nehru suit. The Asian-style suit with a high collar against the neck can cut a dashing figure, particularly with paler linen suits worn at summer weddings.

Waistcoats. Even for the most traditional of weddings, you can get away with a waistcoat that, shall we say, shows off your personality. If you are planning on wearing a cravat, go for a suit or waistcoat with a slightly higher neckline – it will help to keep the cravat under control.

Black tie. For a lot of ladies this is the sexiest outfit for a man, so it could be perfect on your wedding day. Classic and classy and great for an evening wedding with a full black-tie theme.

White tuxedo. Smart black trousers, white pleated dress shirt, bow tie and cummerbund topped off with a white jacket. Very 007.

Lounge suit. This is a more relaxed option for a less formal wedding or for those grooms who feel uncomfortable in the full wedding paraphernalia. Lounge suits are basically casual suits so can be any colour, and you can co-ordinate your tie and shirt with the overall colour scheme. Or don't wear a tie at all. Another bonus of this option is that it's something that you will no doubt be able to use again for other occasions.

Separates. For an even more casual feel you don't have to wear a suit at all. Any combination of separates is fine but check that your venues are okay with your final decision.

Kilts. If you are a true Scotsman you can wear your own clan's tartan and leave your underwear at home. Or if not, simply hire a kilt from Moss Bros and fake your Celtic roots.

Uniforms. Every girl loves a man in uniform, or so they say. If you are in the forces or services you may choose to honour your profession – you certainly won't get any complaints from the ladies.

Bright colours. Whatever you wear, if it is bright, you are a lot less likely to feel like you are about to trip off to work or an interview.

Theme. Reflect any theme that you have running through your wedding.

Team wedding strip. And we're not talking striptease. This is your chance to design your kit for the day, whether that be a variation on a football kit or any other item of clothing that makes you stand out from the crowd.

Wacky. As long as your officiant is happy with your choice you could wear swimming trunks, a boiler suit, catsuit, gimp suit, furry zebra outfit or even a pantomime horse. Let your imagination run riot. If outrageous is your style it is probably worth checking your bride is OK with this and won't turn on her heels and head for the hills the minute she lays eyes on you.

Shoes. While you don't want to turn up in your battered everyday shoes, it can also be crippling to wear new shoes and discover that they rub the skin on your feet until it ends up shredded in your socks. If you can, wear them around indoors a few times before the big day.

THEMES

From the sublime to the ridiculous, a theme for your wedding can make it a unique occasion that everyone will remember for the right reasons.

For some this might just be a consistent style and colour running through the wedding outfits, table decorations, invitations and flowers. For others it means full-on themed dress and surroundings.

Ultimately, a theme can be as much or as little as you want it to be. Pick and choose to design the perfect wedding for both of you. You might even want to mix ideas – a winter wedding with black-tie dress, or a reception in a Bedouin-style tent with a hog roast. Just remember that if you go over the top or buy lots of cheap decorations you are in danger of winning the 'Cheesy Wedding of the Year' award. But carried off effectively, themes can be stylish and have great impact.

Some of these ideas are hard to convey without photos, but let your imagination explore them and you may find just what you're looking for. If you are on a budget simple ideas often go a long way and if you have money to burn then you could think about hiring an event organiser who specialises in themes to create the effect for you.

SUBTLE THEMES

These can add a little touch of something different to personalise your wedding. Subtle themes are good for those on a budget or simply for bringing the whole thing together.

BUTTERFLIES AND/OR FEATHERS

This theme is easier to cater to than many because event companies and wedding specialists like Confetti have butterfly- and feather-shaped invitations, confetti, favour boxes and 3D decorations for tables, chairs and flowers.

Other touches include:

✓ Butterfly or feather detailing on the bridal gown, veil or in your hair

✓ A butterfly or feathered mask instead of a traditional veil could be very striking

✓ Feathers on your accessories, maybe even a feather boa

✓ Feathers or fabric butterflies on wire to use in the bouquet

✓ Butterfly or fairy wings for any very young bridesmaids to flutter around in

✓ Attach fabric butterflies or feathers to the wedding cars, especially if you are driving in convoy

✓ Have your reception at a venue with a butterfly house or aviary or even simply in some open gardens

✓ Decorated banners for the ceiling or walls of your marquee or venue

✓ Themed table decorations; from napkin rings to embroidered tablecloths and shaped cookie favours

✓ Weave decorations into the trees and bushes with fairy lights, especially if you are having an outdoor wedding (if you have kids, stop them getting bored by designing a simple game around finding all the butterfly shapes and any clues or treasures you want to attach to them)

✓ Releasing white doves at the end of your ceremony

✓ Butterfly cakes as nibbles, favours or piled high in place of a wedding cake

✓ Themed cocktail stirrers and cocktail names – you could create the Red Admiral, Painted Lady or Elegant Peacock

✓ Hire a professional face painter to paint different styles of butterflies or birds on the kids

HEARTS AND FLOWERS

As with butterflies and feathers, let your chosen motif flavour every part of your wedding. Plus for a flower theme either use your favourite, a selection or go nice and simple with something like a daisy or rose theme. See the **Flowers** chapter for how to get imaginative with blooms.

COLOURS

The simplest of themes, but choosing a colour can be just what's needed to bring it all together.

CELEBRITY SPOTLIGHT

When Mel B (AKA Scary Spice) married her first husband, dancer Jimmy Gulzar, they asked their guests to wear white, transport for the couple was a white vintage Cadillac, the church was decorated with white lilies and a white tunnel shielded guests from the glare of the press as they walked from the drive to the white reception marquee. And naturally, the bride outshone all in her sparkly white number with feathers.

Fellow Spice Girl, Victoria and David Beckham had a regal touch at their wedding. While it is unlikely that anyone other than them could carry that off, you could always go for the same rich and regal colours of deep purples and reds using lots of plush, velvety fabrics.

If you like this idea but can't decide on a colour, you could always go and get your colour charts done with your bridesmaids to work out what is going to look best with all of you and any complementary combinations. Silver, gold or any primary colours are a great option either on their own or in combination with other colours, because you will find it easy to get decorations to enhance your theme at high-street prices. And crisp white linen is set off a treat by oranges, yellows and turquoises in summer, or raspberries, purples and greens in winter.

Echo your chosen colour scheme throughout your cocktails and drinks, favours, table settings, flowers, bridesmaids' dresses, groomsmen's cravats and ties, stationery and anything else that crops up, even food.

> Colours were the prominent theme at my wedding. My dress was Baileys coloured, my bridesmaids were in a purple-looking fabric, which was actually a weave of dark blue and dark red that changed colour as it caught the light. We carried these colours throughout the wedding, from the flowers, to the ribbons on the invitations, groomsmen's cravats and even to the bowls of sweets and disposable cameras on each table.
>
> Jo, 27

BLACK TIE

A lot of your guests will be very appreciative of this theme because they will be able to buy an outfit they can use again. Everyone gets to don their glad rags and feel in the party mood and black tie will give any event an instant sense of occasion. You can also easily combine this with other themes to create your perfect day.

HATS

Unless you are a close family member or going to a society wedding, a lot of people don't wear hats to weddings any more. If you want to make the occasion more formal you can tell everyone that this is the theme. This can also tie in well with other themes such as a horse-racing day.

Make it a bit more fun by having a prize-giving ceremony during the speeches if you like. You can let your guests know in advance if they are going to be judged on most attractive hat or if there are also categories for originality and appropriateness.

WINTER WEDDING

Create your own sumptuous winter wonderland, whether this be in a fully fledged ice palace or a cosy country-house drawing room, complete with roaring log fire.

OUTFITS AND COLOUR SCHEMES

A white, silver, gold or ivory outfit will look stunning against deep, dark winter colours. Or maybe you want to go for something in a rich, heavy velvet fabric. Reds and greens immediately spring to mind but just because it's a winter wedding doesn't mean you have to go for all the traditional Christmas colours. How about blues, purples and fuchsia pink?

Fake fur will also add a dramatic edge to your winter outfit. If your wedding is near Christmas, you could make up red stoles or capes edged in white fur for young bridesmaids. Or to finish off a snow queen look, how about a sparkling tiara?

You might be getting your dress made up in June but will it suit the weather in January? If you've got a light dress make sure you have something to keep you warm, and if you've got a long train and floor-length dress think about how you're going to negotiate the wet pathways. Buy co-ordinating umbrellas for you and the wedding party to match your outfits and prepare for all eventualities.

CELEBRITY SPOTLIGHT

If budget is no problem, then you have the opportunity to go completely to town and deck your venue out in style. For the premier party of the James Bond movie *Die Another Day* the Royal Albert Hall was transformed into an ice palace.

DECORATIONS

Snowflake motifs, white fairy lights, ice sculptures, church candles and tiny bells will all help create an atmosphere. And silver and gold glitter will add a finishing touch to the tables. Deck the halls with boughs of holly, ivy and whatever other evergreen plants you can lay your hands on.

If yours is a Christmas wedding, you could also have luxury crackers in an assortment of colours, or bags of gold coins instead of favours.

For your very own ice palace have lots of fake fur throws around the room to give people somewhere cosy to sit down and maybe even snuggle up. If you have your hearts set on snow for a magical wintry experience, you can always fake it with a snow machine, while indoor sparklers and fireworks outside will add to the magical feel.

> *I loved the fact that we decorated the venue ourselves. We bought all the decorations and then our whole family and some of our friends just 'decked the halls'. It was great because I'd had this vision of what I wanted the room to look like – all fairy lights, candles and sparkles – but I didn't think I'd be able to put it into words to ensure it ended up the way I wanted. I also didn't think I'd be able to afford the vision I had if I paid someone else to do it! So my sister took me to a trade supplier and we bought all the stuff to decorate the venue at a really reasonable price (and Tescos was unbeatable for fairy lights!). Then we just let rip with our imaginations. It took about ten to fifteen people three hours to get everything done but the effect took my breath away. And it wasn't that expensive. Plus, as it was a Christmas wedding, we all now have enough Crimble decorations to last us a lifetime!*
>
> MARIE, 29

A FAMILY AFFAIR

If you are in a venue with grounds and it has been snowing the kids are bound to be excited, so have someone on standby to build snowmen and co-ordinate sledge rides.

A real fire is a nice touch, especially if you have a secondary room that you envisage your more elderly guests might like to retire to. Big sofas and brandies all round. Later on in the evening, if more of you fancy the idea of sinking into the sofas, send the grannies off to bed and crack open the cigars. But beware – the need to make inebriated speeches leaning on the fireplace could overwhelm anyone at any time.

For some pre-Christmas entertainment, give everyone a chance to sing along with some traditional carol singers when they first arrive at the venue. And who says you can't have Santa at a wedding?

FOOD

✓ Mince pies and rich treats on arrival at the reception. And have nibbles available to warm everyone up; roasted nuts and of course chestnuts or marshmallows ready to toast will go down a treat

✓ Your gut instinct is probably to steer completely clear of turkey and all the trimmings. But stop and think – how many times do you actually have turkey in the run up to Christmas? Maybe it's not such a strange idea after all for a December wedding

✓ Anything hot, cosy and filling will go down well when it's cold outside

DRINK

✓ Mulled wine, hot rum or eggnog

✓ Later in the evening serve real hot chocolate with a jug of brandy to lace your drinks to your personal taste

✓ If you fancy making your ice sculptures more entertaining, they are also available as luge shots for spirits. The spirit shot goes in the top and comes out somewhere else on the sculpture, chilled and either into a glass or straight into the mouths of your more daring guests

BUDGET

Make the most of what's available for Christmas and if you're organised in time, pick up your decorations in the previous January's sales. Whatever you do, don't get carried away with the *Blue Peter* tips – leave the cotton wool alone. That said, if you have children of your own, they would probably be thrilled to help you make wintry decorations for your wedding.

If you can't afford to employ someone to entertain the kids in the snow, nominate someone, give them a carrot, two coals and a scarf and lock them outside with the little darlings.

Winter food should be hot and stodgy, so one giant cauldron of chilli, a casserole, stew or giant shepherd's pie should be fine for everyone (but remember to factor in special dietary requirements).

MIDSUMMER NIGHT'S DREAM

Embrace the magic of the night with a summertime theme to enchant your guests.

> Here come the lovers, full of joy and mirth.
> Joy, gentle friends, joy and fresh days of love
> Accompany your hearts.
>
> A MIDSUMMER NIGHT'S DREAM, ACT 5 SCENE 1, 28–30

OUTFITS AND COLOUR SCHEMES

✓ Either a traditional princess-like wedding dress or adopt a more ethereal, floaty look

✓ Wear a crown of real flowers instead of a tiara, or wild flowers entwined in your tussled tresses

✓ The groom could opt for more natural colours for his suit with a slightly bohemian edge

- ✓ Natural, woodland colour schemes work well with this theme. Choose one to suit your time of year

- ✓ Make it clear on your invitations that you would like your guests to wear something in keeping with the theme rather than formalwear

- ✓ Young bridesmaids will love being dressed as fairies complete with wings and tiaras or crowns of flowers and ivy. They can even have sparkly wands. Complete their look by giving them baskets of flowers or loosely tied posies instead of formal bouquets

- ✓ For true authenticity threaten to dress your groomsmen as Puck and Bottom (or perhaps that's taking it a bit far – unless the stag-night antics mean that they deserve it)

DECORATIONS

Opt for an outdoor reception or bring the outdoors in by using lots of greenery, white fairy lights and maybe even have some fairy motifs dotted about. You can also hire blankets of tiny lights to cover the ceiling and resemble a starlit night sky. The ultimate aim is for your guests to walk into the room or marquee and believe they could have stepped into Shakespeare's woodland fantasy world.

Name your tables after characters from the play and use quotes in the invitations and other stationery. Pinecones, sprayed gold, silver or left natural make great place-name holders. But make sure they are creepy-crawly free! Top wooden tables off with white tablecloths and have plenty of wild flowers in simple vases, jars or pretty bottles dotted around to complete the rustic woodland feel. For alternative favours, give little books of Shakespeare quotes, copies of the play, magic tricks or sparklers.

A FAMILY AFFAIR

- ✓ Keep extra fairy wings and sparkly wands on standby as favours for the kids

- ✓ If you have a number of young children attending, have a woodland storyteller for them in a separate room sitting in an enchanted chair

MUSIC AND ENTERTAINMENT

✓ Make the most of the enchanting atmosphere by hiring a table magician to weave around your guests, amazing them with tricks

✓ As people arrive at the reception or while you are still having your photos taken, entertain everyone with a few actors quoting lines or acting out scenes from Shakespeare's play

✓ Although you'll probably still want a band or DJ, a string quartet or medieval-style band with lute and harp will provide fitting background music until people are ready to start dancing

✓ Fireworks, though not exactly Shakespearean, will give your night a truly magical ending

DRINK

✓ Start with refreshing summer drinks like spritzers and Pimms

✓ Move on to cocktails disguised as magical potions or named after characters from the play

BUDGET

A Midsummer Night's Dream is all about the magic of the night. Organise your wedding or blessing at dusk and then you only have to feed everyone once.

If the cost of bringing the outdoors indoors is too much to bear, then stay outdoors. You can really cut costs by using your own garden for your reception. You could have a blessing there too if you choose and so shift the whole emphasis of the day outside. Just be cautious about your reliance on the weather.

ENGLISH GARDEN THEME

Think Jane Austen-style elegance or 1930s garden party. Whichever appeals to you the emphasis is on that truly English feel, so pick and choose the elements you are most drawn to.

OUTFITS AND COLOUR SCHEMES

Pastel colours are ideal to carry throughout the wedding, especially in the summer. Think Edwardian greens, rose pinks, lavender and lemon yellows.

Princess-line classic cuts, *Pride and Prejudice*-style frocks, and more natural fabrics apply here. Tie your hair up with loose curls to frame your face and entwine flowers in your hair but remember that these days there is no excuse for a grown woman to wear a bonnet. Gents can opt for the Mr Darcy look (wet shirt optional) or light stylish suits. Parasols for your bridesmaids will complete their English lady look.

DECORATIONS

The beautiful English rose would be quite at home in a country-house garden with guests spilling out onto the lawn or the Olde English bride can celebrate in a beautifully renovated barn. If you want to create an English garden feel you can even hire white picket fencing.

Fill your venue with lots of wild and cottage garden flowers. Lavender, sweet peas and roses are readily available, fragranced blooms. If you are getting married in springtime, you can also use tree blossom, catkins and delicate spring flowers such as snowdrops, crocuses, miniature daffodils and violets.

As the dusk draws in, light your venue with striking table centrepieces, such as scented candles in tall candle holders decorated with flowers and ivy. For an authentic barn look, sit people on hay bales (although this will play havoc with the hay-fever sufferers).

A FAMILY AFFAIR

When it comes to favours for the ladies, give keepsakes around the wild-flower theme or pretty bottles of rose or lavender water. Children can have classic English storybooks to keep or bags of old-fashioned sweets, while the gents will be happy with brandy or port miniatures. No stereotypes there then.

MUSIC AND ENTERTAINMENT

✓ If your budget will stretch to it and distances allow, transport the guests between the different locations by old-fashioned horse-drawn carts or hay rides

✓ If you want to ham up the 'English fayre' angle, entertain your guests with a coconut shy, hoopla and a tug-of-war (never mind the grass stains). Top it off with candyfloss or toffee apples

✓ Croquet or bowls on the lawn will give your reception a classic English atmosphere

✓ Once night falls, light up your venue with lanterns and outside have a huge romantic roaring fire. Provide marshmallows for toasting while the band plays or fireworks light up the sky

✓ If you are worried you're going to struggle to get people onto the dance floor, have a barn dance and an enthusiastic caller to make sure everyone does their bit for fear of being singled out

FOOD

✓ At an Olde English or Medieval wedding, an alternative to the big sit-down meal is a hog roast and buffet. Everyone can help themselves and if you want to you can avoid a rigid seating plan. This will create a lovely buzzy atmosphere and will save you planning time

✓ Serve up strawberries and cream to top off your meal or, for a novel touch, have an ice-cream vendor (although preferably not in a multicoloured van with a megaphone on top)

✓ Depending on the time of your wedding, how about a high tea? Delicate sandwiches followed by fruit scones with lashings of strawberry jam and thick clotted cream

DRINK

✓ Real ale, cider and ice-cream sodas will complement the Olde English wedding

✓ Pimms, gin and tonic, chilled white wine and homemade lemonade are suited to the English rose

BUDGET

Hiring an authentic barn and having an informal setting gives you more space to invite more people, especially if you steer away from a sit-down meal. Cover trestle tables with affordable white linen or paper tablecloths and opt for an English fayre buffet. You can even rustle this up yourselves with the help of a few willing volunteers.

> *We just wanted to get married, have a great time with our friends and family, and get on with our new life together without a huge millstone of debt around our necks. In the end, we opted to hire a barn and found one out in Norfolk. It had an electricity supply, so we set up long trestle tables, got a live band, lit the barn with fairy lights, had a huge bonfire outside and fireworks in the evening. Even the food was easy – a pig on a spit with salad, fresh bread and cider, beer and wine to finish it off. Doing it this way kept stress to a minimum. It was really low-budget and everyone had a fantastic time. We wouldn't change a thing.*
>
> ROB AND SARAH, 36 AND 32

HIGHLAND FLING

If you have Scottish blood or even just aspirations to wear tartan, a Highland fling wedding will provide a warm and very lively backdrop for your nuptials.

OUTFITS AND COLOUR SCHEMES

For those with family tartan, you might be heavily influenced regarding your choice of colour but if you have free rein, lilacs and greens conjure up an idea of Scotland and its Highlands.

The groom does not have to wear a kilt for a Scottish theme, but it certainly helps. But will he stand the test of a true Scot? Probably not a good idea if there are a lot of children and grannies present. It is worth noting that if the groom-to-be opts for tartan, nothing else has to tie into his colours as they are stand-alone.

DECORATIONS

✓ Scatter heather, thistles and lavender around your venue for a purple hue and a fantastic fragrance

✓ Use a combination of white and lilac table linen with tartan or lilac and green ribbons

✓ Infuse these colours throughout your wedding stationery, decorations and use lavender flowers to decorate your cake

✓ Scotch whisky miniatures and decorated shortbread favours (your more elderly lady guests might appreciate delicate lavender sachets instead)

MUSIC AND ENTERTAINMENT

✓ A bagpipe player to give you a dramatic serenade at the ceremony or as you enter the reception venue

✓ Learn the Highland fling for your first dance and hire a Scottish ceilidh band to lead you in the dance

✓ Hire some Scottish dancers to come and give you a display at the start of your reception or while your guests are waiting for you to finish with your photo call

✓ Host a mini Highland Games (this is also a great idea for the day after the wedding – that way if anyone puts their back out tossing the caber they won't disrupt the wedding itself!)

✓ A must for a Scottish party is to get everyone up and dancing

FOOD

To be traditional you should go for porridge and haggis. Or you could go for food people will actually eat. How about kedgeree? Scotland has a whole range of its own dishes including cock-a-leekie soup, mashed potatoes, mashed turnips, smoked haddock soup, and it is internationally renowned for its tasty salmon.

DRINK

A wee dram is the key. Naturally it has to be whisky and you could also serve hot toddies at the end of the night.

INDIAN INSPIRATION

Before you do anything else, watch the film *Monsoon Wedding* for inspiration on how to have a British wedding with an Indian flavour.

OUTFITS AND COLOUR SCHEMES

✓ An Indian bride wears red with gold jewellery and embroidery – you can also get henna paintings on your hands and feet, toe rings, a bindi for your forehead, a jewelled tiara and lots of bangles

✓ Nehru suits for the groom and groomsmen

✓ Keep to bright colours – reds, yellows, oranges and pinks – and encourage your female guests to wear saris or heavily embroidered clothing

✓ The tradition for Indian grooms is to wear black eyeliner to ward off the evil spirits

DECORATIONS

✓ Use lots of brightly coloured fabric and gold to decorate your wedding venue. Combine silks, sheer and heavier fabrics for a sumptuous feel. Wall hangings and scatter cushions will complete the look

✓ Seat the bride and groom beneath a canopy decorated with flowers. Marigolds are lucky flowers for Indian weddings. And have garlands for the guests of honour

- ✓ Orange or pink fairy lights and lots of candles in coloured glass bowls or lanterns

- ✓ Use a large but shallow bowl of water on each table and cover the surface of the water with lotus flower or water lily heads and candles. Or use a substitute flower to keep the costs down and achieve the same effect

- ✓ Provide flower petals for confetti and a carpet of petals for the bride to approach her groom during the ceremony

- ✓ Incense on the tables will give a mysterious haze

- ✓ Fun favours ideas include floral garlands, bindis and henna tattoos

MUSIC AND ENTERTAINMENT

A bhangra band is a must and if you fancy doing the 'screwing in the light bulbs' dancing, this could be for you. Belly dancers and a palm reader could provide additional entertainment for you and your guests.

> *Once everyone was settled at their dinner tables for the reception, Simon and I walked into the room with the Dhol (drum) player from the bhangra band we had hired for the evening. He was banging out a bhangra-style beat so that we could kind of dance as we walked and weave in and out of the tables to the top table. It was fantastic – my favourite bit of the whole day!*
>
> SHILPA, 27

FOOD

Have a traditional Indian table buffet for each table to give your guests the benefits of a buffet without having to leave their chairs. Customarily, this will include lots of vegetarian food. Creamy and milk-based desserts such as kulfi (Indian ice cream) can top off your meal.

DRINK

Lassis are traditional, but not bang lassis unless you want everyone to end up starry-eyed.

JAPANESE

Posh and Becks' pre-World Cup party might not have been a wedding but it was an amazingly well-themed Japanese party with no expense spared. Even if you don't have quite the same budget you can pick up plenty of ideas to create a Japanese experience of your own.

OUTFITS AND COLOUR SCHEMES

✓ Use red and white to allude to the national flag, along with black and creams to complement and dilute the scheme and make it feel classy and clean rather than brash

✓ For a complete alternative to western wedding outfits, the bride and bridesmaids can wear kimonos and Japanese silk dresses with make-up inspired by the classic geisha-girl look

✓ High-necked suits in beautiful fabrics for the men

DECORATIONS

✓ Cherry blossom, plum blossom and chrysanthemums are the national flowers of Japan so use these in simple displays. Orchids also have a delicate oriental look to them

✓ Paper lanterns. And lots of them as, the more there are, the more effective they look

✓ Fold serviettes in origami shapes and give origami presents as favours. Origami is the ancient art of paper folding. The wedding tradition is to have 1,000 hand-folded cranes – if the bride and groom do this together, it teaches them the patience, endurance and attention to detail required to make a marriage work. They also symbolise loyalty and honour

✓ Use bold, clean lines in all decorations. Japanese screens can section off different areas of the room or just use them on the peripheries to add to the overall look

✓ Handwrite or print Japanese characters, such as those for eternal love, happiness or understanding, on all your wedding stationery. Replicate this around the room, with wall hangings or banners

✓ Fans make lovely and unusual favours as they are a symbol of happiness and good fortune for the future. Alternatively you could give small silk purses or notebooks covered in Japanese-style embroidery

✓ Willow trees are typical Japanese symbols. Get some willow twigs and leave them natural or spray them in your main wedding colour, tie them and use them as centrepieces on your tables. You can also hire plants to add to your Oriental look and feel

A FAMILY AFFAIR

Arrange for someone to show the kids how to make origami gifts. Or teach them how to write words and their name or initials in Japanese characters.

MUSIC AND ENTERTAINMENT

What could be more Japanese than karaoke? But only consider this if you have a second room to use or limit how long it lasts – once your less tuneful guests have had one too many and think they're Robbie Williams, you'll be grateful you had the foresight.

Alternatively, you could try sumo for a less formal affair. Hire padded sumo costumes and let the heifers loose.

FOOD

The Japanese follow their colour schemes throughout all aspects of their wedding catering. And red and white are the most positive, lucky colours so you can also pull this through to your food and drinks menus.

But while you might love the idea of an Oriental celebration, is it suitable for all your guests? Consider children and guests with different tastes and think before you opt for sushi all round. Traditional dishes include sushi, noodles and rice. Or you could opt for more of a buffet-style selection so that guests can pick and choose for themselves.

Chopsticks and square plates in contrasting colours have a striking effect. To be fully Japanese-style, sit on the floor cross-legged with low tables on bamboo mats – but as always, consider your older guests.

DRINK

Sake, red and white wine or red and white cocktails.

CIRCUS

This is a great opportunity for performers to shine but if you want a tightrope wedding or to say your vows as you swing on a trapeze you'll have to go overseas or settle for a blessing in the UK. This is a slightly more outlandish theme, but you can pick and choose elements for a truly entertaining day. For a more sophisticated angle think Cirque du Soleil rather than village common. Roll up, roll up!

OUTFITS AND COLOUR SCHEMES

Use bright colours everywhere. Red and white to reflect the colours of the big top and primary colours all around.

Just because you have a circus theme does not mean the bride has to look like a clown or overly made-up doll but if you want to, go for it. And maybe your groom likes the idea of playing ringmaster in top hat, red tails, jodhpurs, handlebar moustache and a whip ... Kinky.

DECORATIONS

✓ Think big top instead of a regular marquee. And wind red and white ribbon around all the poles on display

✓ Lots of multicoloured streamers, exploding confetti, glitter and party poppers will all add to the carnival atmosphere

✓ Coloured fairy lights to set the tone for most of the night, but spotlights for speeches

✓ Lots of brightly coloured helium balloons tied to the back of chairs or in the centre of tables – just make sure the strings are long enough that your guests can still see around the room

✓ Clown favour boxes with sweets and party blowers

A FAMILY AFFAIR

Custard-pie throwing and coconut shies are beckoning for a bit of old-fashioned family entertainment. You could add a puppet theatre for the kids and adults who wish they were kids.

MUSIC AND ENTERTAINMENT

✓ Hire stilt walkers, clowns, magicians, jugglers, firewalkers and acrobats

✓ Drum rolls to introduce speeches and a brass band playing as your guests mingle, or you could opt for the more enchanting feel of Cirque du Soleil-style music

✓ If you're really adventurous, strap yourself to a spinning disk, blindfold the groom and give him a couple of knives to throw at you – or perhaps not

FOOD

You can go more highbrow but to stay in theme hot dogs, hamburgers and corn on the cob are a more apt offering, while a candyfloss machine will always be a hit with children and adults alike.

DRINK

Fizzy pop packed with additives so that you end up on the verge of bursting and the kids are climbing the walls. Alcohol is an optional extra, of course.

HAWAIIAN

Aloha! The original beach party, this is *the* wedding theme for summer fun.

OUTFITS AND COLOUR SCHEMES

Vibrant colours all the way for this theme. The guys can show off their best Hawaiian shirts and, if you're really game, you can have grass skirts and bikinis for the hula bride and bridesmaids. Use tropical flowers for your hair, garlands and bouquet, if you have one. Hand out Hawaiian leis galore. Try and get everyone to wear one or at the least use them as napkin rings and hope for the best. Party shops sell artificial flower garlands or you could splash out and go for the real thing.

DECORATIONS

✓ Hawaiian garland fairy lights to string around and add a glow as night falls

✓ Wooden Tiki-style carved facemasks, along with orchids and bird-of-paradise flowers will add to the tropical atmosphere

✓ Sweetie favours in coconut shells on the tables

✓ Decorate tables with tropical fruit, cocktail glasses and umbrellas and use citrus fruits or pineapples with names on cocktail flags to mark the table name or place names

A FAMILY AFFAIR

✓ If it's a hot summer wedding, have a paddling pool and sandpit for kids. Recreate the Pacific beach atmosphere, and we're not talking hankies on your head and deckchairs

✓ Hula Hoops to entertain the kids. Have some extras to accommodate the big kids too

✓ Initiate a limbo game, although watch out for overeager oldies as you don't want to end up spending your wedding night taking relatives to casualty

MUSIC AND ENTERTAINMENT

✓ Music plays a big part in a Hawaiian theme. Live or recorded cocktail lounge music will be perfect to ease your guests into the occasion, with a steel band or ukulele and guitar band for later on to get the dancing going. And don't forget to add a dash of Elvis tunes to top your night off in style

✓ If you don't want a bouquet, throw your lei to the waiting girls instead to see who will be next to tie the knot

✓ A surf simulation machine could be the icing on the cake at your beach party if you can stretch the budget

FOOD

It has to be a barbeque for your seaside soirée. Have a seafood banquet with fresh lobster, shrimp and fish with an array of salads. Dot bowls of macadamia nuts around as nibbles and baked bananas (split down the middle and stuffed with chocolate) and fresh pineapple make a wonderful dessert.

DRINK

Gallons of tropical punch will go down a treat. Use the shell-shaped containers from children's paddling-pool kits to put punch in. And make some elaborate and sexy fruity cocktails. Try Mai Tai, Blue Hawaiian or coconut cocktails with obligatory umbrellas and mini palm trees.

BUDGET

If your wedding won't be complete without a theme but you have a tight budget, this is a good option. You can have a home-cooked barbeque rather than bringing in caterers and a lot of the accessories will be easy to find at affordable prices in party shops.

MASKED BALL

This can be a really sophisticated and elegant choice. For the ultimate example look to the Venice Festival held every February.

OUTFITS AND COLOUR SCHEMES

✓ Opulent, rich colours with lots of highly textured fabrics

✓ This theme works especially well with black-tie and Oscar-inspired glamorous outfits. Or if you want to be really elaborate encourage everyone to hire full fancy dress for a sumptuous eighteenth-century extravaganza

✓ The bride should obviously be the belle of the ball, so think about having a mask specially made to ensure that it is completely unique and matches the bridal outfit. And ask your guests to avoid a certain colour so that the two of you are the only ones wearing it. The groom could take his inspiration from Beckham and wear an ivory suit, or settle for a white rather than a black tuxedo

✓ Masks for everyone. Have a few on stand-by for forgetful guests

✓ If this lacks the fairy-tale element that you are after, you can always go for a Cinderella-style ball instead. A wedding meringue will go down a storm

DECORATIONS

Low lighting will add to the intrigue. Have candelabras on each table or clusters of smaller candles with freestanding candelabras around the room. Alternatively, plump for a period venue with high ceilings, chandeliers, ornate decoration and a grand ballroom. You can also hire Venetian-style statues and balustrades which, when carefully chosen, will really add to the Italian feel.

For more of an Oscars theme, have a red carpet at the entrance complete with poles and red ropes.

A FAMILY AFFAIR

Although this could be fun for kids, if you do intend to invite a lot of them be prepared for the fact that it won't be quite as sophisticated as you might have in mind. Keep them occupied by encouraging them to make their own masks starting with templates and using glitter, feathers and sequins. Make it a competition and present a prize for the best one.

MUSIC AND ENTERTAINMENT

- ✓ Everyone wears masks until you are married, then reveal themselves at the same time – ideal for an evening wedding or a blessing after dark

- ✓ For the Venetian carnival-style masked ball, hire masked stilt walkers, mime artists, jugglers, magicians and a wandering two- or three-piece band of musicians

- ✓ A string quartet or other classical music will provide the perfect background music

- ✓ Prepare in advance and learn to waltz for your first dance

FOOD

Canapés. Keep the time spent sitting down to eat to a minimum or have your meal later on in the evening to retain that sense of mystery for as long as possible.

DRINK

Only champagne will do to start, darling. And red wine decadence for later on.

BUDGET

So that no one is put off at the idea of hiring extortionate fancy-dress costumes, stick to the black-tie and ball-dress option or opt for formal dress and give your guests more leeway.

1930S AND '40S

A fantastic opportunity to launch into a theme that will appeal to old and young alike. And you have the option of breaking the bank or achieving an authentic look by having a wedding reception on a budget, as it would have been in the 1940s.

OUTFITS AND COLOUR SCHEMES

✓ Uniforms or pretty girl-next-door look for the ladies. Don blouses with padded shoulders, layered skirts and don't forget to draw the pencil lines up the backs of your legs

✓ For the glamorous, there's the forties film-star look. Dress to show off an hourglass figure to die for

✓ Zoot suits or armed forces uniforms for the guys

DECORATIONS

✓ Use names of bands of the time, army references, movie stars or film titles for your table plans

✓ If you are hiring a marquee go for a khaki army tent and line the walls with parachute silks. With a combination of white and khaki colours, a single deep red rose on each table will look really striking

✓ If you don't like the idea of the parachute silks, what about 1940s film posters or the shot of lovers on the station platform with the steam train in the background? Doctor them to put the faces of the bride and groom on the bodies or recreate the look from scratch. You can also hire backdrops of Spitfires in flight

✓ Issue menus on ration cards and provide dance cards for the ladies

✓ Candles or handfuls of simple flowers in jam jars

A FAMILY AFFAIR

Really involve your older guests by asking them to bring along their photos of themselves in that era and see if they will be willing to wear their wartime medals.

For extra authenticity slap the kids' hair down with a bit of spit.

MUSIC AND ENTERTAINMENT

✓ For speeches and announcements, use an authentic 1940s vintage microphone

✓ Employ a pianist to play favourites of the time for a touch of class. You could even have your first dance to a classic like 'Anything Goes', 'I've Got You Under My Skin', 'I Get a Kick Out Of You', 'As Time Goes By', 'Let's Do It (Let's Fall In Love)', 'They Can't Take That Away From Me', 'Embraceable You', 'Love Is Here To Stay', 'Someone To Watch Over Me', 'I Got Rhythm', 'Blue Moon' or 'Night And Day'. Cole Porter and Gershwin galore

✓ Dances of the time were the jitterbug, rumba, tango, samba, conga and not forgetting the Lambeth walk, so initiate these or have a dance teacher who can take to the floor for an hour or so to show everyone how it's done

✓ Swing-band music such as Glenn Miller was another favourite so, if you have the budget, hire a full band to entertain the troops

✓ You could also hire Judy Garland and Bing Crosby look- and sound-a-likes to sing to you, or Fred Astaire and Ginger Rogers look-a-likes to dance for you

FOOD

Meat and two veg. Food can be simple, especially if everyone is expecting rations! Treat them to a banana between two for dessert. And if you don't want a sit-down affair, buffet stations can be set up on army crates.

DRINK

Port and sherry.

BUDGET

Because it is the wartime era, it's a great excuse to make do with what you've got. You do not have to go out and spend a fortune hiring plush chairs and tables – use a higgledy-piggledy collection with white tablecloths.

Budget venues are an option because a lot of older village halls will have the atmosphere of an old dance hall and may even have been used as one in the past. Look for wooden floorboards, open rafters and a raised stage at one end.

1950S AND ROCK 'N' ROLL

For inspiration, settle down in front of *Grease* on the telly with a bag of popcorn, milkshake and paper and pen to take notes.

OUTFITS AND COLOUR SCHEMES

✓ Girls – rolled-up jeans and bobby socks or circle skirts and petticoats. And remember that poodles were *the* decoration of the time. Or get your twin sets out and add a dash of gingham. Sweep your hair up into a cute cheerleader ponytail

✓ Guys – pull on your leather jackets, tight white T-shirts and jeans with turn-ups and comb your hair into a quiff. And give your outfits an Elvis spin if you are fans

✓ Take the *Grease* theme further with your bridesmaids as the Pink Ladies and groomsmen as the T-Birds

✓ Or go for the alternative fifties-style and have a beatnik theme – black and tight all the way. Don't forget the berets and neck scarves

✓ Use pastel colours throughout with a particular emphasis on candyfloss pink. For the bold use red, black and white

DECORATIONS

✓ We're talking fifties diner with Formica tables and chairs and silver barstools with red tops

✓ Musical notes should inspire confetti, images on stationery and wall decorations

✓ Use bands or records from the fifties as table names for your seating plan. And vinyl records for place mats with the centre as the name card

✓ Decorate the walls with posters from the era

✓ Have a jar of gobstoppers or aniseed balls on each table instead of favours. Or yoyos, the toy of the era. Alternatively, plastic pocket combs for the men and wedding Love Heart sweeties for the ladies (0800 970 0480, www.lovehearts.com)

MUSIC AND ENTERTAINMENT

✓ Book a Teddy-boy band complete with quiffs and double bass. You could even have a live rendition of 'Love Me Tender' for your first dance

✓ Hire a Wurlitzer jukebox so that guests can pick and choose their favourite tunes

✓ Enlist the help of a dance teacher to lead everyone in rock 'n' roll, the hand jive and the mamba. Another option is to reawaken the Patrick Swayze or Jennifer Grey in your guests and get them *Dirty Dancing*

✓ Also think about hiring a caricature artist to capture everyone in their fifties style

✓ You can even go as far as having all your waiters and waitresses on roller skates

✓ It has to be a classic Cadillac for your wedding transport

FOOD

We're talking fast food; burgers, fries and ice-cream sundaes. Plus popcorn to nibble during the speeches.

DRINK

Strawberry and banana daiquiris or milkshakes, ice-cream soda and cola floats for the non-drinkers.

MORE INSPIRATION FOR THEMES

BEDOUIN

With cool, light and bright fabrics in rich hues of reds, oranges, pinks and yellows adorning Bedouin-style tents, this relaxed theme still manages to have an air of majesty and intrigue about it. Draw inspiration from the desert sunsets, sand palaces, market bazaars or a lush oasis. And tap into the sandpit and flying-carpet angle to keep the kids amused – an enthusiastic storyteller with a copy of *1001 Arabian Nights* should do the trick.

As the evening wears on, entertain the adults with belly dancing and food, drink and music with a distinctly North African feel. For a more fun angle, you can offer camel rides – well not rides exactly, but believe it or not you can hire a 'bucking camel' (as opposed to a bucking bronco).

BUBBLES

Another more subtle theme that can blend seamlessly through all elements of your wedding preparation. Carry the theme of circles through all the stationery. Have a bubble machine, bubbles on the tables, sparkling wine, champagne and fizzy cocktails and mini champagne-style bottles of bubbles as favours.

CASINO

James Bond-style, bring Monte Carlo to you. A black-tie do finished off with a private casino for everyone to have a flutter. Plenty of event companies specialise in these evenings for corporate events and as long as you don't use real money you don't need a licence.

> I've got more than one ideal wedding scenario, whether hubby-to-be and I are rich or not.
>
> The simple one would be to start with a breakfast with the family, then get married and have a late lunch with others and then a dinner with mates – shifts of guests gathering round the same table, if that makes sense. Of course, it would have to be a square table so that I could hear what everyone was saying. And obviously my husband would have to be an orphan!
>
> Second idea is to go to Sweden to the Ice Hotel with a small number of guests. I would arrange to have them picked up in a sled with husky dogs and then have an evening ceremony lit by candles followed by a black-tie do and plenty of vodka on the rocks. Just like the James Bond movie.
>
> Or finally, I would love to go to the Sahara Desert and set up camp in the old-fashioned harem, Bedouin style. About five days should do it. Lots of parties and getting married at some point in the middle.
>
> HENRIETTA, 32

HALLOWEEN

We all know the Americans are very into Halloween and lots of people in the UK are catching on. If you do this British style, then you'll have everyone dressed like old hags, witches and warlocks. If you go with the American ideal you need to fish out your old *E.T.* video to get some ideas for wild, wacky and totally unrelated fancy-dress themes.

Light your venues with tea lights inside pumpkin heads and have roaming wizards performing tricks to add to the magical atmosphere.

HORSE-RACING DAY

Name your tables after horses and use silk colours as your inspiration. Or go the whole hog and head for the races. Either hire a box or just take a picnic along for a simple wedding celebration.

> *I would love a summer or spring wedding. At the reception I would have trestle tables, a high tea like the Mad Hatter's tea party with lots of paper lanterns, big colourful teapots, tea plates of scones, pots of jam and cream, champers, cucumber sandwiches, dolly cakes and meringues in nibble size, not forgetting the Eat Me, Drink Me slogans on favours and glasses.*
>
> REBECCA, 28

MEDIEVAL

This is becoming quite a common theme now so ferret around on the Internet for ideas. Spit roasts, chain mail and swords, damsels, mead, knights in armour, men in tights, court jesters, chivalry and a good bit of jousting.

MEXICAN

If you're both great fans of Mexican food and bright colours, this could be for you. Use lots of bright and vivid colours with Spanish-style flamenco-inspired dresses for the bride and bridesmaids. Use chilli-shaped fairy lights and the colours of the Mexican flag (red, white and green) to decorate your venue. Have a piñata for the kids (who cares if it's meant to be for birthdays?) and salsa dancing to get the party going (think about hiring a teacher to get to grips with the basic steps). You can even get tequila belts for waitresses so they can wander around offering shots to people. One supplier that offers this is Shooter belts (www.shooterbelts.com).

1980S

Big hair and bad clothes. Who wouldn't be surprised if your first dance was a break dance?

1920S

Girls dressed as flappers, with headbands, fringed dresses, dolly shoes, long strings of pearls, rosebud lips and cigarette holders. Dance the Charleston and the cancan.

SOUTH-EAST ASIAN

Ideal if Thai, Vietnamese or Indonesian culture, food or fashion appeal. Perhaps you both travelled extensively round the area and have fond memories that you would like to relive on your wedding day. Maybe you even had a legal ceremony or are planning on taking your honeymoon in one of these countries. Alternatively, if Chinese culture holds a special appeal for you, light up your reception celebrations with Chinese lanterns and a dancing dragon.

SPORTS DAY

A real family affair if you have a lot of kids. This is also an excellent budget idea for informal weddings because food can be picnic style or lunch buffet. A lot of villages have cricket houses on the green that are available for hire at very reasonable rates – they will have a kitchen, loos and plenty of room for everyone inside in case it rains.

THIS IS YOUR LIFE

If you love the idea of getting everyone involved in your wedding, then give them all the chance to contribute to a *This is Your Life*-style wedding. Informal anecdotes about the bride and groom will help the families and friends get to know each other and the group to bond. And you'll get more variety from a mixture of short stories than just a few long speeches. Just prepare yourselves for the fact that you could end up being the butt of a lot of jokes.

UNDER THE SEA

Beautiful sea nymphs, mysterious mermaids and sophisticated shimmering goddesses in silver and aquamarines. If you don't want to wear costumes, just use the green and blue hues to create a marine or nautical theme. Ditch flowers altogether or entwine anemone flowers or the spiky gerberas that resemble anemones around seashells, pebbles and driftwood. Use fish bowls as vases or, depending on your guests, as cocktail glasses. You'll certainly have a few drunken sailors around then. Decorate tables with star-shaped confetti for starfish, write names on pebbles in place of name cards and put favours in shell-shaped bowls.

REALITY CHECK

Weddings are very expensive for everyone involved and it is a once-in-a-lifetime opportunity to do things your way. You need to decide how important a theme is for you and how far you want to take it. Is a theme how you want to remember your wedding or, indeed, how you want it captured for posterity? If you are asking all of your guests to dress up, is it something they are likely to be able or willing to afford to do? If not and the theme is make or break for you, you might want to ask them to spend their money on their outfits rather than on wedding gifts, or risk that they might not be able to fork out the cash to come.

INVITATIONS AND STATIONERY

Clearly, things have changed somewhat.

Your choice of stationery will be the first official indication that helps to set your guests' expectations as to the kind of wedding they are being invited to. So what message do you want to give exactly?

> Traditionally, the bride's parents (as hosts) sent out the invitations six to eight weeks before the wedding and replies were sent back to them. The upside of this is that the gift list could be sent from a bride's mother to guests without seeming presumptuous. Invitations would also be sent to couples, harking back to the days when married people would attend together and unmarried women would be frowned upon if they were out in public without a chaperone.

With divorced parents and couples getting married later and paying for their own weddings, there is not the same basis for this etiquette.

So, does everything have to be so complicated? Not to mention expensive?

INVITATION WORDING

> Conventional practices suggest that invitation wording is in the third person and varies according to who is 'hosting' or paying for the lion's share of the wedding, such as:

Bride's mother and father are paying – Mr and Mrs [bride's father's first name and surname] request the pleasure of your company at the marriage of their daughter, [bride's first names], to Mr [groom's first name and surname] at [venue] on [date], and afterwards at [reception venue].

The bride and groom are paying – [Bride's first name and surname] and [groom's first name and surname] request the pleasure of your company at their marriage at ...

When addressing the invitations, etiquette suggests married couples should be addressed as Mr and Mrs [husband's first name, surname]. Or if they have kids; Mr and Mrs [husband's first name, surname], [child 1 first name] and [child 2 first name]. On the envelope, formal invitations should only be addressed to the wife, however, using the 'Mrs [husband's first and surnames]' format.

The RSVP address is traditionally that of the person or people hosting the wedding, but it is fine if you choose to delegate this role to someone else. You should also include a phone number for quick replies and any queries.

Divorced parents – Mr [bride's father's first name and surname] and Mrs [bride's mother's first name and surname] request the pleasure of your company at the marriage of their daughter ...

KEEP ETIQUETTE IN CHECK

The problem with these rules is that they seem inflexible. What if you think of your stepfather as your real father? Or someone else is paying for the wedding but you are doing all the organising and want all the invitations to come from you? And do you use 'would like to invite you to the wedding of' or the more formal 'request the pleasure of your company at the marriage of' or 'request the pleasure of the company of [guest name] at the marriage of'?

In short, there are no hard-and-fast rules. Etiquette should only exist to make life easier. If you don't want to follow it, then don't. You could send an invite asking everyone to 'Swing on over to our place to see us tie the knot' if that is more your style. All you have to think about is the message you are giving to everyone and if that is consistent with your ideal wedding. But also remember to keep this in perspective – invite your guests in whichever way suits you. People are coming to share your special day with you, not judge your stationery.

VARIATIONS

There is an overwhelming array of options for how you produce your stationery:

Bespoke, unique. Scan wedding stationery catalogues for inspiration and then work with a supplier or on your own to design a unique look. As a result the unit cost is likely to be higher. Some printers will also print your guests' names on the stationery for you – the downside to this is that if you have 'extras' or last-minute changes it can be expensive to amend the odd one and you might end up making corrections by hand.

Personalised, printed. A catalogue item that prints the wording specific to your wedding. These are fairly reasonable, starting from just under a pound per invitation. Prices vary depending on detail, the degree to which they are handmade and quality. Again, some suppliers will also print the guests' names on the stationery with the same downside as above.

Pre-formatted, shop-bought. These are the most reasonably priced option because they are mass-produced and have a standard message with blanks for your personal information. You can get them at the usual high-street stationery outlets such as WHSmith.

Handwritten (and even handmade). For that personal touch. Probably only practical for smaller weddings unless you have a craft god or goddess for a best mate or a lot of time on your hands.

There are also more than just invitations to consider when you are commissioning or planning your stationery.

'Hold the date' cards. Although your elderly relatives are not booked up months in advance, your friends could well be, especially if you know lots of people who are getting married or if you are inviting people from overseas. Practicalities and final arrangements will mean that you probably cannot send out the official invitations months in advance of the wedding, so 'hold the date' cards are a great physical reminder that you can send as soon as you know your date. Where possible, have them made in the same style as your other wedding stationery but don't worry if this isn't possible – a postcard, email or phone call will do just as well. It's not the end of the world and the 'hold the date' cards are just functional at the end of the day. Anything on top is a bonus.

> *We're both South African although Anna's parents now live in the States and we live in the UK with friends in all three countries. Because we're getting married in Johannesburg we wanted to give our guests plenty of warning. So we're sending out official invitations six months before the wedding, but in the meantime Anna's parents have already sent out 'reserve the date' pre-invitations to give everyone twelve months' notice.*
>
> ROB AND ANNA, 26 AND 27

Reply cards. Take out the hassle factor by including reply cards with the invitation that capture all the basic information about 'would be delighted/cannot accept', dietary requirements and a song request. If you are inviting some guests to the evening only, consider getting different sets of cards printed so as not to rub in the fact that they are not invited to the ceremony and wedding breakfast. And to make things even easier for your guests you can go to the lengths of pre-printing the address on a reply envelope or postcard, stamping it and writing your guest's name on it. All they have to do then is fill in the information that you do not already know.

Orders of service. While not obligatory, if you have a lengthy ceremony your guests might like to know what is happening when, especially if they need to give responses. This can help people keep their attention, especially if their mind starts to stray, because they know exactly how long things will go on.

Place name and table cards. If you have free seating, you do not need to worry about this one. Or if you just want tables numbered 1–10 the venue may well already have the cards. But if you want to have a bit more fun, you can liven up your tables with some imaginative names. For some great ideas, see the **Reception Logistics** chapter.

Thank-you cards. Never mind etiquette, it's just polite to thank people for joining you to celebrate your wedding. Your wedding might be the most important day of your life, not theirs. Show them how much you appreciate them being there by sending them a thank-you card and perhaps include a photo that sums up the day for you. You should send out thank-you cards within a month of returning from your honeymoon and if you are going away for a long time, you need to get inventive. There are more ideas in the **Thank Yous and After the Wedding** chapter.

Loose leaves for your guest book. An alternative to the guest book circulating at the reception is to send each guest a loose leaf out in advance so they have time to think about what they want to say. Let them know if there is anything in particular you would like them to include in their message, for example, 'top tip for a happy marriage' or 'best day of their married life'. Ask them to send it back to you in a reinforced envelope so as not to bend the page or bring it with them to the reception. Then you can compile all the messages in your guest book.

ALTERNATIVES

Don't feel that you have to have stationery with ribbons, engraving, embossing or curly writing. Here are a few ideas for doing something different:

> *Because we were having a beach wedding and we wanted to keep it low-key and fun, we printed up our invitations on beach towels. Everyone thought it was a great idea and it really grabbed their attention. Plus people were clear from the outset that it was going to be a casual party and were even able to use them on the day.*
>
> LOUISE, 33

If it's flat, you can print on it. Leaves for a woodland wedding, old vinyl records for a rock 'n' roll theme, beach towels for a wedding with a poolside reception, or CD cases with a CD of music you plan to play at the ceremony or reception (give them a chance to learn the lyrics and tune in advance).

If it's not flat you can still print on it. Although professional printers may wince at the idea of getting information directly onto curved surfaces, you can have transfers made up or handwrite the details. This means that things like seashells, glasses and silver balls are all fair game.

Let your imagination run riot. Depending on your budget, if you can imagine it, you can have it for your stationery. Printing on clear acrylic means that you can have any shape you want to complement the theme of your wedding. Envelopes also come in a variety of sizes and colours, so you will be able to find something just right for you.

Sing it. You could always record your invitation on a CD for a really alternative angle.

Professional HTML email versions. If your friends and family are not terrorised by the digital age then whiz-bang techie invitations could be for you.

Get creative. Make your own. You don't have to be an artist for this very original and personal touch but it can be a bit unwieldy if you have more than 50 or so guests. Scour what's available for inspiration, or here are some simple but effective ideas:

✓ Spray a jigsaw and put two interlinking pieces on each piece of stationery

✓ Buy copper or silver wire from a craft shop and bend it – you can make hearts circles, stars, squares and triangles and mount them on another fabric or piece of card before you put them on the card itself

✓ Tie ribbon around your stationery items, whether they are flat, folded or rolled. Or thread it through punched holes. This is a very effective way to pull colour schemes together

✓ Haberdashers also sell individual fabric rosebuds, glittery decorations, coloured cord and braid and feathery chains. Even buttons can make a great difference. Or what about an invitation that has to be unzipped?

> *I wanted to make my own stationery because I knew it would be cheaper and I had a very clear idea of how I wanted it to look and I hadn't seen anything close to it in the usual places. I really enjoyed making them and had a great sense of satisfaction when I sent them out knowing that I (and a few family and friends) had created them and that they were just how I wanted them. It was a personal touch that really paid off as I think I did all the stationery, including place names, for £65 and yet many of my guests commented on how professional they looked.*
>
> Jo, 27

✓ Solid blocks of colour against pale backgrounds are simple and effective. Use metallic copper, gold or silver leaf for a striking look

✓ Invitations don't need to be folded. For something different have flat invitations

✓ Buy blank cards. You can print your wedding information onto a separate sheet of quality paper and hold it inside with a piece of ribbon running the whole way around the spine

✓ Only use one or two types or sizes of font to keep the finish as professional as possible

✓ Theme your invitation as a flight ticket, menu or holiday postcard for something slightly different

CONSIDERATIONS

PROOFREAD EVERYTHING. The smallest detail, such as a missing digit in a date or phone number, can make a massive difference. Have at least two people that you know have a good eye for detail look all your stationery over before you go into mass production. Find out whether your printer will show you proofs at no extra cost and if they will charge you for any last-minute changes or error corrections after the proofs have been provided.

Shop around. It is worth looking at what's available. You can get wedding stationery from high-street shops and stationers, print up your own styles or order them from specialists. Prices, lead times (the time from your order being placed to you receiving the finished invitations) and styles vary dramatically, so make sure you are clear about what you want.

Theme. Your stationery is a great chance to reinforce this.

Invitations for all. Send invitations to everyone you want to attend, including all attendants, bridesmaids, the best man, officiant and your parents if they are not the hosts.

Timings. Will you write a finish time for your reception on your invitations? If you think you would like to stay until the bitter end and maybe continue the celebrations with whoever is left in the venue bar, then avoid committing to a time. 'Until midnight' means that some guests who stay until midnight just to see you off will be disappointed if they have to leave before you do.

Be explicit. State clearly exactly who you are inviting to your wedding, especially if it is not 'and partner' or 'and children', otherwise you might have a few surprises on the day.

Reception only. For reception-only invitations you can change the details accordingly and avoid any confusion or hurt feelings by including a brief explanation. For example: 'Due to the small size of the church we have to limit the numbers and so hope to see you at the reception. Thank you in advance for your understanding.'

No children. Similarly, if you are excluding children, the explanation could be: 'Due to the small size of the venue/our need to keep the wedding small, we have limited the invitations to over-16s only. We plan to have a more family-orientated party after the wedding. Thank you in advance for your understanding.' You can also use the opportunity to invite them to your home as a family or give notice about having a kids' party at a later date if it is appropriate. It's a simple practicality that can save on misunderstandings in the long run.

Surprise! If you are planning a surprise wedding for your partner, make sure you are clear that people should not risk letting the cat out of the bag. You could theme your invitations and get them printed with 'Shhhhh' or 'Surprise!' to make your motive obvious.

Double weddings. An interesting twist. How many names can you get on an invitation? And include the words 'double wedding' if you anticipate any confusion. In theory, the couple closest to the hosts should be listed first or, if they are both children of the hosts, list the eldest first.

Send out all your invitations together. If this is possible for you it helps to avoid offending anyone who feels that they have only been invited to make up numbers when someone else can't make it. See the **First Things First** chapter for who to invite.

When to send. Don't feel constrained by the six- to eight-week guidelines if you don't think that is enough. Or, if you want to keep numbers low you might want to issue last-minute invitations – just make sure that everyone you definitely want to be there has an 'unofficial' note in their diaries. Do still send all official invitations at the same time in order to avoid offending anyone.

Tourist info. If you are anticipating your guests having free time in the day or they are travelling long distances, delegate someone to research and provide them with information about any other tourist attractions in the area. They might like to make a short break of it.

Musical requests. This is your opportunity to ask your guests to put forward songs they would like to hear played at the wedding. If this appeals then you also need to include a separate form for this with the invitation.

Inclusions. Your invitations will probably be your last official contact with guests before the wedding, so make sure you provide your gift-list details (but don't be so presumptuous as to include the actual gift list), dietary requirements request, directions, accommodation information, dress code and any other relevant information, such as reply cards, confetti, music request forms and loose leaves for your guest book.

Confetti. If you have a theme for your wedding and are going to include glitter or flower-petal confetti as a table decoration, put a few pieces into each invitation to tie in with your theme from the outset. But don't go too mad with it – ideally your guests should think it's a lovely added touch and give them an idea of your theme, rather than making them wish they'd never opened the envelope!

Online updates. If your guests are comfortable with technology you can set up your own website with all the details for your wedding. You can either send an email or card with the login details. If you are not a technical wizard yourself, companies that supply this service include www.simplywedded.co.uk. Use your own site to let guests know information about your choice of venue, directions, transport arrangements and to allow invitees to RSVP online. You can add some background about the people involved and also arrange your hen and stag parties without even picking up the phone.

BUDGET OPTIONS

Email invites. It saves on postage and stationery but is reliant on having a fairly IT-literate group of friends and family and would also really struggle to set the tone of the wedding unless it is done professionally. Plus, you are asking people to absorb outfit, travel and possibly accommodation and pressie costs to attend, so some people will find it less compelling to come or make an effort if they don't even get a 'proper' invitation.

Savings? As a guide, the average cost for 100 basic personalised invitations is £100–£120. Bearing this in mind, although making them yourself is a very personal touch, it is also very time-consuming and depending on the quality of card and decorations you buy it can be quite hard to make any substantial savings this way. Stationery wholesalers, haberdashers, craft shops and wedding stationery specialists will have a range of decorations and card at reasonable prices to create unique designs. But if budget saving is your main motivation you should shop around and do the sums before you undertake this task.

Batches. Will your printer charge you more if you split your order into two batches – 'hold the date' cards, followed by all other stationery?

SHOP AROUND

There is a vast range to choose from and the larger suppliers such as Confetti (www.confetti.co.uk) will always have very competitive prices for catalogue designs because they mass-produce their 'personalised' stationery. They also have very contemporary designs, but if you want something more unusual you should contact a few independent suppliers for their brochures:

- ✓ Bride and Groom Direct (0800 316 2016, www.brideandgroomdirect.co.uk)
- ✓ Diddy Gilly (0161 643 8548, www.diddygilly.co.uk)
- ✓ Handmade By 'me' Ltd (01273 905 041, www.handmadebyme.co.uk)
- ✓ Heather Marten (01590 672 778, www.theweddinginvitation.co.uk)
- ✓ Hitched (01455 636 297, www.hitched-stationery.co.uk)
- ✓ Katie Druett Designs (020 8392 1685, www.druettdesigns.co.uk)
- ✓ Libra Designs (01234 376 165, www.libra-designs.co.uk)
- ✓ Little Cherub Design (01642 783 027, www.littlecherubdesign.co.uk)
- ✓ Mandalay Wedding Stationery (020 8691 6100, www.mandalayweddinginvitations.co.uk)
- ✓ The Letter Press of Cirencester (01285 659 797, www.letterpress.co.uk)
- ✓ The Silver Nutmeg (0845 130 1132, www.thesilvernutmeg.com)
- ✓ The Whole Caboodle (01803 813 726, www.whole-caboodle.co.uk)

CAPTURING
THE OCCASION

Give some thought to how important the photos
and video are to you.

If you like the idea of gazing lovingly at these memories of the day when
you are both octogenarians, then don't skimp too much; it's not worth the
risk of not getting what you want.

 The standard wedding photo session sees you spending at least an
hour posing rigidly for traditional wedding shots outside the church,
or somewhere else with beautiful grounds, with your photographer
fiddling with their light meter for hours on end as you find a thousand
new ways to say 'cheese'.

If you're not really a photo person, then consider cutting corners. This
is one area where it is important to take other people's feelings into account
– you might not be bothered about photos or a video but maybe they are
very important to your incredibly proud and emotional parents and 90-
year-old granny.

Above all, relax and (try to) enjoy having your photos taken on the day,
even when you are on the 99th shot.

PHOTOGRAPHY – WHAT ELSE IS ON OFFER?

Before you drift into accepting the standard wedding style, think about
the type of photo you want to go for. If you opt for the full photo package,
then these are photos that may haunt you for years. Think about how
quickly they'll date. And do you want soft focus, obviously 'posed for'

shots, a storybook of the day, or natural and spontaneous style shots. If you're not sure, pick a photographer who can demonstrate that they are capable of doing a mixture. And if you would like them to be a bit creative with their shots then let them know.

Reportage shots. These relaxed, spontaneous-looking photos are increasingly popular. Photographers will often offer this option, even in combination with some more traditional shots.

Digital cameras. Your photographer can take endless pictures, either posed or natural, without having to fork out for expensive film. Using a high resolution on a good-quality camera will produce excellent results and having the pictures in this format means you can pick and choose easily on a computer and even retouch anything you don't want to see. Bear in mind, though, that it can be difficult to negotiate ownership of the original files.

Colour and speed options. When you look at a photographer's portfolio, ask them what kind of film they work with. You can have colour, sepia, black and white, colour tints, sharp or soft focus or even a slow shutter speed to indicate movement. Black and white have a reputation for being more timeless and classic but if you have put a lot of effort into your colour scheme you will probably want to reflect this in your official photos.

Disposable cameras. Per unit these are fairly cheap (especially if you buy them in bulk) but it is all relative and buying 40 cameras and developing them is going to ramp up your costs. They also come in a variety of colours to match your colour scheme. If you leave them scattered around your reception, in addition to having a professional photographer, you will often get your most natural, spontaneous shots that will really reflect the mood of the day. You will also get to see a lot of what your family and friends got up to while you were circulating and caught up in 'wedding business'. If you like this idea, put a note on each camera to let people know you would like them to be your unofficial photographers for the day and capture the memories you might miss.

BUDGET OPTIONS

Evening wedding. Avoid having to pay your photographer for a whole day.

Student photographers. This might sound a bit risky for your wedding day photos but it depends how much importance you put on them. Contact local colleges and browse through a few portfolios. You never know, you may strike gold.

Extra copies. Ask everyone with a camera on the day to send you a copy of their photos when they get the pictures developed or downloaded.

CHOOSING A PHOTOGRAPHER

It goes without saying that you can't beat recommendations. If you're lucky you will find someone good in your area, but if not a photographer from further afield may be willing to travel (although this may mean that you incur extra costs for their travel, accommodation and expenses). Also speak to your chosen venue to find out if they have a working relationship with specific suppliers that they regularly use, which could also mean a discount.

You'd be pretty crazy to do it, but never book a photographer without seeing their work! Take some time to visit them and ask to look at whole sets of pictures from their most recent jobs as opposed to just the standard portfolio – that will just be the best of your photographer's work to date. Look at the moments they have captured and their attention to detail and trust your instincts. Book as soon as you can if this is top of your list of priorities, as the best photographers will be booked up well in advance. Once you have found the right person for the job get confirmation of the details in writing.

As a guideline, professional photographers tend to quote in the region of:

✓ £800 for half a day (3–4 hours) and 200 reportage-style images

✓ £1,000 for 6 hours and 250 reportage-style images

✓ £1,500 for 8 hours and 300 reportage-style images

These are just sample costs from the market and so you should get comparative quotes from national and local suppliers. Choose a style you like, write down all the details and base your competitive quotes around this specification.

If it's important to you, you can choose a photographer who is professionally qualified and a registered member of the British Institute of Professional Photographers (01296 718 530, www.bipp.com) or The Guild of Wedding Photographers (www.photoguild.co.uk).

Some considerations for your wedding photography are:

Time involved. Ask the photographer how much time you will need to put aside for photos and bear this in mind when you're looking at their portfolio. You don't want to spend all day posing for shots, so you'll have to balance that with the calibre of work on offer.

Guest photos. Standard line-ups often focus on the wedding party with one or two big group shots, but if you want pictures of specific guests, make a list of exactly which couples or groups (with or without you included) you would like captured on film and ask your photographer to include them in his running order. Remember, people are not mind-readers – you need to let everyone know so that the guests you have in mind don't disappear before time because they don't realise they are needed.

Location, location, location. Think in advance about where you want to have your 'mantelpiece' photos taken. Even if you want to have natural shots, you can have them taken in a specific location. Go and visit places you have in mind – if you use a local photographer they should also be able to give you pointers. If your photographer is not local then make sure they are able to familiarise themselves with your chosen setting prior to the day. There's no reason why you can't have your photos taken somewhere completely different to your church or venue – but do think about the logistics of getting everyone there.

Contingency plan. If you've planned to have all your photos taken in the beautiful gardens of your venue and it tips with rain on your wedding day, is there somewhere inside that will provide a good backdrop instead?

Choosing your pictures. Ask the photographer what format they will use to present the photos to you after your wedding so that you can choose your favourites. Some will show you transparencies, others contact sheets of your pictures. Make sure you are happy with how you will have to make your decisions.

Presentation. How will you receive your final selection? Your photographer might provide you with an album, you might have to pay extra for it, or you might want to choose your own. Alternatively, you can pay for a CD of all the images and print out as many as you like in your choice of size.

VIDEO AND DVD – WHAT'S ON OFFER

This can be a very expensive choice and in essence, as with photography, you get what you pay for. Once you start involving professionals, prices vary drastically and so do standards. Again, as with many other aspects of a wedding, if you want a professional production that you could screen at your local cinema, it is possible at a price. But you also need to think about how comfortable you are spending that kind of money, the purpose of the video and how likely it is that the audiovisual equipment you hire will turn your wedding into a complete circus.

When making your selection, view some past work and look out for the following:

✓ Focusing – make sure the film is *always* in focus and not slipping from clear to blurry throughout

✓ Wobbling – a professional may well use a tripod but check their finished products are not shaky and stay level at all times

✓ Colour – look for an even colour throughout (this is easier if you pay particular attention to the white, it should stay constant and not have a coloured tinge to it)

✓ Sound – hissy, crackly sound is not good, so make sure your professional is clearly thinking about the pictures *and* sound

✓ Overdoing it – too many special effects, too much zooming, too many extreme close-ups, too much of one shot … you get the idea

For something a bit retro, Reel60 use original 1960s cinefilm, complete with that grainy look (0845 226 7220, www.reel60.com).

BUDGET OPTIONS

The cheapest alternative is a relative or friend with a camcorder – this will give you a roundup of the day and serve to jog your memories to bring back the events of your wedding. If you do go for this option here are a few points to bear in mind:

✓ Make sure your budding cameraman is fully acquainted with the camera before the wedding so they don't spend half the day asking everyone where the record button is

✓ Let them know what kind of shots you are looking for – do you want the whole ceremony captured or are the festivities of the reception more important to you?

✓ Think about extra battery power and tapes or memory if you need the camera to last into the night

✓ It may seem obvious, but remind your cameraman not to get in too many guests' way – you don't want disgruntled great-aunts tutting their way through your ceremony

✓ Don't use the zoom too much or you will feel like you are on a fairground ride when you settle back to view your video

✓ Ask your celebrant or registrar for permission to film the ceremony

✓ Think about capturing some vox-pop comments from various guests during the day – you are bound to get some priceless moments of friends and family being wannabe presenters

✓ Worst-case scenario – if the video is really that bad you could always make £250 by sending a clip into *You've Been Framed*

> *We decided that we couldn't justify the expense of a videographer on top of a professional photographer and so one of our guests took a home video of the whole day. The result is great – the photos are ideal for the mantelpiece but the video is a fantastic reminder of the day as it really captures people's personalities. I think they played up to the camera less self-consciously because they knew the person who was taking the film. We're planning on getting it transferred to DVD in the next couple of months and then we can send it out to people and split it into sections more easily.*
>
> MARILYN, 23

OTHER OPPORTUNITIES TO CAPTURE THE OCCASION

Engagement photos. You don't have to wait until your wedding to have your first professional photos together. Studios around the country offer packages for very stylish yet natural shots. Forget the soft focus and posing with your head at an angle.

Portrait. Commission an artist to recreate your favourite photo on a canvas.

Warhol-style. If you are a dab hand with computer photo packages scan in your favourite shot and create some personal modern art.

Caricatures. Capture your personalities in your wedding garb. You could even use the images on your thank-you notes.

Really capturing the moment. To ensure that you have a special shared memory etched on both your brains, take ten minutes together away from everyone else to tell each other exactly how you feel. Or perhaps make a conscious effort to remember your first dance. Alternatively, you could follow the films and have the bride slap the groom round the face at the altar to ensure he remembers the moment for ever! Or perhaps not.

Love letters. Put a few moments aside before you go to your ceremony to write down your exact thoughts and feelings at that time. You should each seal them and then exchange them on your first anniversary.

CARS AND CARTS

Make an entrance and be whisked away with style and panache . . .

 In Olde English tradition, a bridal party would either walk to the church or use horse-drawn carriages. More modern traditions have extended to vintage or luxury cars, from Aston Martins to Jaguars, Bentleys, Daimlers, Mercedes and Rolls-Royces.

So what else is available?

First off, don't let yourself be limited to what instantly springs to mind. The reality is that if it is mobile, you can use it for a dramatic entrance, exit or both.

Tandem. Looking sweet upon the seat of a bicycle made for two?

Boat, yacht or canoe. For waterside weddings. Or if you want to be really unconventional and it is appropriate for you, sit in a double kayak on the back of a trailer if you like!

Motor scooter. Disappear off on twin scooters or tie it in with a mods and rockers theme.

Motorbike and sidecar. For an alternative retro look.

Helicopter. Especially if your groom thinks he's James Bond or if you are going to blow the budget on a wedding spectacular with all the trimmings.

> When Jim gets married this summer, the lads are going to club together for our gift to him and provide him with an entrance to remember. We've hired a helicopter and pilot for the day and are going to take him to the manor house venue in style. It's OK by them, although they did draw the line at us arranging to have him parachute in.
>
> DAVID, 28

Horse. Just don't get too carried away and go for the true Lady Godiva look. Or you could go for a horse box.

Black cab. For city-chic style but this won't carry much novelty factor if you are actually in a city filled with black cabs.

Hot-air balloon. Not only Richard Branson can use them. They're not exactly a quick method of transport but they are definitely eye-catching and if you have a small group of guests you can arrange to have your wedding breakfast for up to sixteen people up in the air.

Camper van. Why not?

CELEBRITY SPOTLIGHT

When the king and queen of light entertainment, Vernon Kay and Tess Daly, married in a modest ceremony in Vernon's home town near Bolton they didn't need any fancy cars to whisk them away. Instead the newly-weds opted to drive themselves to the reception in an old-fashioned VW camper van. A down-to-earth, retro and fun alternative with lots of personality. How apt.

Sports car. Either to transport both of you or, if it is your groom's dream to drive a Porsche, Ferrari, MG, Lotus Elise or Lamborghini, he could use it to get to the venue in the first place – brides are not necessarily the only ones who get to travel in style.

Pink Cadillacs, Mustangs, Corvettes. American beauties to make you purr.

Stretch limousine. The ultimate in gauche style.

Roller skates, Rollerblades, skateboard or a scooter. Who knows? You might think it's a good idea.

Harley Davidson. You easy rider, you.

Tractor and trailer. For the laid-back, simple hay-and-gingham atmosphere of the country.

CELEBRITY SPOTLIGHT

Former Catatonia singer, Cerys Matthews, decided on a 1930s theme for her wedding to her record producer fiancé. Friends and family all got into the swing of things by dressing for the occasion. Cerys also decided on a rather unique arrival as she pitched up in a trailer towed by an old tractor.

Themed convoy. If you have executed your theme with military precision throughout the rest of your wedding plans, then it is only to be expected that you will want to put your mark on the wedding convoy. Give your guests something to attach to their cars. Then travel in convoy to the reception venue the way the French do – they all toot their horns en route too.

Red double-decker bus. Practical and with a very British-cum-*Summer Holiday* flavour. You can even get an open-topped bus if you are feeling optimistic about the weather.

Parachute. This is possible but incredibly tricky depending on your experience, flying allowances in the area you are getting married in, venue restrictions and supplier discretion. If this really does appeal to you then contact a local parachute or skydiving club as soon as you can so that you can see exactly how you could go about making your dream a reality.

Rickshaws and trishaws. For a flavour of Asia and an environmentally friendly option to taxis. Suppliers are cropping up all over the UK and even some charities that run rickshaw fundraising events are flexible about being hired for weddings, so check the Internet for up-to-date information.

Karma cabs. For a kitsch Indian experience travel in a customised Ambassador car sumptuously decked out, complete with an eccentric driver.

Vintage minibus. An alternative to a traditional coach or double-decker bus, some companies have *Heartbeat*-style coaches available for hire. This gives you a practical way of transporting about 16 people in a vehicle with lots of character.

Military vehicles. Again, very alternative considering you are not really supposed to be going into battle and also great for supporting a 1940s theme. Do check with the venue though – they might not be best impressed if the weight of a tank breaks up their tarmac. You may have to opt for a camouflaged jeep instead.

Emergency services. There are now private companies that offer hire services for both fire engines and ambulances. Or perhaps this is more appropriate for your hen or stag nights?

Train. Not only can you hire various types of train to get you all from A to B, but you can also look into having your reception on board.

TV and film favourites. For a chariot that everyone can relate to and have a laugh at, you could mimic something from popular culture for a more light-hearted approach.

> *I arranged to have the Only Fools and Horses three-wheel van drive us away from the reception as a necessary surprise for my wife (otherwise not likely to have been acceptable!). I had also kept it a secret from all my family and wedding guests so that the reaction when it pulled up outside the venue was great to watch. The car had been provided by a local theme car agency but it was owned and driven by the chairman of the Only Fools and Horses Appreciation Society. As a member of the society I was pleased to meet the chairman in the flesh and probably bored my new wife with conversations full of Only Fools and Horses banter. Most amusing was the fact that this chap had assumed that Cassandra was a nickname for my wife on account of my fondness of the show. It is, of course, her real name, which she was keen to point out. My abiding memory of the journey was sitting cramped in the back of the van waving through clouds of exhaust as we departed the reception. The car never seemed to get above 30mph for the whole of the 15-mile journey to our hotel although I think other vehicles nearby were slowing down to catch a butcher's. Nice little runner – never to be forgotten – and I think if Cassandra is honest she got a bit of a kick out of it too.*
>
> NIGEL, 23

PRACTICALITIES

We have not listed an endless directory of suppliers here because this aspect of the industry is always changing and the most popular means of promotion are the Internet and the local telephone directories.

In terms of other factors you should consider:

Best deal. As always, get a selection of competitive quotes. Local suppliers are nearly always going to be cheaper, especially if the alternative is to cover their travel and (possibly overnight) expenses.

Guarantees. If your chosen vehicle is unavoidably out of order on the day, what guarantees or back-up options can the hire company offer you? Where relevant, have your own back-up too in case you are let down at the last minute.

Viewing. Wherever possible, view the vehicle before you agree to the hire. Then you can get an accurate idea of size, colour, cleanliness, smell and other things you cannot ascertain from a photograph.

Colour. If colour co-ordination is very important to you, think about how the vehicle will fit in with your existing scheme. Avoid an ivory car with a white dress and vice versa, because white can make ivory appear grubby in photos.

Outfits. You might love the idea of a tandem or twin scooters but if you've paid a small fortune on a lavish dress, do you really want to risk getting bike oil on it and catching it in the wheels? Similarly, if you have a meringue to rival Princess Diana's, is there going to be room for you both and that dress in the Ferrari?

Getting decorative. If you would like to decorate the vehicle, find out if the company will charge you extra and whether they will take care of it or if they expect you to. A lot of companies are understandably resistant to anything that could possibly mark the bodywork or upholstery, including fresh flowers, confetti and anything like silly string or spray snow.

Busy periods. Vehicles that are wedding specific are often in less demand on weekdays and so are sometimes discounted. Conversely, if you are getting married at the weekend, they will be in much higher demand, booked up months in advance, so if you have got your heart set on something specific you should make a booking as soon as possible.

Confirmation. It is always a good idea to double-check information. Reconfirm your booking a month before your wedding and a week before send the company any maps, schedules, addresses and contact numbers that the driver might need.

Contact details. As the driver is on the move, ask for his mobile number a few days before the wedding. That way, if your wedding 'car' is late you have a way of getting hold of the driver before ripping your immaculately prepared hair out.

Sole use. Check to make sure you are going to be the only booking for that vehicle for that day. If not, evaluate your options.

Theme. Other than colours, are there any other transport options to reinforce your theme?

Starring role. Some brides want shots of themselves, their bridesmaids and the person giving them away on arrival at the church or register office. If the vehicle is going to be pivotal in the photos make sure you agree with the driver to allow time for them. If it isn't, then be proportionate about the importance you place on what you arrive in – in theory no one should be outside to see you anyway. So make the decision based on what is important to you.

Rain or shine. If you have open-top transportation or are planning on walking have a contingency plan in case it rains.

> *I am getting married in May and in the midst of wedding planning at the moment. The only thing I've had to compromise on is how I get to the church – I wanted to walk as we're getting married in our local village, just down the road from my parents' house. My mum's talked me into arranging the wedding cars for the whole day in case it rains. It hasn't cost us any more and now I've got peace of mind that I won't have a muddy hemline and shoes. Plus, if it's sunny I'll walk anyway. Fingers crossed!*
>
> ZOE, 29

Traffic updates. If you've got a long way to travel, check with AA Roadwatch, the RAC, Teletext or local travel services to make sure that you allow enough time in case of traffic jams. This is even more important if you are not the only wedding at your venue – your timeslot might be limited. If necessary, waste time when you get there.

> *We arranged for a double-decker bus to pick my mum, bridesmaids and me up from the house and take us to the church. Then we used the same bus to take everyone who didn't have transport to the reception venue. It was great fun, really practical and an excellent way of kicking off the party.*
>
> JANET, 31

Transport for your guests. Plan how your guests are going to get from A to B, especially if a lot of them are not driving. Let them know if you are expecting them to walk so that they can be prepared. If necessary, delegate someone to organise transport beforehand. Work out how many cars you have and buddy people up or arrange a minibus or coach to make sure you've got the problem covered. If you're laying this on in place of taxis, the guests may also be willing to contribute.

BUDGET OPTIONS

You need to decide how important your chariot is in terms of your complete wedding experience. If it's not high up on your list of priorities, why not drive yourselves or go back to the very traditional way of doing things and walk?

Alternatively, a swanky taxi can be just as effective as a wedding limo, so shop around. Companies that specialise in executive taxi cars may be busy in the week and give preferential treatment to their account customers, so check their booking details and guarantees. If you know of local companies it's always worth giving them a try because they might be more flexible about allowing time to add decorations if you want to and may also be able to let you see the car before the big day. As we mentioned, traditional wedding car companies don't tend to be as busy mid-week so you may be able to negotiate a discounted rate. There's no harm in asking.

And, of course, if you are getting married and having your reception in the same venue, you could easily get away with no wedding transport at all.

FLOWERS

Whatever your beliefs, flowers can add colour, vibrancy and freshness to your décor on the day.

THE BRIDAL BOUQUET

First of all, decide if you want a bouquet. To stop yourself fidgeting, you could always hold a bag or your young bridesmaid's hand instead.

If you would like to carry flowers you have more options than you might think when it comes to shape and size. Think about your dress and what will best complement your outfit and body shape.

Not surprisingly, the tradition of the bride carrying flowers was another thing that people thought would ward off even more nasty evil spirits (seems like there were a lot of them around in the old days). People believed that strong-smelling herbs would send them packing. This even extended to including garlic in the bride's bouquet. The rituals in Roman times involved the bride and groom being adorned with floral garlands that came to signify blossoming fertility.

Round or nosegay. Flowers are tied in a cluster. The type of flowers used can affect how formal this looks.

Waterfall or cascade. Full and dense at the top narrowing down into a flow of foliage at the bottom. This style can look very elegant, wistful and even slimming.

Shaped. Bouquets can be shaped into a crescent or even a heart. The crescent in particular can look quite dramatic.

Single flower. Carry a simple single stem, perhaps with a bow or piece of foliage. This works better with more striking and bold flowers such as tropical varieties.

Hand-tied. More natural and less formally arranged. Stems are left bare and the flowers are tied loosely with a piece of ribbon or raffia.

Arm. An elegant display draped over your arm can flatter your outfit, particularly if you have detail on the front of your dress that you don't want to cover with a traditional bouquet held in front of you.

Basket. A shallow basket with flowers arranged in it for that country-garden look. A popular option for young bridesmaids.

Ballerina. This option was popular during the war as flowers were scarce and the bouquet is largely made up with tulle, netting and just a few strategically placed flowers. It may sound strange but can be simple and effective and may be an option for a themed wedding or for those on a tight budget.

Wrist corsage. À la Carrie in *Sex and the City*, this is a good alternative for those who want a floral aspect to their outfit but want to be hands-free.

WHAT TO DO WITH YOUR BOUQUET AFTER THE CEREMONY

Throwing the bouquet is a well-practised tradition that is another focal point for your guests to enjoy. You can put an alternative spin on this moment by loosening the ties on the bouquet and allowing the flowers to fall individually, therefore avoiding the mad grapple and allowing all the girls to get a souvenir. Alternatively, if you have light flowers, make up your bouquet from a collection of smaller posies. Or maybe you have a girlfriend that you know is desperate for it so you want to give it to them specifically.

Guys also have their own version of this tradition by throwing the bride's garter to a waiting crowd of bachelors. Whether or not there is as much of a scramble to catch it remains to be seen.

If you want to save your bouquet after the wedding you can have it dried, preserved, framed or pressed.

Not all flowers will take kindly to being dried or preserved though, so consult your florist if this is important to you.

FLOWERS FOR THE WEDDING PARTY

BRIDESMAIDS

Depending on their age and your taste, bridesmaids often also have bouquets to hold. Little ones may be better off with mini baskets or even a single flower could look cute. Older bridesmaids could have smaller or simpler versions of your own bouquet or wrist corsages that reflect the colour scheme.

GROOM, BEST MAN, FATHERS AND USHERS

All the men in the wedding party traditionally wear buttonholes but it's up to you if you follow this tradition. These are often a single flower that reflects the bride's bouquet but could mirror the colour of her dress. Roses and carnations are particularly popular but your florist will be able to offer you some alternatives. Whether buttonholes work largely depends on what the groomsmen are wearing for the occasion. You may think garlands are more fitting for your style.

The groom is meant to wear a buttonhole from the bridal bouquet as a mark of respect and admiration for his bride. This comes from the medieval tradition of a knight wearing the colours of his lady to demonstrate his love.

OTHER GUESTS

If you want to go all out you may want to supply buttonholes and pin or wrist corsages for all of your guests as a special touch. This will look great in the photos and could be an alternative to favours. Nominate someone to hand them out as guests arrive at your venue.

OTHER USES FOR FLOWERS

TRANSPORT

Depending on your budget you could run garlands along the edges of the windows or fittings, have arrangements on the back shelf or posies and single flowers in prominent positions. Or go the whole hog and surround yourself with your favourite blooms.

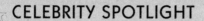

CELEBRITY SPOTLIGHT

When ex-All Saint Natalie Appleton married Liam Howlett of the Prodigy in the South of France she opted for a floral theme. Dressed in a full-length cream dress, Natalie arrived at the church in an open-top vintage car filled to the brim with flowers.

CAKE

Let the person who is supplying your cake know about your colour scheme and choice of flowers in advance so that they can incorporate this into their design. This could range from simply a couple of flowers placed on the top, to flower heads being packed together and facing out of the gap between the cake tiers, or a display entwined around the base and up around the tiers.

HAIR

Lacing flowers in your hair is a lovely natural touch and can look very feminine and fairy tale or very striking. Discuss with your hairdresser the effect you would like to achieve and also consult your florist as to which kind of flowers would work best. They will be able to let you know which flowers will last longer under the conditions of your wedding day so you don't end up with them wilting on your head by late afternoon. Consider a similar look for your bridesmaids to create an effect en masse.

TABLE DECORATIONS

Flowers make gorgeous centrepieces for table settings and can be elegant or extravagant. Instead of standard arrangements you could have shallow trays of flower heads resting on crushed ice or floating on water. As an alternative to pricey vases, use unusual items such as tin cans or milk bottles filled with pretty wild flowers. Or how about using small pot plants instead of fresh-cut flowers so that they will continue to grow after your day? Have simple hand-tied posies for all the ladies – these can be given instead of favours and also look lovely on clean white napkins as part of your decoration.

Once the lights go down, you might worry that your expensive displays will lose their effectiveness. Avoid this by interspersing the flowers with candles and putting cut-glass beads in amongst the petals so that they catch the candlelight and twinkle into the evening. Or use storm vases for church candles with flowers placed around the base inside.

ROOM DECORATIONS

If you love the idea of flowers everywhere then why limit yourselves to tables? You can also entwine garlands around the backs of your chairs, room fittings or hang them in rows around the walls. And if you want to add some beautiful scents use lavender, freesias or roses in your displays.

CONFETTI

Flower-petal confetti is pretty, natural and environmentally friendly too. Rose and bougainvillea petals are especially popular as they are light, biodegradable and still hardy enough to keep their shape. Contact Bougainvillea (01404 811 467, www.passionforpetals.com) for ideas and a whole range of colours. You could sprinkle petals down the aisle or make your own paper cones to hold the petals so that they can be handed out easily as you leave your ceremony.

CHOOSING A FLORIST

If you are using flowers quite extensively and you are no expert, then using a professional can save you time, money and hassle in the long run. They will have experience in how to decorate different venues, which flowers are most suited to your requirements and possible options for weddings.

There are a few things to consider before you go ahead and book:

- ✓ As always, try to get some recommendations from friends and take the time to get comparative quotes before you book

- ✓ Ascertain how experienced the florist is with weddings. How many do they service per year? Will yours be the only wedding they are catering for on your wedding day?

- ✓ Have a look at photos of their work and if possible visit their shop to see whether their displays are to your liking. If you visit on a Friday afternoon or Saturday morning you may be able to see their wedding displays for another client. Florists are designers and as such have different styles. They may be very contemporary or very traditional, so go for someone who reflects your tastes

- ✓ Ask how much they charge for their time and for the flowers. Some will charge a daily rate for their time and then buy flowers wholesale, whereas others will charge according to the flowers and styles of displays you choose. Make sure you are aware of any hidden costs such as hiring equipment like vases, urns, stands or arches

✓ Can they come and see the venue before the day so that you can discuss where you need flowers to go? How will the flowers be transported to the venue? How long will the florist need to set up?

✓ As with all wedding plans, book as early as you can, especially if you are getting married in high season. Four to six months is usual

✓ Have your preferred colour scheme in mind before you try to find a florist, as this will give them the starting point they need to plan. Supply photos of your outfit if you can or swatches of material

> It's important to work on your colour choices for the flowers. Many people try to work to certain varieties of flower, or pick a flower by name. For example there are hundreds of variety of red rose. If you pick 'Red Velvet' and on the day the flower auction has none or the grower changes, you may be devastated. However, if your florist knows the exact colour and texture of flower you are after they can use their expertise to make a substitution and most brides will never even notice the difference. Flowers are individual, living, growing, dying things. It's not the same as the DJ not turning up or the venue being double-booked. Leave it to the professional florist who knows their flowers and they can create the beautiful bouquets you dream of with the blooms available.
>
> JO-ANNE KING, FLORAL DESIGNER (01962 880 871, WWW.JOANNEKING.COM)

BUDGET OPTIONS

Flowers may be a necessity in your eyes but it can be very expensive to create the effect that you have in mind. They can seriously ramp up your wedding budget. As with all aspects of your planning you will need to weigh up your priorities. Some budget-saving ideas are:

Church helpers. If you are getting married in a church then it is likely that there will be members of the congregation who have been doing the flowers there for years. Taking advantage of this could save you money and they will know what works well in the space you have. Do check out their handiwork in advance though, just to make sure you are happy with what they have to offer. Your minister will usually discuss the floral arrangements with you early in your planning stages.

Blooms on the move. Arrange displays in moveable pots or on stands, then you can have them transported from your ceremony venue to the reception venue so you get maximum value.

Ready-made. Getting married in a venue that is commonly used for weddings could save you money as standard floral arrangements may be included in the price.

Create your own. Another option for other venues if you have a bit of artistic flair is to decorate the place yourselves or with the help of a creative friend or two. Keep it simple and buy flowers wholesale if you can. You could even go on a flower-arranging course.

Keep it simple. You don't need to have flowers everywhere. Simple arrangements go a long way and will look very elegant. You can also pad things out with greenery and ribbons to save money on blooms.

Overall effect. Do you want lots of little displays that may be fairly ineffectual unless they're strategically placed or one big display that no one can miss, or something in the middle? Think about how you are spending your money for maximum effect and satisfaction.

Cheap labour. You could also approach your local agricultural college or night school floristry class. Would any students like to prepare the bouquets as a project? This does obviously come with some risks attached, but you may get lucky and find someone who will offer you a cheap and cheerful option.

Local garden centres. Some now offer a floristry service that can put the high-street prices to shame. Check out the options close to your venue.

Seasonal variations. You can get most flowers for a price at any time of year. Choose flowers in season for the best value for money.

Native flowers. Flowers that are grown in the UK will generally be cheaper than those that have to be imported.

BYOF. Bring your own flower. Ask your guests to bring a specific type or stems from their gardens to create your flower displays on site.

MORE FLORAL CONSIDERATIONS

When choosing your specific flowers here are some points to bear in mind:

✓ If you are upset by the idea of all those flowers going to waste after the event then encourage your guests to take them home at the end of the night or donate them to a local hospital or old people's home

✓ How long do they last? Will they wilt as soon as they are picked or exposed to any kind of heat? If so, consider ordering more than one set of flowers to be able to refresh them at some point during the day, especially if they are pivotal to your look

✓ Is their scent overwhelming and does their pollen stain?

✓ Would you like an independent floral consultation? For some advice, ask a horticulturalist or impartial expert

> *At my second-cousin's wedding they didn't have any flowers but had an Eastern European tradition where each guest brought a single flower and they ended up with a massive bunch, which eventually made up the bridal bouquet.*
>
> LOTTIE, 29

✓ If you use garden foliage to decorate your venue, spray it with an insect repellent and leave it outside for an hour or so to avoid surprising your guests with any unwanted visitors

✓ Hay-fever sufferers should let their florist know to avoid using plants with pollens you know you are particularly sensitive to. Or use silk flowers instead

✓ Keep your theme unfussy by opting for one type of flower throughout your day

✓ Is yours the only wedding that day? If not, be prepared for the possibility of pre-arranged floral decorations 'to suit all couples' at the venue. If you have something very specific in mind then think about avoiding very popular days

FLOWER REFERENCE TABLE

Realistically, most brides will put the colour of their flowers above what they mean according to old wives' tales but going with a meaning might make it a bit more unique.

 The Victorians attached meanings to different flowers. Lovers would send coded messages using specific blooms and some brides still incorporate them into their wedding flowers today.

Name	Season	Common colours	Meaning
Alstroemeria	All seasons	Cream, orange, pink, purple, red, white, yellow	Aspirational
Amaryllis	Winter, spring	Pink, red, white	Pride and splendid beauty
Anemone	Winter, spring	Cerise, purple, red, white	Fragile
Antirrhinum (snapdragon)	Spring, summer, autumn	Burgundy, lavender, pink, purple, white, yellow	Presumption
Apple Blossom	Spring	Pink, white	Hope
Aster (Michaelmas daisy)	All seasons	Lilac, pink, purple, white	Contentment and variety
Calla Lily	All seasons	Burgundy, orange, pink, white, yellow	Delicacy and modesty

Name	Season	Common colours	Meaning
Camellia	Spring	Blue, pink, red, white	Graciousness
Carnation	All seasons	Pink, red, white, yellow	Pink = gratitude, red = admiration, white = innocence/ purity, yellow = cheerfulness
Cherry blossom	Spring	Pink, white	Spiritual beauty
Chrysanthemum	All seasons	Bronze, pink, red, white, yellow	Bronze = excitement, pink = friendship, red = sharing love, white = truth, yellow = secret admirer
Cornflower	Summer	Blue, white, pink	Delicacy
Daffodil	Winter, spring	White, yellow	Joy and devotion
Dahlia	Autumn	Orange, pink, purple, red, white, yellow	Dignity and elegance
Daisy	Summer, autumn	White, yellow	Simplicity and innocence
Delphinium	Summer, autumn	Blue, lavender, pink, purple, red, white	Boldness
Forget-me-not	Spring, summer	Blue	True love and don't forget me
Forsythia	Winter	Yellow	Good nature
Freesia	All seasons	Orange, pink, purple, red, white, yellow	Innocence and trust
Fuchsia	Summer	Fuchsia pink	Taste
Gardenia	Summer	White	Purity and ecstasy
Gerbera	All seasons	Orange, pink, purple, red, white, yellow	Radiant and joyful
Gladioli	Summer, autumn	Cream, green, lavender, lilac, orange, pink, purple, red, terracotta, white, yellow	Ready armed(!)
Gypsophila	All seasons	Pale pink, white	Pure of heart
Heather	Spring, summer, autumn	Lavender, white	Good luck
Holly	Winter	Green, red and white	Foresight
Honeysuckle	Spring	Coral, pink, white	Rustic love
Hyacinth	Winter, spring	Pink, purple, white	
Iris	All seasons	Blue, purple, white, yellow	Message and faith
Ivy	All seasons	Green	Matrimony
Jasmine	Winter, spring, summer	White, yellow	Amiability
Larkspur	Summer	Pink, purple	Fickleness
Lavender	Summer	Lavender	
Lilac	Spring, summer	Purple, white	First emotion of love

Name	Season	Common colours	Meaning
Lily	All seasons	Orange, pink, red, white, yellow	Majesty and elegance – but have also come to symbolise death
Lily of the valley	Spring, summer	White	Return of happiness
Lisianthus	All seasons	Cream, lilac, pink, purple, white	
Love-in-a-mist	Summer, autumn	Blue, pink, white	
Lupin	Summer	Blue	Imagination
Marigold	Summer	Orange, yellow	Grief and trouble, although some think it means good fortune
Mimosa	All seasons	Yellow	Sensitivity
Nerine	Autumn, winter	Pink, white	
Orchid	All seasons	Cream, orange, pink, purple, red, white, yellow	Beauty
Peony	Summer	Pink, purple, white, yellow	Bashfulness
Phlox	All seasons	Pink, purple, white	
Poppy	Summer	Pink, red, white, yellow	Pink = kindness, red = extravagance, white = antidote/sleep, yellow = wealth
Primrose	Spring	Yellow	I can't live without you
Rhododendron	Spring, summer	Orange, pink, purple, red, white	Danger!
Rose	All seasons	Coral, cream, orange, pink, purple, red, white, yellow	Pink = admiration, red = love, white = heavenly/purity, yellow = friendship
Stephanotis	Winter, spring	White	Happiness in marriage
Stock	Spring, summer	Burgundy, cream, pink, purple, white, yellow	Lasting beauty
Sunflower	Summer, autumn	Yellow	Adoration and hope
Sweet pea	Summer	Lavender, pink, purple, white	Delicate and lasting pleasures
Tulip	Spring	Burgundy, cream, orange, pink, purple, white, yellow	Declaration of love, hopeless love
Wax flower	Winter, spring	Pink, white	Susceptibility
Zinnia	Autumn	Red, white, yellow	Absent friends

RECEPTION LOGISTICS

Time to celebrate!

If you are still in doubt about how you want to celebrate your marriage and are holding out against the traditional big party, have a look back at the **First Things First** chapter for some alternative ideas.

In terms of the traditional reception party, there are choices you can make to do it differently.

THE RECEIVING LINE

The benefit of the receiving line is that it means that everyone feels that they at least got to say hello to you both, especially if they do not see you very often or have come a long way. It also means you don't have to spend the rest of the reception trying to get around to talk to everyone and working the room instead of being able to enjoy the party.

The reality is that you can have any combination of people that you want. You may have stepparents, children or other people pivotal to the wedding

Conventionally, the hosts of the wedding line up to welcome guests to the reception and the receiving-line order reflects the tradition of the bride's parents picking up the lion's share of the tab:

1. Bride's mother
2. Bride's father
3. Groom's mother
4. Groom's father
5. Bride
6. Groom
7. Chief bridesmaid (optional)
8. Best man (optional)

who you would like to join you. Or if you have financed the wedding without any other help then you might not want anyone else to act as 'hosts' in the receiving line with you. You do not have to feel restricted by convention but whatever you choose, again, the key is to communicate that choice to everyone it might affect to avoid confusion.

CONSIDERATIONS AND ALTERNATIVES

Time is a factor in whatever you decide about your receiving line – the longer the line-up, the longer it will take to get through your guests. Instead, you might choose to greet your guests:

Row by row as you leave your ceremony venue. This is quite unusual and depending on the number of guests you have could take a long time. It also means that you will tend to take one side of the venue each, your 'own' side, so will not be introduced to any guests that you still do not know from the other side of the family.

Outside the ceremony venue. You will probably be the first two people out of the ceremony venue so in theory you can wait at the door and greet people as they leave after you. But this is not practical if you want to stay in the venue for your wedding photos because some of your guests may not stay for the whole photo shoot. And it also doesn't allow for additional people coming to your reception that you are not inviting to the ceremony (although if a reception has a sit-down meal and even more guests arriving later then this is often the case anyway).

Between the ceremony and the reception. You will need to think about whether or not to entertain your guests if you are having photos taken or if your official reception is not due to start immediately. You could just ask them to while away an hour in the venue bar or you could lay on a cocktail reception, wine tasting or other activity in the interim. Then you can mingle with the guests once you are free in a less formal setting. In order to ensure you make everyone feel appreciated, keep a mental list of who you need to talk to.

Traditionally, a wedding reception is a formal dinner affair and, as such, has a 'status' attached to where people sit. Wedding seating plans were also designed so that the two families could have the chance to get to know each other in a convivial setting.

The conventional top-table seating order from the left is; bridesmaid, groom's father, bride's mother, groom, bride, bride's father, groom's mother, best man.

Variations on this are:

- *Move your parents so that they are next to their partner, rather than their new in-laws*
- *When both sets of parents have remarried; groom's stepfather (or swap with groom's stepmother), bride's stepfather, bridesmaid, groom's father, bride's mother, groom, bride, bride's father, groom's mother, best man, bride's stepmother, groom's stepmother (or swap with groom's stepfather) – in this case, it can really help to have more than one best man and more than one bridesmaid on the top table too*
- *If the groom's parents have remarried; best man, groom's stepmother, groom's father, bride's mother, groom, bride, bride's father, groom's mother, groom's stepfather, bridesmaid*
- *If the bride's parents have remarried; bride's stepfather, chief bridesmaid, groom's father, bride's mother, groom, bride, bride's father, groom's mother, best man, bride's stepmother*

The seating plan tradition goes beyond the top table. In theory the reflection on status extends to seating all your guests, as those that are closer to the family should be seated nearer to the top table on the lower table numbers.

At the tables. Once all your guests are sitting down, the bride and groom can move from table to table to chat to them. The downside is that it is harder for you both to take time to enjoy your meal but because the top table is usually served first, you can take advantage of gaps between courses and tackle a couple of tables at a time.

By chance and in the speeches. If you want a more informal setting with no receiving line at all, then that is fine too. In this case, it would be polite and courteous to make sure you thank as many guests as possible in person for coming and thank them in your speeches.

On paper. Although it does not allow for personal introductions, if you have time or inclination you can give something to each of your guests such as an individual note at each person's place setting so that they know you are pleased that they came.

SEATING PLANS

ALTERNATIVE SEATING LOGISTICS

So much of this aspect of wedding etiquette is outdated. In modern society, couples may see their friends every week and their relatives rarely if ever at all, apart from at other weddings and funerals.

You should plan your reception logistics around what will give you the best memories on the day. Some ideas are:

Themed seating plans. These are great fun and also avoid having table numbers that distract your relatives away from wondering about why they are on table 82 while your friends are on table 2, right next to you. Use significant places, times or events in your relationship, or tie the table names into your wider theme e.g. butterfly types or Shakespearean plays, football or other sports teams, song titles, a tube map, Bond movies, *The Lord of the Rings* characters, colours, jockey silks and racecourses, countries or memories. Anything that means something to you and will be a talking point for your guests is ideal. And you can have some fun designing the seating plan in the same way. If you love the idea but doubt your creative ability then rope in the experts. There are a few companies doing this now including thetableplanner.com (01737 226 597, www.thetableplanner.com).

No seating plan. Free seating is great if you have a buffet or more chairs than people. It can also work well when all your guests know each other but can detract from the atmosphere if you have a crowd that need shepherding. It is also not a good idea if you know that certain guests clash – free seating takes away your ability to control where they sit. The upside of this is that you can definitely avoid the whole expense of place names, place-name holders and seating plan maps. And because the formality is removed, there is even less of a reason to have favours (although these should be optional anyway).

A round or 'two-sided' top table. It can be quite dull sitting at the top table, especially if you only sit people down one side. At best you get two people to talk to, while the people on the end only have one person. Meanwhile, you have a full view of everyone having fun and get to feel a bit like a goldfish on display. Instead, either have a round top table or an elongated table with people down both sides to be able to have more banter over your meal. Those giving speeches should be sat facing the whole room so that they don't have to move around when the time comes.

Do away with a traditional 'top table'. The top table will just be wherever you decide to sit. This might be especially appealing if you have divorced families. It also gives you the chance to sit with your mates if you want to.

Matchmaking opportunities. Don't worry about making sure your families are getting to know each other if they are unlikely to meet again. Instead, sit your guests with people they would like to spend more time with or people you think they might get on well with. And being as a lot of people meet their future partners at weddings, use the opportunity to put all your single friends and family on one table together and play matchmaker.

Seating rules. If you know you have twice as many men as women, then print up a notice at the door to the dining hall that advises guests that they cannot enter unless they are in threes of two men and one woman. Set up tables in multiples of three. This will get your guests mingling and 'boldly venturing' a lot faster than they might usually dare. Or for groups of even numbers, ask men to sit to the left of the ladies to ensure that the tables end up mixed.

CONSIDERATIONS

Ultimately, seat people in the way you think is most comfortable for everyone. That way, all your guests can relax and enjoy it rather than being traumatised with having to make conversation with someone they've never spoken to before, or stopped speaking to, just because tradition says they should.

If you do need arch enemies to sit together or near each other, let them know your plans and reasons in advance and appeal to their better natures to put aside their death stares and catty comments for the day.

Finally, ask your venue for advice and recommendations on seating plans that they give to all events. They know what works best in their venue and their gems of information might spark off some more ideas for you.

MORE RECEPTION LOGISTICS

Venue liaison. If you don't have time to check yourself, you need to delegate someone to ensure that everything is squared with the venue. They may also need to be responsible for signing off any additional requirements and saying when a free bar should draw to a close.

Honeymoon provisions. If you are not planning on going home before you go on your honeymoon, then someone will need to ensure your cases are secure and waiting for you and they should also be able to store your wedding outfits until you are able to pick them up.

Timings. Even for a 'simple' wedding, you should draw up a rough schedule with timings. This is important to make sure that you can achieve everything in the day that you need to. Run your ideal schedule past all the suppliers involved in your plan – they are the experts in their field and will let you know if you are being realistic.

FOOD AND DRINK

Eat, drink and be merry!

From budget options for 20 to banquets for 400, these handy hints can help you to plan how to do it in style.

 Most people will have experienced the traditional 'wedding breakfast'. This is the first meal after the couple are married and is now incorporated into the wedding reception. Drinks tend to be bucks fizz or Pimms on arrival, half a bottle of wine per person with the meal, additional allowances for non-drinkers and a glass of champagne or sparkling wine for the toasts. Food is usually a three-course sit-down meal, quite probably of the dried-up variety, and a vegetarian option. The main course is often chicken because most people will eat it. And for this wondrous concoction, you have to allow anywhere between £25 and £120 per person.

TIMINGS

Whatever time of day you get married, bear in mind that you will need to wine and dine your guests for the rest of the day, unless you clearly state that the reception has a start and finishing time. This will affect your food and drink budget and so if you are hoping to keep costs down, have a wedding later in the day and a reception that starts in the early evening.

But even if you are on a budget, be considerate to the needs of your guests. They may have travelled a long way and so basic hospitality is a must. Don't leave them wilting while you are having your photos taken or are performing other duties. If it is hot they will be gasping and will need some sustenance to stay on form. This doesn't have to be flash but it does need to keep them happy, especially if you are expecting everyone to be in high spirits late on into the night.

You also need to think about how much people are drinking in the course of a day and make sure you have food available to balance this so that you are not scraping people off the floor at 3 a.m.

And finally, give some thought to when you are going to be having your meals and how your toasts will fit in around this. See the **Speeches and Toasts** chapter for more ideas.

STANDARD CHOICES

Early on in your food planning you will need to make a choice about what type of food you want to serve to your guests, and how you want to serve it. It needs to be right for your guests and for you too.

Send a 'special dietary requirements' form out with the invitations, as you will need this feedback before you finalise your arrangements. It may even help steer your choice if you have very diverse requirements. Most caterers are happy to have a provision for vegetarian meals at short notice, but meals for vegan guests or those with religious restrictions, wheat, gluten, nut or dairy allergies normally take some more planning.

SELF-CATERING OR PROFESSIONAL CATERERS (INCLUDING RESTAURANTS)?

Your choice may be dictated to you by the venue you choose. Some of them rely on making a large share of their profits from in-house catering and so if you want to deviate from this, you may be charged a premium unless you can negotiate otherwise. Outside caterers will need to see a venue before the big day so that they can let you know of any access problems or additional equipment they will need. They vary in terms of whether or not they are willing to clear up or how late they will stay, so being clear about the facts and getting recommendations from other people are very important in finding the right caterer for you. Also, you should insist that you sample the dishes that you choose prior to the day. They often have a selection of menus to help you create one in your price range and should be able to advise you on dietary options and the cost of hiring linen, cutlery, glassware and waiters where required. Ultimately, hiring in the professionals and handing the job to someone else should leave you free to plan other parts of your wedding.

Alternatively, self-catering can be cheaper and more flexible but it can be a big task to take on and you need to think about whether you or your close family want to enjoy the party or be worrying about food, washing up, hiring extra cutlery, crockery and glassware, clearing away and freezer and fridge space. You shouldn't underestimate the military precision in planning a sit-down meal for a large number of people and so need to allocate tasks early on and perhaps have a dry run to ensure you have got all bases covered. A self-catered buffet is an easier option but it still means a lot more work than if you hire caterers, clearers and serving staff, even if it means them coming to your home.

STYLE OF MEAL

Whatever you choose, bear in mind the relevance of the season – in the depths of winter people tend to feel a lot hungrier than in summer and will appreciate a substantial hot dinner. In summer, a lighter meal will be more popular.

There are three more-conventional options:

Formal sit-down meal. This is a minimum of a three-course meal and involves either plate service or silver service at the table. Usually, there is a set menu that only varies for those with special dietary requirements (which caterers need to know in advance) and so this tends to cater to the most popular options. If you want to, you can go for a more exotic menu, but do be aware of people's likely tastes. For an additional fee, some venues will give your guests the choice of two or three dishes. In this case, you can keep prices lower by asking people to confirm their choice of meal in advance of the day so that the caterers have exact numbers and do not have to build in a 'wastage' budget. Make sure you have plenty of serving staff so that food quality doesn't suffer while it is left on serving hatches and your guests don't get frustrated with how long it takes for it to get to them. You should have a minimum of one waiter or waitress per table of eight to ten for silver service.

Finger buffet. A much less formal meal that consists of light, easy-to-pick-up food while the guests are often left to stand. Although this can be a lot cheaper, because it saves on space and expensive meals, it is not necessarily a good option for a wedding that involves a cross section of ages. Some people feel they need to sit down to eat and, after a long day, the food is often too light to satisfy everyone's appetites. The general lack of seating in the room can also make it harder to encourage people to mix in the way you would like and speeches have to be kept to a minimum as your guests will not find it comfortable to stand still and balance plates and glasses for a long period of time. If you do opt for this type of buffet, have enough chairs for a minimum of a quarter of your guests so that they can sit down in rotation if they need to. And look into hiring glass holders that hook onto plates to give people a free hand.

Hot or cold fork buffet. This option combines the other two; people can help themselves but then return to tables to sit down and eat. It might not sound very glamorous but a buffet will keep most people happy because, as long as you have a good selection for all tastes, they can choose food that they like rather than pushing a quail or spicy number around their plate in the hope that it will disappear. And it gives you the option of branching out from the standard melon, chicken, chocolate cake option. This also gives you the freedom of choosing a flexible or fixed seating plan. Budget wise, you save on paying for additional waiting staff but you must also think about how long it will take. If you have more than 50 guests, a second buffet line-up will mean that your guests aren't waiting for ever to get to the food. Also be sure that it will be replenished regularly so that no one feels they are getting the leftovers. Your master of ceremonies can co-ordinate people getting to and from the buffet. You can either go airline-style (mothers with small children first), or ask people to go up table by table. If you have themed table names and place settings, you can have some fun around this too and keep everyone entertained until it is their turn.

MOUTHWATERING OPTIONS AND THEMED FOOD

Even if a largely traditional meal is for you, there is no reason why you cannot get inventive about the extras or go for something completely different. Your food should reflect the rich textures and flavours of the day.

Colours. Keep it simple with one or two colours as the main themes through your food. Oranges and yellows can look really fresh against white linen for a summer wedding and give you lots of opportunities to introduce citrus flavours, yellow pepper, carrots, yellow courgettes, neutral-coloured foods like fish or chicken and beautifully laced desserts – not forgetting passion fruit. Use any combination of colours in the same way, but bear in mind that natural food colours are usually more appealing to the adult palette than luminous and fluorescent hues, not to mention the effect additives can have on hyperactive children!

Individual table buffets. Have the best of both worlds – choice without having to leave your chair. Serve individual buffets, course by course, to each table. With a collection of dishes and no queues, everyone can eat what they like and while it is still hot. From Greek meze to Spanish tapas, shared Chinese, Thai or Indian buffets, this is also a great way to introduce an international flavour to your meal.

> We had a traditional Indian table buffet. It worked really well because it had all the advantages of a sit-down meal but food was brought to the tables and topped up so that our guests could eat as much as they wanted and what they wanted. That was great because it made sure that everyone was satisfied. And the other bonus was that it encouraged interaction without people needing to leave their tables.
>
> SHILPA AND SIMON, 27 AND 30

Mexican. With burritos as big as your head and salsa to spice up your guests, top it off with a tribe of musical *banditos* making their rounds of the tables giving red roses to all the ladies. Plus have a piñata for the kids to tie in with a Mexican theme.

> Because we're having a summer wedding we fancied something seasonal and a bit alternative. A barbeque lets people choose what they want from a hot buffet rather than just eat what they are given and it's cheaper per head than a formal sit-down meal. We think it's a great idea – flexible, easier to prepare and serve, and means less time for sitting down and more time for dancing.
>
> JAMES AND STEPH, BOTH 30

Barbeque. Stay fresh outside in the balmy summer heat. If your venue has adequate grounds they may be able to arrange this for you or you can book caterers specifically. But do make sure you have shelter and an indoor space should the weather take a turn for the worse on the day.

Table fondue. Give each table a selection of fondue pots and things to dip for a varied, unusual and convivial meal.

World food buffet. For real variety, provide a buffet with serving tables inspired by the cuisine of different countries. If you have been great travellers, each could be based on your memories of those places. Again, it is a good idea to have an English table for those with less adventurous tastes.

Seafood banquet. Fresh lobster, Dover sole, oysters, mussels, tiger prawns and crab. No expense spared.

Chocoholic's paradise. From chocolate fondue to chocolate-dipped strawberries. If Willy Wonka is your all-time hero, then this could be for you. You can hire a single large chocolate fondue to serve about 100–300 people for around £500. Check out www.thechocolatefondue.co.uk or www.the originalchocolatefountain.com for fondues and www.chocolatechatter. co.uk for personalised chocolates.

Sweet tooth. Let everyone play at being big kids. What about a candyfloss stand, ice-cream machine and toppings, cake or toffee-apple stall? You can also tie this in with an English-style wedding, circus or country fayre theme.

Picnic. For really laid-back, summer style, a picnic is an informal option that can suit any budget. If you want to go for the top-end options, laden your hampers with champagne, strawberries, salmon, lobster and caviar.

DELICIOUS DRINKS

If you do not have any reason *not* to serve alcohol at your wedding, then you should do – it helps to get the atmosphere warmer and more lively as people lose their inhibitions and chat like old friends to people they have only just met. That said, you should also factor in and make an effort with those who are not drinking much alcohol, are driving or are teetotal, especially on a hot summer's day.

When you are planning your drinks, consider these ideas:

Wine tasting. As a warm-up to your wedding, or if your immediate families haven't spent much time together to date, organise a wine tasting at a local wine supplier to give them time to get to know each other and help you select the wine for your reception.

Wine order. Before you confirm your final wine order, think about what food you are serving. But more important than all the 'what you should drink with what' is what do your friends and family actually tend to opt for out of choice? On average you need to budget for a minimum of half to three-quarters of a bottle of wine per person (this also allows for non-drinkers). But again, use your personal knowledge of your guests to be realistic.

COCKTAILS

If you fancy yourself as a Tom Cruise then you should have fun coming up with your own recipes that you can name especially for the reception. Alternatively, get someone in to organise it and have fun at the tasting session before the big day. The selection below comes from www. cocktailmaker.co.uk. At Cocktailmaker, they design and then supply cocktails throughout the day, from a nerve-steadier when the bride is getting ready, to a celebratory tipple in the wedding car after the ceremony, to novel ideas for the guests on arrival. They are happy to create drinks to suit any theme, a signature cocktail just for you or their popular menu for weddings is:

Royal Wedding: Kirschwasser, peach schnapps, orange juice, champagne – a marriage of differing tastes that cries out for a sparkling finish.

Nuptial: Gin, Kirschwasser, Cointreau, lemon juice – not to be taken lightly. Orange, lemon and cherry with a bit of added strength.

Confetti Punch: White rum, sparkling wine, orange juice, white grape juice, lemonade, strawberries – an orange/wine flavour to this one; prepared in a bowl, served over ice.

Wedding Belle: Gin, Dubonnet, cherry brandy, orange juice – one for the ladies, definitely the belle of the ball.

June Bride: Gin, *crème de fraises*, lemon juice, Gomme, egg white – whatever the name, whatever the month.

Sparkling Southern Bride: Gin, Maraschino, lemon juice, champagne – a sparkling drink indeed!

Bride's Bowl: Cognac, cherry brandy, gold rum, lemon, orange and pineapple juice, fresh pineapple and orange, champagne – the ingredients are combined in a bowl with marinated fresh fruit. After chilling, the champagne is added and a little ice.

Bridesmaid Cooler: Gin, lemon juice, Gomme, Angostura, ginger ale – a Cooler is a long drink similar to a Collins. It originated in the 1880s and is never shaken, only stirred.

Wedding Cake: White rum, Amaretto, Coco Lopez, single cream, milk, pineapple juice – blended and served with chocolate-chunk floats. A sumptuous cocoa and nutty-flavoured drink.

Honeymoon: Calvados, Benedictine, lemon juice, orange Curaçao – apple, orange, lemon and herb flavour. Served over crushed ice.

Honeymoon Paradise: Blue Curaçao, Cointreau, lemon juice, champagne – blue in colour, lemon and orange overtones. A great champagne cocktail.

Welcome drinks. Veer away from traditional welcome drinks at your reception. How about gin and tonics, Pimms, Bellinis, punch, cocktails or even ice-cream sodas?

Virgin drinks. By having imaginative non-alcoholic options you will keep the drivers happy and kids love to think that they are drinking grown-up drinks so virgin cocktails will go down especially well because even non-drivers might not want to drink all day. You should also make a selection of soft drinks and some sparkling-wine alternatives available.

Champagne. Create a more interactive, opulent experience by placing champagne fountains strategically around the room.

Liqueurs. Think about whether you want to offer liqueur coffees or straight liqueurs at the end of the meal. You could include this at the end of a buffet as long as you are confident children will not be a hazard. Or put some miniatures or full-sized bottles on each table according to taste. The most popular after-dinner spirits to consider on their own or with coffee are brandy and whisky. Tia Maria, Frangelico and Bailey's are also popular in coffees. Or port, Pernod, Sambuca and lemon liqueurs are popular on their own.

BUDGET OPTIONS

You don't have to starve and dehydrate everyone to avoid blowing a fortune on your wedding catering. Here are some pointers to get you thinking.

FOOD

Avoid wastage. If it's just finger food, order three buffet places to cover four people. It will be enough to keep people going and mean that everything you order is eaten.

Contacts. Tap into anyone you know in the catering industry for ideas.

Student fare. Ask at your local colleges that run chef or catering courses and see if they offer wedding catering. But before you rub your hands in glee at the money you'll save, check out the standard of fare and service you can expect.

One meal only. Have an evening wedding so that you only need to feed everyone once. But if you are planning on eating late, let everyone know with your invitations so that they know to stock up on food at lunchtime.

Home-made buffet. If you're really up against it in terms of time and money, you could ask everyone to bring a dish to the wedding.

Keep food simple. If you know people like it, then why not?

⭐ CELEBRITY SPOTLIGHT

When Kate Winslet married Jim Threapleton, she won the hearts of many budget-conscious brides by opting for traditional British sausages and mash in her local pub for her reception, despite her millions. If she can do it then, in the right setting, it can be a good alternative for anyone.

> *I went to a wedding in an abbey last summer. It was all fairly conventional, right up until it was time to eat. The bride and groom had arranged for a fish and chip van to dish up meals for everyone. It was a fantastic idea – really novel and it also saved money and washing up!*
>
> LOTTIE, 29

Split the group. Only invite a small group of people to a sit-down meal, either at home, in a restaurant or at the venue, and arrange to meet everyone else later. But this may mean a lot of hanging around for those not invited, so make sure you have provided a list of alternative things for them to do in the meantime.

Serve your wedding cake for dessert. Then your heart is not broken when no one has any room left to eat it after a three-course meal. Plus this could be justification for getting the cake you really want.

Meal ticket. If the only way you can afford a reception is for people to pay for their own meals, then do it. You will find out who really wants to be at your wedding and can ask people to do this instead of presents so that they don't have to feel out of pocket. This one could really offend the traditionalists and your parents might be upset as they feel it reflects on them. Handle the subject sensitively and hopefully they will all understand.

> *When we got married, Jason's parents were insistent that we invite more of their extended family than we had done. Because we were getting married on a budget (not to mention having a baby on the way) we compromised by saying that they had to cover the cost of any additional places we agreed to. It was a bit tense at first but in the end, after a few controlled conversations with the in-laws, everyone was OK with it.*
>
> HELEN, 29

DRINK

The first thing is to consider how important alcohol is to your wedding and, if it is of great importance, how much is enough? The alcohol budget for a wedding can be extortionate and even if you go on a booze cruise you may still be charged corkage. Having said that, a booze cruise can be a real money-saver as long as your venue has reasonable (or no) corkage fees.

> *We did a lot of hunting around to find a venue that would let us bring in our own alcohol at a reasonable corkage charge. Fees varied hugely from place to place – they ranged from £2 to £15 for our champagne. Corkage on wine was usually less. If venues do try and charge you silly amounts per bottle then I'd recommend buying those really big bottles! (Except that I think a lot of places are on to that idea now.) It did save us a bit of money but to be honest overall it was all a bit of a faff.*
>
> MARIE, 29

Other money-saving tips include:

Use sparkling wine or Proseco instead of champagne. Champagne is simply sparkling wine from the Champagne region (although if you do want the real thing, think about buying direct from a vineyard in the area). Alternatively steer away from bubbles altogether.

Advance purchase. For the wine connoisseur, if you are organised enough and someone wants to buy you an engagement present, you could ask for wine that will be at its peak in the year you get married.

Non-drinkers. Factor in those people who will be driving and so not drinking – this will ensure you don't have loads of booze left over at the end of the night if you are bringing in your own. This is also a practicality so that everyone has something to drink throughout the night.

Restricted free bar. Limit it to the cheaper range of drinks e.g. house wine, draught beer and soft drinks. That way, people can choose to accept your hospitality or to put their hands in their pockets for more luxurious tastes.

Don't have a free bar. If people have to pay for their own drinks they tend to pace themselves more and make the effort to hold on to their half-full glass.

Individual glasses. For weddings where only one drink is served for most of the time, like punch or wine, you can give everyone their own personalised glass instead of favours. Then they will feel more compelled to hold on to it and wastage should be dramatically reduced. But depending on the quality of the glasses, they might set you back a bit.

Be the barman. If you are really strapped for cash, go on a booze cruise or to a bulk wine merchant and then ask someone to man the bar for you. You can even ask guests for suggested 'donations' per drink. You'll need to check for the licensing laws at your venue and double-check with national licensing laws at that time. UK law means that it is illegal to sell alcohol without a licence.

Shop around. Get the best prices for drinks and find out if your supplier will refund any unopened bottles. Some suppliers will also provide additional glassware at a reduced hire cost or for free hire on bulk purchases. You will be charged for any breakages or unreturned glasses.

Serve punch. Don't go crazy and make it the most potent thing anyone's ever tasted, but you can make up basic cocktails using a couple of core ingredients. Prepare one that's sweet and one that's drier to appeal to the widest possible audience, and have some iced beers on stand-by too. If you make it available in containers around the room then that can count as your free bar – once it's gone, the paid bar opens. This works well at summer weddings when guests are keen to sample refreshing alternatives to wine and beer. Or at winter weddings have mulled wine.

SPEECHES AND TOASTS

Many couples still go by the traditional order for speeches, as they provide one of the focal points of the reception.

Guests look forward to hearing what the wedding party will have to say and especially to seeing whether or not the best man will completely stitch up the groom. But there are other options for the modern wedding.

ALTERNATIVE IDEAS

You don't have to do things in this order if your circumstances make it tricky or awkward. Or perhaps you just don't like the formality of the whole thing. You may have a super-shy best man, a bridesmaid who's dying to have her say, a groom who thinks he's a comedian, or the mother instead of the father of the bride giving the speech about her daughter. So look at your own situation and think outside the boundaries of tradition.

Give speeches before the meal. That way nervous speakers can relax and enjoy their food. But make sure your guests aren't famished as their minds may start to drift. One way around this is to have speeches after the starter or have nibbles and drinks on the tables while they are going on. This is also a good option if your speakers are likely to be half-cut by the time the meal has finished.

Speeches are a central element of a traditional reception and are usually given after the meal and before the cutting of the cake. In the usual scenario the toastmaster or best man will get the audience's attention and introduce:

The father of the bride – who will usually tell a couple of nostalgic and cute tales about his daughter to introduce her to her in-laws, say a few words about the groom and welcome him to the family. He will also thank the guests for coming and propose a toast to the happy couple.

The groom – who will say thank you on behalf of himself and his new wife to the guests for their attendance and gifts, his parents for his upbringing and the bride's parents for granting him permission to marry their daughter and for hosting the day. He will then thank everyone involved in organising the wedding, including his best man and the bridesmaids. At this point many grooms will propose a toast and give gifts of flowers, jewellery or champagne to the mothers and bridesmaids.

The best man – who thanks the groom on behalf of the bridesmaids, who are obviously too demure to speak for themselves. He extends his congratulations to the newly-weds and thanks anyone that the bride has requested be mentioned on her behalf. Then he traditionally reads out any telegrams and good wishes from those who could not attend. It is also his job to act as the groom's spokesman to introduce him to the bride's family. Finally, the real fun begins as he tells some 'carefully chosen' stories about the groom's past.

The speeches end with the best man or toastmaster announcing the cutting of the cake.

At my cousin's wedding last year, they had all the speeches before we sat down for the meal so my uncle could enjoy it without worrying about making a speech. Which, when you think about it, makes a lot of sense considering how much a wedding breakfast can cost – you might just as well enjoy it rather than be scared witless!

LOTTIE, 29

Allow the girls to speak too. Bridesmaids, mothers and the bride all have the option to give speeches. It may traditionally be the boys who get to do all the talking, but guests will be interested (and pleasantly surprised) to hear what the girls have to say. Because of the break with tradition (although ladies' speeches are becoming more popular) you are also free to say what you like as there is no set pattern. So you can tell anecdotes and be as witty or as slushy as you like. The bride can also get the opportunity to thank her bridesmaids, parents, new husband and guests herself.

> *When I was bridesmaid to my best friend, she asked me to give a speech at her wedding. If her hubby was allowed a best man's speech, she wanted a bit of the spotlight for her amusing anecdotes too! I hate public speaking and so said no initially, but on the day before the wedding I changed my mind. It was easy to come up with stories about her but giving the speech was terrifying. The plus side was that a wedding audience is a fantastic crowd to talk to because they desperately want you to do well. My friend was really chuffed and I felt so exhilarated once I'd done it. Definitely no regrets.*
>
> LOUISE, 28

More than one best man. You may really want your oldest friend to be your best man but also another friend or brother to give a speech; there is no reason why you can't indulge both. Get them to liaise to make sure there isn't too much overlap in what they want to say.

Have an open floor. Either on its own or in conjunction with the key speeches, and invite anyone to speak. Let your guests know in advance that this will be the case and they will have time to prepare what they want to say. Think about a way to control this though or you could be listening to speeches all night!

Place your bets. Keep it light-hearted and have a sweepstake to guess the total length of the speeches or finishing time. All bet a pound or fiver and the winnings get split fifty-fifty (at least!) with the bride and groom. But be prepared for hecklers.

Get away from the top-table setting. If you are having a more free-form reception with people milling around without table plans, the speeches can take place with speakers simply standing up on chairs to be head and shoulders above your guests.

Toasts. If you want to involve someone who is too petrified to make a speech, proposing a toast is a way for them to meet you halfway. Or to avoid the speeches going on for ever, keep them to a minimum and ask some people to give toasts instead.

> *Why do people ask their friends who can't speak publicly to speak publicly? I've been to a few weddings where the speeches were either: a) too long, b) not funny or c) both a and b. There's so much pressure on having to have a set of speeches. Why do you have to have them at all?*
>
> DAVID, 33

Don't have any speeches. You might not want them or feel the need.

> *We wanted a low-key wedding that ended in a huge party. Neither of us really wanted speeches to be a part of that. I think our parents were a little bit disappointed at the time but they soon got over it.*
>
> HELEN AND JASON, 29 AND 30

STARTING POINT FOR SPEECHES

When asked to give a speech many people will freeze with fear and from that moment spend the lead-up to the wedding day obsessing about the detail of what they are going to say. Most people in this situation would rather the ground swallow them up than stand up in front of a room full of people expecting to make them roll around with laughter. There are lots of websites and books on the market dedicated to wedding speeches to help you out if you are lost for words. However, here are a few pointers to stop your speech taking over your life:

Relax. Easy for us to say. But breathing deeply into your abdomen and relaxing your shoulders will help immediately as it will slow your heartbeat down and will send 'relaxed' messages to your brain. Concentrating on this will stop you stressing about the situation you are in.

It's not about you. Well, it is, for a brief moment of the day, but in the whole scheme of things your speech is just a small element of the day, so allow this fact to take some of the pressure off.

The guests are rooting for you. The one great thing about giving a speech at a wedding is that your audience are on your side. These are friendly faces, not a rowdy public audience waiting to challenge you. Unless you are the best man, in which case don't rule out the odd heckle.

Prepare. Your speech will be a lot easier and a lot more coherent if you are well prepared and have some notes. So (however tempting it is) don't bury your head in the sand. Do some research and planning what you want to say and in what order. Make sure you have notes with you on the day, but as you get in more of a flow you may even find yourself ad-libbing.

Practise. It may seem obvious but don't be afraid to rehearse (and not just in front of the mirror so you can reassure yourself by laughing at your own jokes). Ask your partner or an honest friend to listen to you a few times so that your confidence in what you are saying grows and they can help you to rephrase things or add little comments.

Jokes. A few well-timed quips will keep your speech rolling, but don't be tempted to launch into a long joke that has no relevance to the day – you're at a wedding not in a comedy club.

> I had two best men and expected one to struggle with his speech. As it turned out, he was a knockout. He kept it simple, played it straight and knew where to draw the line. His opening was: 'Hi, my name's Mart and I'm an alcoholic ... [dramatic pause] Whoops! Wrong meeting!' and it flowed from there. His speech appealed to everyone and he had some great anecdotes in there from our past.
>
> DAN, 27

Think about how you'll feel afterwards. Don't dwell so much on how you feel before the speech, think about how you will feel once you've sat down at the end. You will be glad you had a chance to add to a memorable part of a special day.

Know your audience. Being a little risqué never hurts but think about what your audience can handle. Go for Disney-style innuendo rather than full-blown details. You don't want to have any shock revelations that make Granny's mouth purse up like a cat's bum.

Distraction techniques. A few props will get your audience's attention and can help the speaker feel more secure in front of a crowd as all eyes will be on the props and not them. Childhood or college photos are a good starter. You may even be able to dig out some choice video footage of the bride, groom or both from years gone by. One best man we spoke to had made up a whole brochure of photos cataloguing the groom's past and had printed one for every guest. He hid them until his moment came and then surprised everyone as he handed a pile out to each table, reaching the bride and groom last so that they wondered what on earth he was passing around. An alternative to this would be to stick photos or props under guests' chairs so that they can reach for them on cue.

Be soppy. Not all speeches have to be about making your audience roll in the aisles laughing. In fact, playing it straight and removing the pressure to make people laugh will make your life a lot easier. Wedding speeches are a perfect chance to get slushy and really express your feelings whatever your role.

Only have one to steady your nerves. A drunken slur on the wedding video is something that will haunt you for life and no one will thank you for it either.

Create an anchor. Rugby player Jonny Wilkinson clasps his hands out in front of him before he kicks. He has worked on identifying this physical action with a positive memory/feeling from a past experience; as he clasps his hands the feeling comes back to him so that he can perform at his best. Recall a time when you felt exactly how you want to feel when you are giving the speech. When you can really remember it and feel it, pick a physical action such as pressing your thumb and index finger together and repeat it until you are convinced that you identify the action with the feeling. Then, when you are due to give your speech, execute the action to recreate these feelings again.

Still quaking in your boots? However you are feeling, do your best to smile and *enjoy* the experience. Speak slowly and clearly, make eye contact and keep breathing! You may be stepping out of your comfort zone but face the challenge and be proud of yourself when you achieve it.

Emergency measures. There's every chance your speech will go well and people will thank you and congratulate you on it. However, if you do have a moment of crisis, freeze completely or say something wholly inappropriate, resist the urge to run out of the wedding or to drown your sorrows in a bottle of whisky in the corner – do your best to laugh it off. Everyone in the room will understand how you feel. Apart from perhaps the oldies, who you've just shocked into never talking to you again.

CAKE

Let them eat cake

Ancient Romans would bake a cake from barley or wheat and use it in the same way as we use confetti today. It was believed that if it was broken and the crumbs sprinkled over the bride that it would bestow fertility on the couple. Then someone had the bright idea to stop wasting all that cake and eat it instead.

The wedding cake as we know it has developed over the years but started life as a pile of small cakes or biscuits – guests would bring their own and add to the pile. The bride and groom would be challenged to kiss over the top of the tower of cakes and if they could, without knocking it down, they would have a lifetime of prosperity.

Folklore has it that the daughter of a baker was to be married in St Bride's church in the middle of London. Her father created the first wedding cake in the image of the church to commemorate her wedding day and this led to the traditional, tiered, white wedding cakes that we know today. This church is clearly visible from the south bank of the Thames, just west of St Paul's Cathedral.

If you do opt for the classic three-tiered fruitcake, some couples save one tier of their cake for the christening of their first child. It is also said that you should keep the top layer to celebrate your first wedding anniversary. That won't leave much cake for the actual wedding day!

CAKE-A-BOCKER GLORY

Thankfully the traditions of barley and wheat cakes and piles of dry biscuits are long gone, and even the days of royal-icing-covered tiered cakes seem to be numbered. These days (if you choose to have a wedding cake) if you can imagine it, you can have it. What is clear is that you are no longer limited to fruitcake.

If you are in doubt about your many options, check out the online picture catalogues of some of the specialists in making wedding cakes. Or to really see what you're letting yourself in for, visit one of the national wedding show exhibitions, where there are plenty of extravagant and sophisticated cakes to choose from. There's everything you can think of from very elaborate and diverse individual cakes stacked on tiered stands to bride-and-groom figures sat on suitcases, replicas of the top table, fairy castles, fairy cakes, patriotic statements, sweetie-covered sponges, profiterole mountains, cake tiers alternated with layers of flowers or simply alternate tiers of lemon, passion fruit, carrot or chocolate cake.

You can keep it very classic and simple, or you can create a unique novelty cake that reflects your personalities. Specialist companies will consult with you and can then bring your ideas to life. We heard of one couple who had a cake iced as the exterior of Harrods, as that was where they had bought their rings.

> *Wedding cakes have changed enormously. Ten years ago, brides wanted hundreds of tiny small sugar flowers, loads of frills and cakes on pillars – not anymore. Brides have not only latched on to the 'American' idea of a stacked (one directly on top of the other) wedding cake, but chocolate wedding cakes are the very latest phenomenon. They have become so popular because at last here is not only an alternative to a three-layer fruitcake that gets left but it can also be used as a dessert. The reassurance therefore that not only will your cake still have that 'wow' factor but it will actually get eaten!*
>
> TRACEY MANN, WWW.TRACEYSCAKES.CO.UK

There are no hard-and-fast rules about your wedding cake, or indeed whether you have to have a cake at all. You could simply have your favourite sweet thing, be it a coffee and walnut sponge, giant Battenburg, or a wedding-sized version of your favourite dessert. There's no real reason why your cake-cutting moment can't be the two of you digging a spoon into a massive bowl of tiramisu or slicing into a hazelnut roulade. In fact, there are plenty of caterers who will arrange a dessert, for example a strawberry mousse cake, to look every bit as stunning as a traditional wedding centrepiece.

It is customary to cut the cake after the speeches but it might be easier to cut it before if you want it as soon as possible so that the caterers have plenty of time to slice it up (especially if the father of the bride can talk for Britain). It can then be passed around without too much of a gap in the proceedings.

Alternatively, ditch the cake-cutting ritual altogether and opt for designed cookies or individual cakes. They come in all shapes and sizes and can be personalised to your individual requirements.

If you are not following the conventional order of meal and speeches then cut the cake (or dig into your dessert) whenever you see fit. Just make sure you let everyone know when this is, as it's another classic photo opportunity for your guests.

CONSIDERATIONS

✓ Don't just consider people's diets for the meal. If you know that some of your guests have allergies, then you could get one tier made up as a gluten-, dairy-, nut- or wheat-free cake

✓ You can buy individual mailing boxes (www.confetti.co.uk) for sending wedding cake out to your guests after the day. If you include your thank you cards with this it is a great finish to the wedding

✓ Cupcakes are also a great option if you think a lot of people have had their noses put out of joint because their offspring were excluded. Personalise some for the kids that were not invited so that the parents have something to take home to soften the blow

✓ If you are getting married overseas and taking your cake with you, choose one that will travel well – only two tiers max. If it has elevated tiers then construct the height on site. Or you could just save yourself the hassle and buy a local cake in your resort

✓ Hark back to the lost tradition of trying to kiss over the cake for a lifetime of prosperity. Let your guests know what you are doing – it is a nice touch and will reassure them that you haven't gone potty as you get butter icing all down the front of your outfits

BUDGET OPTIONS

Bake a cake yourself. Ignore the old wives' tale that this brings bad luck; it was just a gaggle of gossips who made that up anyway. If you think you'll be rushed off your feet arranging other things, ask someone to do it for you. Perhaps they would prepare it for you as their wedding gift? If you are having a fruitcake, invest in a good storage tin and it can be made well in advance.

Pitching in. How about a tower of little cakes, home-made and iced individually with your initials, something relevant to you both personally or to your theme? You could even have a cake-making day in the lead-up to your wedding and invite the children of family and friends to all pitch in. Sure to be a very messy affair, but it will create a very personal tower of cakes.

Sweetie time. If you want a more fun cake, use basic sponges with butter icing and decorate them liberally with Jelly Tots and other little sweets.

Pudding. As mentioned, you can combine your cake and dessert so that you effectively get two for the price of one.

Cheat. Lots of big food stores, including Asda and Marks & Spencer, now sell white iced 'occasion' cakes in a variety of sizes. You can either stack them directly on top of each other or buy the white pillar sets. This should only set you back about £35–£50 as opposed to £200–£900. A real budget saver and you can personalise them in your own theme. You can also hire cake stands from any cake shop.

Compromise. If you want to hedge your bets because you don't trust your own decorating skills, buy or make the cakes but get someone else to decorate them for you. Or vice versa.

DECORATIONS AND FINISHING TOUCHES

You may think that minute detail doesn't bother you, but when you start planning don't be surprised if you suddenly become obsessed with what colour ribbon to tie around napkins and other frivolities.

It's those little things that make the day complete and can also cost a fortune, so this chapter discusses all the added extras to make your wedding unique.

CAUTION! BUDGETS BEWARE

There is a very real need for a good sense of judgement around how far you go with the finishing touches. Sometimes simplicity can be more effective than pricey extras that go completely over the top and triple your reception budget. Alternatively, a couple of expensive details can be a lot more striking and memorable than the equal amount spent on a bulk shipment of cheap tat.

Yes, the detail can make the difference, but learn to recognise when something is pivotal to your experience on the day as opposed to being something that no one is likely to notice. What is much more important is the overall effect. You can save money by making things yourself. But the only real way to save money is to be willing to reassess your ideas as to what you would like. You don't have to give up on your dream – just find different ways to achieve the same effect. For example, if you want a starry look and have your heart set on a blanket of lights for the ceiling of your venue, consider whether a liberal sprinkling of candles and fairy lights will achieve the same magical effect. You could buy tens of thousands of tea lights for the same price as some professional lighting effects.

If you are the creative type and want to make the decorations yourself to keep everything as personal and unique as possible, look around at what is available from wedding décor companies and also visit art shops, haberdashers and craft shops to find out what is possible.

While you are striving to create your ideal wedding, consider adjusting your standards or expectations; you can be happier with less. It is all about positive thinking, not getting carried away to an extent that you will regret and not getting stressed or blowing your budget for the sake of small details. To help you keep things in perspective, make a list of your ideal wedding reception, work out the cost of each line item and then tier it according to 'must have', 'would like' and 'not necessary'. And have fun choosing.

COLOUR CO-ORDINATION

When it comes to choosing the main colours for your wedding, it can be daunting knowing where to start. To help, use an artist's colour wheel to see which colours work together. As a general rule, you can use colours that are very close to each other in the wheel or directly opposite as complementary colours.

Black, white, metallic colours, such as gold or silver, and neutral colours like cream tend to go with all options. Ultimately, nothing beats seeing the actual colours together – you will just get a feel of whether it works or not. And once you have decided on the colours you want, make up a swatch of samples to carry around with you so that you can snap up impromptu purchases with peace of mind.

CONFETTI

Normally guests will bring their own confetti to a wedding and it must be used in accordance with the rules of the particular venue. These often state that it must be biodegradable or kept to a certain area to minimise the cleaning up.

Alternatively, if you want to have a certain look in your photos, for example with colour co-ordinated, feather or rose-petal confetti, then you can let the guests know on their invitations that 'confetti will be provided'.

Throwing rice at the bride and groom was an ancient custom in which the grains were believed to bestow fertility on the happy couple. Confetti originates from Italy, where nuts and grains covered in sugar were thrown at couples for the same reason.

FAVOURS

Favours are a prime example of the wedding industry gone potty. It was all well and good when you could give someone five almonds and they would be happy, but the stakes have been raised. Favours are now an art form.

Traditionally, favours are given to all the guests as a memento of the day and token of your gratitude to them for coming. Until recently, these would have been a very affordable five sugared almonds in a box or purse. These represent health, wealth, fertility, long life and happiness.

The first thing you need to decide is whether to have them or not. If you have a very small budget for them, rather than get something you are not particularly happy with, consider not giving favours at all. They are not 'make or break' so only have them if you want them, not because you feel you have to. But don't be tempted to go for something that looks cheap – this can compromise the overall effect of other more expensive elements of your wedding.

INSPIRATION FOR FAVOURS

Flowers. If your table decorations involve putting a single rose or posy in each place, especially for the ladies, then treat that as a favour.

Sweets. Always popular, either as favours or in a container in the centre of the table. And for an added touch, colour co-ordinate them. This also gives your guests something to nibble on to keep the hunger pangs at bay until the food is ready. Choose from family packs of sweets, jelly beans (or the adventurously flavoured Jelly Bellys), lollipops, designer chocolates or personalised chocolates. Love Heart sweets with wedding messages are also popular as favours or to scatter on the table (0800 970 0480, www.lovehearts.com).

Iced biscuits. You can personalise them with a logo, your names, initials, date of the wedding or whatever else appeals to you. Again, if you're on a budget, this is something you could delegate to an over-eager relative who doubles as a domestic god or goddess. If you are not lucky enough to know someone who fits this bill, then there are plenty of suppliers now offering this service.

Miniatures or cigars. These are favourites with male guests, but avoid giving out cigars unless you can afford good ones – people can tell the difference. And miniatures of whisky are a great way to top off a Scottish theme.

Fortune cookies. These are becoming mainstream and the real bonus is that you can design your own message or messages. Hey, if you've got exciting news, maybe a baby is on the way, this could be the ideal way to tell everyone in one go!

Fortune-tellers. To avoid edible favours, make up the folded fortune tellers that you used to play with as a child. You have to pinch it with forefingers and thumbs from behind and move your fingers together and apart again a chosen number of times, then reveal the fortune under that number or colour as revealed in the mouth of the paper folds.

A lasting favour that will grow with your relationship. This can be anything as simple as tulip or snowdrop bulbs, a pot plant, small sapling tree or even a bonsai. Just make sure they are small if you are going to put them on the table or your guests will not be able to see each other or you through the forest.

Lottery tickets or scratch cards. Original, and you can guarantee that you can get them for a pound, plus the cost of an envelope if you think that is necessary. Later on in the evening you can read out the winning numbers for that day and see if any of your guests have been lucky.

Hangover cures. Painkillers and a hangover remedy for the next morning. But this might not be appropriate for all of your wedding party and is definitely not a good idea if you have a lot of children around who might mistake them for sweeties.

For children. Give a small toy or fun box instead of a favour. A Kinder Surprise, bubble bottle, colouring book and crayons will not only be a thoughtful touch, it should also keep them entertained.

Event fever. If your wedding is coinciding with another event that everyone knows about such as the FA Cup final, world championship events or royal weddings, favours are a fun way to allude to that event and a great take-home present. Use the team colours for sweetie bowls, the ball shape for little individual cakes, or personalities involved for inspiration.

Luxury. For the top-end budgets, give a voucher for the hotel beauty or leisure facilities to be redeemed the day after the wedding. Or what about a small bottle of perfume or cologne?

Packaging. The array of boxes, bags or purses that you can choose from is extensive. You can get boxes that are straightforward, themed, handbag shapes with a snap clip, themed for kids, material-covered, embellished with roses or gems – anything you can think of really. And the purses come in any colour or fabric you can imagine. Considering how much it would cost you to make them yourself or have unique ones specially designed, they are also very reasonably priced as a bulk stock item, so if your motive for going home-made on the packaging is budget, don't bother.

Themes. Check out the **Themes** chapter for ideas to get you started.

There are lots of companies specialising in wedding favours. The list below is by no means exhaustive, so if you don't find what you are after at the right price, keep looking.

- ✓ Bomboniere by Manancourt (01780 751 926, www.bombonierebymanancourt.co.uk)
- ✓ Confetti (www.confetti.co.uk)
- ✓ The Card and Favour Company (01425 476 606, www.thefavourcompany.co.uk)
- ✓ Forever Memories (01384 878 111, www.forevermemories.co.uk)
- ✓ Passion for Petals (01404 811 467, www.passionforpetals.com)
- ✓ The Last Detail (0845 6 804 084, www.thelastdetail.co.uk)
- ✓ The White House (01905 381 149, www.the-whitehouse.uk.com)
- ✓ UK Wedding Favours (01282 850 032, www.ukweddingfavours.com)

PLACE-NAME CARDS

There are hundreds of types of place-name cards and holders available in all shapes, colours and sizes. But again, at between £2 and £10 a pop, these can add a fair amount to your reception budget and that is not counting the printing costs. Something to keep in mind is that if you can write on it or cut a slot in it, it can be used to mark place names.

If you are interested in printing place-name cards, see the **Invitations and Stationery** chapter. Some of your other options include:

Handwrite place-name cards. Rather than print them. This makes it much easier for you to make last-minute changes without it being obvious.

No card holder. Just fold the card so that it can stand on its own. You can add extra decoration with a bit of ribbon, glitter, a flower petal, feather or other decoration. Alternatively, fold the napkin so that it forms a pocket and insert the name card tied to a single flower with ribbon for a simple, stunning effect.

Pebbles. Buy a bag of medium-sized pebbles from your garden centre and write your guests' names on these. You can get standard white or black markers or use a colour to tie in with your theme. Put each pebble on top of a napkin and maybe drape some ribbon around it to add some colour. This looks great and is very budget friendly.

Food for thought. Back to the 'if you can cut a slot in it, you can use it' idea. This goes for anything from oranges, lemons, limes, apples and exotic star fruits to marshmallows. The effect is fabulous because not only is this very unusual, you can also choose things with great colours to complement your theme and stand out against the table linen. For an extra touch add some ribbon or raffia. But before you go out and buy 150 oranges, use the exact pen and card you will use on the day and have a test run to check that the ink will not run.

Natural inspiration. Nature provides you with ready-made place holders such as pine cones. Dry them out in a garage or shed in advance of the wedding and spray them with insect repellent to make sure you don't have any six- or eight-legged visitors joining your reception uninvited. Then you can spray them to colour them. It's best not to go too far with pine cones in terms of additional decorations, because otherwise they can end up looking a bit like something a seven-year-old brings home from school. Done well, they are perfect for an autumn wedding or a wedding with a woodland theme.

Get inventive with your guests' names. Either keep them in your theme or pick out a characteristic ideal for that person. And so John 'guvnor' Smith and Margaret 'randy' Brown are born. This should give everyone a bit of fun and give people something else to get the banter going.

Name cards double as trivia cards. Use the back of the card to write an interesting fact or Q&A about you, weddings, the family, the other guests at that table or your theme. It will give everyone something to kick-start conversation, especially if they don't know each other.

Themes for seating plans are discussed in the **Reception Logistics** chapter and can be tied in with both place cards and table decorations.

TABLE DECORATIONS

Every issue of every wedding magazine has amazing photographs of wedding tables and they are stunning. You can easily achieve these looks too, but they are not cheap. Be prepared to pay the price and set your budget before you get stuck in to the suppliers. How much money are you willing to spend per head on table decorations?

> For me, it came down to what was cheap but effective. I wanted simplicity but elegance and something that tied in with the colour theme. Finding little artificial flowers that were the same colour as my bouquet was a real inspiration, so we made some small wreaths to go round the candles in the middle of the tables and then we sprinkled dried bougainvillea leaves over the plain white tablecloths, which I think looked fab. To top it all off we had bowls of sweets in the same colour themes, as everyone knows I love sweets and it solved the whole problem of favours.
>
> Jo, 27

There are lots of ideas out there for all types of budget.

Napkins can be folded or 'ringed'. Napkin rings can be hired from event and catering companies but can also double as keepsake favours if you have them printed with the date and details of the wedding. For very simple and cheap napkin rings, just tie them with quality ribbon. Save money where you can.

Bloomin' lovely. There are lots of ideas in the **Flowers** chapter. One is to use small wooden or glass boxes that mirror the shape of the table. Then cut the stems off your flowers and pack the heads in really tightly for a tidy, colourful and fragrant centrepiece. Evergreen shrubs can also be used. Liven up the colours with fabric, ribbon, single flowers, crystals or coloured pebbles. Or use clusters of small pot plants that can double as favours for people to take home with them – this also avoids the wastage of a room full of flowers that will be dead in a day or two.

Colour co-ordination. Don't forget that although table linen usually comes in white for weddings, you could go for a bolder colour like a fuchsia pink or deep red and then use your finishing touches to add complementary splashes of colour.

Table confetti. Shaped glitter confetti is incredibly popular. Sprinkled on the tables it can be very effective to reinforce your theme and also catch the lights to give the evening some sparkle. Selections come in a variety of colours and range from stars to bells, cupids, hearts, butterflies, 'just married' text and lots more. You can also include a couple of pieces of the confetti in each invitation as you send them out. Alternatives to glitter confetti are feathers or small coloured pebbles.

Wired decorations. Wired ribbon or material butterflies on wire can be attached to table displays. But stick to your theme to keep things clear and simple.

Disposable cameras. As discussed in the **Capturing the Occasion** chapter, a great way to get reportage shots of your guests without having to pay your official photographer for them is to provide disposable cameras on the tables and collect them at the end for developing.

Photo stand. Collect willowy twigs from trees in your garden, spray them in a colour that complements your wedding colours, tie them with ribbon and prop them up in the centre of each of your tables by using a stand or vase. Then attach photos of the guests at that table and favours to the display. Just don't make it so large that people can't see around it!

A treat in your glass. When you set the table, fill wine glasses with party poppers, streamers and sweets.

Simplicity. If you want to keep it simple, just loosely wind bits of ribbon around the cutlery, glasses and napkins, through invitations, orders of service, place cards, thank you cards and as additional decorations in the flowers and bouquets. It's cheap, quick and effective.

Shapes. Don't feel restricted to round white plates or silver cutlery. If you think that coloured crockery will enhance your overall look then you can hire it from event and catering companies. Plates can also be rented in triangle, square and shield shapes that look especially effective when used with one of the other shapes of plate.

LIGHTING

This is probably the most important factor in creating an ambience at any event. Visit your venues at the time of day that your ceremony and reception will be and see the effect of the lighting they currently have. If you can afford it, you might want to employ a lighting specialist to give you advice. If the problem is that the lights are too glaring, see if you can replace them on the day with lower wattage, soft-finish bulbs, or turn them off and party by candlelight. Low lighting is also fantastic for hiding a multitude of sins in a venue – you would have to be lying on the floor to notice cigarette burns and drinks stains in a packed room with only candlelight and fairy lights to see by.

Just make sure it is bright enough so that your guests can see what they are eating (unless you are going for the 'dining in the dark' experience). If you have spotlights, rather than point them at your guests you can direct them at focal points such as the cake or flowers, letting the light diffuse into the rest of the room. Lighting options include:

- ✓ Candlelight – create a feeling of intimacy in an otherwise dimly lit room. Use church candles or clusters of tea lights as part of the decoration on the tables or thinner candles in candle-holders or freestanding candelabras. Another option is floating candles alongside flower heads, petals or glitter confetti. Any of these can be very effective, especially for evening or winter receptions. But do exercise some caution if you are planning on having a lot of children around – ditto for hideously drunk people

- ✓ Fairy lights – draped around balconies, windowsills, mirrors, staircases and dado rails

- ✓ Rope lights – similar to fairy lights, but you can wind them around poles with a lot less likelihood of them getting tangled

- ✓ A blanket of stars – event companies offer star-cloth ceiling linings. For added sparkle or to bring the outdoors indoors, this is a great alternative

- ✓ Nets of lights – for draping over shrubs or trees or hanging on walls

- ✓ Rustic – for less formal lighting, put tea lights in jam jars and hang them from the rafters

ROOM DECORATIONS

 As you would expect, the obsession with old wives' tales has also been evident in the traditional choice of wedding decorations: bells ward off evil spirits and horseshoes (provided they are the right way up) are symbols of good luck.

Thankfully, you have a lot more choice now.

Ice sculptures. Still a source of fascination for people. You can get figures, pistols, fish, trees, animals, shells or anything you can imagine. And you can also arrange to have a hole drilled through the middle so that later on, when the party really gets going, you can pour shots of drink in the top and get people to catch them at the other end (see also 'Winter Wedding' in the **Themes** chapter).

Backdrops. To transport your guests to another place. Tropical beaches, flames, mountains, golf courses, fireworks, city scenes or clouds are just a few of the options.

Decorating the chairs. This is currently a very popular look and ranges from full chair covers to swathes of fabric tied around the chair backs. If you want to achieve this look yourself then consider how much the fabric will cost you and how much hire costs are by comparison. Do not try and cut corners by cutting back drastically on fabric because the final effect will be compromised. If budget is a concern, then consider going for a sash or a corsage effect of evergreen and a single flower tied to the back of the chair with a long length of ribbon, or just go for a thick ribbon rosette. Hire costs are approximately £4 for the cover and sash tie if your venue is supplying chairs. Alternatively, you can just hire some good-quality chairs for about £3 each and avoid the chair covers altogether.

Celebrity style. If you want to go for a red carpet reception you can hire carpet and barrier post with red rope from The Hire Business (0844 800 7508 or 0161 724 4888, www.thehirebusiness.com).

Extras and special effects. Event hire companies can also supply you with confetti sprayers, bubble machines, smoke generators, snowstorm machines, potted plants and shrubbery, statues, outdoor heaters, picket fencing and different types of flooring.

Photo walls or boards. Prepare a collage of photos of you both as youngsters, either as one collage or two separate ones. This gives all your friends a bit of a laugh and lets your family reminisce. If you have time, or are looking for another job to be able to delegate to someone, go the extra mile and prepare a collage that has photos of all of your guests from the past, preferably with you as a youngster too. There is usually a fair amount of hanging around at weddings so this will help to entertain the troops and make them feel a part of your past and your future.

Space fillers. If you feel like you haven't got enough decoration prepared to give the venue a make-over, cheap additions to fill out the space are ivy and other evergreen plants that you might be able to get from the gardens of friends and family. And balloons (again, wedding specialists have a range of colours), ribbons and streamers can be effective.

Professional help? Decorating a room can be a daunting task if you really want to transform the space. You can do it on your own if you are organised, realistic and creative, or if you want help with all or part of your décor there are now a plethora of companies specialising in decorating the tables and chairs as well as the venue itself. They are professionals used to working with ample budgets and the looks they create tend to be fantastic. Realistically, if you want exactly what they are offering you are probably best to get them to do it unless you're willing to invest a lot of time yourself and have access to some very cheap material stocks. On the other hand, if you are happy to compromise then you might be able to do it more economically yourself.

Before you sign up your chosen supplier the usual rules apply – get at least two other comparative quotes, ask for recommendations, visit another wedding they are working on to see their professionalism in action and check the fine print of the contract to make sure it serves your interests as well as theirs.

GUEST BOOK OPTIONS

Because it can be tricky to find the time to have a deep and meaningful talk with all your guests, a guest book means they get to leave you a thought that you can read when you have some time to digest your day.

Usually, a book just circulates at a wedding reception and people sign it as and when it reaches them. Some other possibilities include:

Themed messages. Ask the guests to write a message that includes either their definition of marriage, their top tip for a happy marriage, their favourite memory in their own relationships or something that will capture the sentiment of the day.

And here's one I prepared earlier. Give your guests time to think of something meaningful to write rather than rushing it. Send out blank pages with the invitations for people to write on before they arrive and then compile everything in a guest book after the reception. This is definitely a job to delegate to someone central in the family.

Personalised pottery. With the boom in pottery painting comes a new alternative. Visit your local pottery-painting shop and choose a plate to keep it simple or go for a six-piece dinner service if you fancy. You can ask your guests to sign the unfired pottery at the reception and then take it back to the shop to have it fired and glazed. *Et voilà*, you have a working reminder of your wedding for everyday use or display.

Photo messages. There are various ways you can do this:

✓ Photo wall or board – pictures of the bride and groom throughout their lives, including photos of important memories with friends and families too. Provide a wide border around the photos and ask guests to sign this board instead of a book. But do give some thought as to how you will get it home, store it and be able to access it easily to reminisce about the day

✓ Bring your own – ask everyone to bring a photo that captures the epitome of your relationship with each other or your relationship with them. They will have already had to give some thought as to why that photo means what it does and so when they arrive, stick the photo in a guest book and ask them to write a message alongside it. Only write on the right-hand pages because otherwise the photos will get indented from the handwriting on the back

✓ You've been framed – when people arrive at the reception, give someone the job of taking Polaroids of them. Then stick the photos in a 'memories' book and ask the guests to write a few words against their photos. This will provide you with a snapshot of each person on the day and is especially useful if you do not know the names of everyone in each other's families yet

Blank canvas. A variation on the photo wall is to hang a large blank canvas and ask people to sign this. You can divide the canvas up into smaller boxes like the donation walls in museums if you think space will be at a premium or if you would like it to be symmetrical. Depending on the size of the canvas you might just want names and a couple of words or you might have space for anecdotes and drawings. Either way, you end up with one or two canvases of wedding memories that you can either hang in your home or give to your parents or grandparents.

EXTRAS

Just in case you are still hungry for more ideas to personalise your reception:

Useless fact or question cards. For each table to get the conversation going. To make it more interesting, make them 'scruples'-style questions.

Sparklers. You can get heart-shaped sparklers from wedding specialists.

Doves. Doves are known to mate for life, making them a classic symbol of unity. Try www.wingsforlove.co.uk or www.whitedoverelease.co.uk.

Wedding day kit. If you know that your mums will be at their wits' end with nerves on the big day, give them and yourself a goody bag with herbal Rescue Remedy, nibbles for the hectic wedding morning to ensure you do not feel faint by the time you get to the ceremony, breath freshener and a facial spritz.

Mementos. Another nice treat for you, your mums and your bridesmaids are hand-decorated keepsake boxes, photo albums, guest books and bride's notebooks.

CONSIDERATIONS

If your ideal wedding involves a low-stress day and run-up to the day, then keep your attention to detail under control unless you can afford to pay someone else to worry about the finer points of the plan. It's true that these details really can make a difference but keep it all in perspective – your day will be fantastic whatever happens because you will be in such a euphoric blur that you'll only really remember the big picture. It's best if that doesn't involve a tantrum over the distribution of the glitter confetti on the tables.

Unfortunately the service industry in Britain still has some way to go to ensuring total customer satisfaction. Accept that you are highly unlikely to get 100 per cent of the results you want on your enquiries, or maybe even on the day, and then you can only be pleasantly surprised.

To spread the cost of your wedding, buy non-perishable favours as far in advance of the wedding as possible and get organised about any themes you want a year in advance of your wedding, then you can scoot around the shops and buy decorations on special offer because they are about to go out of season. Even the wedding companies will have sales to sell off summer stock before the winter months. And a great idea is to snap up lots of glittery and glass decorations in the January sales. Christmas decorations come in all colours and can give a great lift to a table display or room decorations at any time of year. And fairy lights will be a real bargain.

RECEPTION MUSIC AND ENTERTAINMENT

When it comes to wedding entertainment the traditional choices immediately spring to mind:

✓ A string quartet for the start of the reception as guests are received and take their seats

✓ Dave the DJ, complete with glittering disco ball and flashing traffic lights for the 80s retro knees-up

✓ A band whose lead singer bears more than a passing resemblance to Adam Sandler in The Wedding Singer.

As with every aspect of planning your ideal wedding, you do have options for your reception entertainment. And you can even take this opportunity to enhance your theme that little bit more.

STYLE OF MUSIC FOR THE RECEPTION

If music is the main form of entertainment at your reception, you have one initial choice to make: live band, DJ or a mixture of both?

From now until your wedding, you will find yourselves turning into talent scouts – taking contact details from anyone you see or hear about that impresses you.

LIVE BAND

Live music has a whole different feel to a one-man DJ set. Plus, a live band can create more of a sense of occasion. Bear in mind that they may have a limited repertoire of songs and will tend to be more expensive than a DJ. A selection of the types of acts available include:

- ✓ Jazz
- ✓ Barn dance
- ✓ Seventies funk
- ✓ Rock 'n' roll
- ✓ Big band
- ✓ Salsa
- ✓ Tribute bands
- ✓ Scottish ceilidh
- ✓ Steel band

DJ

A good DJ will be able to play pretty much any request and can even play the exact set that you plan. Guests can choose songs in advance and spontaneous requests are more likely to get played. Alternatively, you could go for:

- ✓ Two in one – DJ and karaoke, barn dancing or anything else you want
- ✓ Headline – for bigger budgets, hire a club or radio DJ
- ✓ Decade specific – for a throwback to the halcyon days of yesteryear

PRACTICALITIES

For advice on contracting a supplier, have a look at **First Things First**.

See them in action. There is a huge range of ability, reliability and equipment out there, so don't just book the first act you find. Try to see the band or DJ in question playing live at another function to see if they can fill a dance floor. A lot of bands also have demo CDs.

Hiring through an entertainment agent. It may cost more but they should be able to offer you a back-up plan if for any reason your chosen act can't make it.

> " We always have a contract, whether we work directly for the
> bride and groom or via an agency or party organiser of some kind.
> The contract protects not only us but also the bride and groom. It is
> not unusual to be phoned at the last minute by a bride who has
> been let down by a band that has not been formally booked by
> contract.
>
> CHRIS BARTON, WWW.CHRISBARTONBAND.CO.UK

Set lists. Many will have set lists that you can view to state your preferences
about songs before the night and some will learn a specific track if you
ask them.

> " We are due to be married in a couple of months and we've
> asked each of our guests to nominate a song they would like to hear
> played at the reception. We've let them know that we might not be
> able to play everything, but it means that we have a good list to work
> through with the band and on the day they will read out who chose
> each song and why before they play it. We hope it will make
> everyone feel really involved.
>
> JANET, 31

Set up and space. Bands tend to take up more space than a disco so make
sure your venue can accommodate a 16-piece band before you book it.
Check how long they will need to set up on the day and cross-reference all
your plans with the venue.

Power. See if you need a separate generator for the band in case they are
liable to overload the system.

Sound restrictions. Are there any limitations on noise levels or a curfew?

Special effects. Some venues do not allow the use of smoke or fog machines as these may set off alarms.

Specifics. Venues will often ask to see a Public Appliance Test Certificate for the act's equipment to ensure that their kit is in full working order. They may also request a Public Liability Certificate, which confirms that your act is insured. Make sure they have both of these when you book them or you may find yourself without entertainment at the last minute.

Back up. Whether it's your first dance or a particular song that you definitely want to hear during the evening, to be on the safe side, make sure you have your own copy in the right format at the venue to avoid last-minute disappointment.

> Try to warn your DJ if there are stairs at the venue and no lift! Or if it is difficult to park close by. Things like this will affect set-up time because health and safety can't be compromised.
>
> Couples will often give me a list of tracks that they would like to hear but are just as likely to let me know what they don't want played. This obviously helps me out a lot as a starting point and they can also feel free to request any extra songs on the night. Ultimately you can trust a professional to know what will work best to get your party going. Although one of the most unusual requests I've had was from a mother of the bride who wanted some Moroccan belly-dancing music so that she could surprise everyone with a belly dance for the bride and groom!
>
> JASON GRIFFITHS

BUDGET OPTIONS

Cheap as chips. If you are on a tight budget don't be tempted to go for an act just because they are cheap – make sure you are happy with the quality of their work first.

DIY. If you can't afford a DJ or a band, the obvious option is to supply your own mix CDs or an iPod playlist. If you make them yourselves you might have some dodgy links between the songs if you are not an expert, but if you don't mind then your guests won't care. Or you could buy a few compilations.

Ready made. Have your reception in your favourite bar, club or at an outdoor concert so that you can rely on the music from the venue's sound system.

No music. Maybe the venue is not appropriate for music, or you just want to concentrate on the conversation instead. How highbrow.

FIRST DANCE

Whether you can't wait to take to the floor and sway around in the spotlight or you can't think of anything worse than having to dance with everyone watching you, you have choices:

CELEBRITY SPOTLIGHT

Being celebrities, Charlie Sheen and Denise Richards have their images to think of. To avoid the embarrassment and discomfort of being stared at for their first dance, they made sure they enjoyed it and entertained their guests. The sly couple had been taking dance lessons and set the dance floor alight.

Take dance lessons. Imagine the look on everyone's faces when you step out onto the dance floor like the winners of *Strictly Come Dancing*? Search online for choreographers or dance teachers in your area, or contact your local dance school or leisure centre to see what services they offer. You may only need a few hours to spruce up your steps so you can wow the crowds.

Do something different. You needn't shuffle round the floor spinning in circles. Do the hustle. Cha cha cha! Who wouldn't be surprised if your first dance was the salsa, a tap dance or even a bit of moonwalking, *Dirty Dancing* or break dancing?

Say no to a first dance. If the idea of being in the limelight for any longer than absolutely necessary will ruin your day or you don't want the formality of a first dance, then don't do it. But however much you try to stick to your guns there will always be someone who will try to drag you onto the dance floor, so you will need to be pretty resilient to resist.

Meet them halfway. Just dance for half a song. Let everyone get their piccies but ask the DJ or lead singer of the band to invite everyone to join you halfway through and prime your closest allies so that they do this (especially if you have a song that goes on forever).

A first dance for everyone. Ask everyone to join you from the start.

Who says it has to be slow? Go for a more upbeat first dance and shimmy around the dance floor with or without your mates for company. How about dancing with all the chicks and bucks from your hen and stag nights?

Voices of angels. Alternatively treat your guests to a first song instead. Take to the floor with a mike and belt out a rendition of your favourite tune, either solo or as a duet.

CHOOSING THE RIGHT TRACK

You may immediately know the right song for you, but if you're looking for a little inspiration for that special track then don't get too hung up on it – you've got ages to decide. The following list is to get you thinking or you could even go for the same song that your parents had. For more contemporary choices, spend a little time browsing iTunes.

CLASSICS

✓ 'Our Love Is Here To Stay' - George and Ira Gershwin

✓ 'Let There Be Love' – Nat King Cole

✓ 'She' - Elvis Costello (or the Charles Aznavour version)

✓ 'The Look of Love' – Dusty Springfield

✓ 'Fly Me To The Moon' – Frank Sinatra

✓ 'The Way You Look Tonight' – Tony Bennett

✓ 'It Had To Be You' – Harry Connick Jr

✓ 'The Nearness Of You' – Etta James

✓ 'Have I Told You Lately That I Love You' – Van Morrison

✓ 'Wonderful Tonight' – Eric Clapton

✓ 'All Time High' – Rita Coolidge

✓ 'Unforgettable' – Nat King Cole

✓ 'Still The One' – Shania Twain

✓ 'Baby I Love Your Way' – Peter Frampton

✓ 'Something' – The Beatles

✓ 'Everything I Do' – Bryan Adams

✓ 'Every Breath You Take' – The Police

SING-ALONG SPECIALS

✓ 'Can't Take My Eyes Off You' – Andy Williams

✓ 'Angels' – Robbie Williams

✓ 'Nobody Does It Better' – Carly Simon

UPBEAT

✓ 'Isn't She Lovely' – Stevie Wonder

✓ 'You Sexy Thing' – Hot Chocolate

✓ 'How Sweet It Is To Be Loved By You' – Marvin Gaye

✓ 'It Must Be Love' – Madness

✓ 'Walking On Sunshine' – Katrina & The Waves

✓ 'You're The First, The Last, My Everything' – Barry White

✓ 'Feel Like Making Love' – Bad Company

✓ 'Get What You Give' – New Radicals

✓ 'I Believe In A Thing Called Love' – The Darkness

SLIGHTLY SILLY ...

If your sense of humour is to have a laugh at every opportunity, then one of these might be first on your list. And for the rest of you, if nothing else, hopefully they illustrate the importance of listening to the lyrics of a song the whole way through before you choose it as your first dance.

✓ 'Bat Out Of Hell' – Meatloaf

✓ 'I Will Survive' – Gloria Gaynor

✓ 'I'm Not In Love' – 10cc

✓ 'Respect' – Aretha Franklin

ENTERTAINING YOUR GUESTS

Providing some different activities or attractions will certainly make your wedding particularly memorable and will ensure that no one is left loitering waiting for you to reappear. But if you start putting things on in too many rooms, you might lose some of the atmosphere. Avoid this by making sure that everything is brought back to the one main room at some point in the evening. Again, remember that the guests have ultimately come to see you both, so if you are unsure, go easy on the peripheral entertainment. Let them get their fill of the happy couple.

Wine tasting. It will get them in the swing of things and get the party underway. You could give people tickets for the tastes to avoid anyone being under the table by the time you get back to the celebrations. Don't forget the non-drinkers, though, and have an alternative for them. This can give your wedding a lovely continental feel, especially if you are sitting outside. Get even more *Français* by having a vineyard as your setting, an accordion player and delicious French cuisine.

Table magicians. You can hire a magician through an entertainment agency for part of your wedding. They will roam around breaking the ice amongst your guests with tricks that will amaze and get everyone talking.

A caricaturist. Just think how people gather around when you see one of these guys on the street. Guests won't be able to resist seeing how the mother of the bride looks in the caricaturist's eyes. Try www.caricaturist.co.uk as a starting point.

Table games. If you think your guests will be without food for a while, or perhaps you doubt their ability to make conversation with strangers, there are some great card games designed as icebreakers. You don't need a game per table, just a dozen or so cards to get things off to a good start. Games ideas range from trivia questions, to guessing a celebrity's name on a card, to having to express a personal preference between two outrageous courses of action.

Singing waiters. Comical and highly talented, your guests will cringe as the 'waiters' inappropriately sneak up onto the stage and end up being amazed by their incredible renditions of show tunes, operatic classics and rousing patriotic favourites. Check out www.thethreewaiters.com for more information.

Comic waiters. Pretend waiters who act accident prone, trip up and shock the guests. This could be your act of defiance if you've been cornered into having a wedding you don't want!

Background music. Create a refined atmosphere or a more informal one by choosing your music accordingly. This is also a great way to warm up the ambience in a room and make it easier for people to make conversation.

Karaoke. You know your crowd the best so will know if this is a good idea. It could be disastrous if everyone is absolutely dire but also highly amusing to have everyone singing their hearts out to your favourite tracks. You could limit the range of songs to those that mean something to you to keep it personal. Prime a couple of people who you know can actually sing so that your guests do get at least a few less-painful renditions.

Fundraiser. In France, during a wedding reception there is a game where the bride sits on a chair in front of everyone and pulls her garter down to her ankle. The men bid money to get her to raise it in the hope of catching a bit of leg, while the women pay to have her pull it down again. Another option is the idea of a 'money dance' found in some cultures, where every man who dances with the bride must pin money to her dress. Since we've no longer got the one-pound note, this could be a worthwhile venture!

Jamming. Are your guests a musical bunch? If they are, have the instruments they play on stand-by. Alternatively, let them know in advance of the wedding how much it will mean to you if they would prepare something.

Stage show. Either hire some budding actors or take to the boards yourselves to perform a scene from your favourite play or film.

Outdoor activities. For an all-day outdoor reception, think about a lawn sport such as croquet, rounders, French cricket or *boules*.

Go continental. Just as the meal is finishing off, ask your tuneful toastmaster to kick off a rousing chorus of a well-known song. This is great if you have a split crowd that will pit their musical talents (and volumes) against each other.

Fireworks. These are a very popular option, especially for country weddings. It totally depends on your circle of friends and family as to whether the novelty factor has already worn off or not. Whatever you do, choose one fantastic firework in place of 50 average ones. Your guests are much more likely to prefer having a short-lived extravaganza and then getting back to the party rather than being bored rigid staring at an unimpressive display for an hour.

WHAT TO DO WITH THE KIDS?

You need to be realistic about this if you are going to invite children. There is a reason why lessons are so short when kids are young. With attention spans of about 20 minutes, they are hardly likely to survive the meal, much less the speeches. So it's a good idea to employ distraction tactics. This will also allow their parents to enjoy your day with you as well. Check with the venue if they can offer or have:

A children's entertainer or clown. Have them take up residence in an adjoining room complete with games, balloons and treats.

Face painting. This can work especially well if it ties into your wedding theme as children will feel a part of it.

Videos. It may sound like a cop-out, but if you have a long period of time where children may get bored then a well-timed showing of the latest Disney classic or something similar may be in order.

Bouncy castle. Always a winner, just make sure all the adults don't push the kids out of the way to get on there first.

Children's table. If they are old enough then think about giving them a table to themselves (or perhaps that is just asking for trouble!). Make sure they have food that they like and will eat with minimum fuss, even if it means corrupting your perfected wedding menu with a few plates of fish fingers and chips.

> *When my daughter got married, she asked me to think of ways to entertain the kids. I got together brightly coloured gift boxes to match the overall wedding colour scheme and put crayons, a colouring book, bubble kits, a balloon and a small (and not noisy!) toy in each one. It definitely helped to keep them entertained during the meal and speeches.*
>
> JILL, MOTHER OF THE BRIDE

Jackanory. A storyteller dressed up in a magical costume to tell bedtime stories as the night draws in.

Mobile crèche. These are available, for example VIP Mobile Crèche Service (www.vipmobilecreche.co.uk) or the Mobile Crèche Company (www.mobile creche.co.uk). But make sure that if you are asking your guests to leave their children with anyone that you have a full set of checked references from them. All staff who run the crèche on the day should also be able to give you their valid police-check and childcare certificates for inspection. If you are short on space, some mobile children's entertainers even use their trucks as play rooms that can park up outside.

Goody bags. Instead of favours.

BODY BEAUTIFUL

Time for some pampering . . .

Six months ahead of your wedding, visit a beauty consultant to find out what is available. If they are enthusiastic about their work, they are bound to try and flog you more than you might perceive you need, but you can also pick up some good pointers from them.

SKIN

Facial skin. Blitz those zits. If you are planning on a detox diet then time it so that it finishes at least a month in advance of the wedding because initially it can make your skin worse. And drink lots of water to flush any remaining toxins out. If your skin problems persist, see if your doctor can provide you with any further options.

Body skin. Especially if you have a strapless or backless dress. Smooth out any irregularities with daily exfoliation and moisturising. If you are planning on a natural tan then watch out for unsightly strap marks. Otherwise, you could look into fake tan treatments; always try options you are considering at least a month before your wedding to avoid any disasters on the day.

Hair removal. You know what works for you. But do be cautious about trying anything new close to your big day in case you develop an allergic reaction.

HAIR, HANDS AND MAKE-UP

Again, it is all obvious stuff really. Treat yourself to a pedicure (especially if you are wearing open-toed shoes), manicure, eyebrow shaping, make-over and trial 'how you want your hair' day etc.

In-store make-overs are very reasonable or free. Most of the beauty counters in the big department stores or independent outlets will give you a make-up consultation lasting about an hour for around £10–£20. This fee can be redeemed against any products you buy, so the consultation effectively becomes free. Choose a brand you think you would like to buy, or pay for the consultation.

Similarly, some hair salons will offer a special pre-wedding service where you and your entourage can go and be pampered while you try out different styles. You have lots of options for your hair including dyeing it, wearing it up or down, wearing a tiara, Alice band, coronet, hat, veil, wig, hair extensions, combs or even lacing it with beads, gems, feathers or flowers. The hairdresser's is also a great place to chat about your ideas with someone who is equally enthusiastic as you about your hair and may have experience of other people's weddings to share with you.

With both hair and make-up, keep trying out new things until you find something you are happy with. Take photos of your headdress, outfit, flowers and colour swatches so that the consultants know what they are working with. They can advise you and create a hairstyle that incorporates your requirements. Don't feel obliged to go with the first thing you are offered – this is the look that will immortalise you for years, after all.

But what if you are the type who likes to create a stir and get dramatic reactions? One bride we heard about wanted to have long hair for the ceremony and, unbeknownst to anyone else, had arranged to have her hair cut short between the ceremony and reception. She loved the response she got – especially the fact that she could still shock her husband.

In terms of practicalities, on the day make sure that you have allowed enough time for the beautification process and that you have the mobile phone numbers of any hairdressers or make-up artists you are expecting. Make a social event of it and avoid worrying about getting anywhere other than your wedding. Splash out on a bit of pampering at home and let everyone come to you for the ritual of getting ready for your wedding. Feel like a princess, steady your nerves with a tipple of champagne and, if you can afford it, treat your mum and bridesmaids to a bit of pampering too.

BUDGET OPTIONS

✓ Instead of hiring a make-up artist and hairdresser to come on the day, you could recreate the look from your consultation yourself on the morning of your wedding. If this is the case, either take along one of your bridesmaids to learn the art while it is being done or take some photos to remind you of the steps. And have a practice run before you commit to doing it without a professional

✓ You don't have to buy everything new. It is a lovely idea and a lot of women justify buying a batch of quality make-up for their wedding. But it is all about priorities

TO DIET OR NOT TO DIET

...That is the question.

Realistically, you need to think about the kind of person you are. Will you find it easy to lose weight and fit a healthier lifestyle, diet and exercise regime into your life? Or do you know that you become a horrific monster overnight once you've decided to lose weight?

If the former applies, then great, give it a shot. If you're of the monster category, then you are going to have enough stress in your life over the next couple of months, so you need to be clear from the outset about what tack you are going to take. And there's always body-shaping underwear to hide a multitude of sins.

If you do want to get into better shape, then bear in mind that cutting food out of your life teaches your body to do more with less: it stretches out what it's got to make it last and as a result your energy levels will fall. So this is definitely not an option for anyone under stress, let alone a bride-to-be!

If you would like advice on which diet you should follow, call your doctor's surgery, the British Dietetic Association (www.bda.uk.com) which can provide names of qualified dieticians, or visit www.medicdirect.co.uk/diet for information on how to diet sensibly and a comprehensive list of your options.

Alternatively the Nutrition Coach offer three-month or five-week wedding detox plans to prepare you for your big day (www.thenutrition coach.co.uk/wedding-detox-programme.htm).

EXERCISE

We've heard it time and again: exercise is the only option for losing weight, getting rid of the flab and toning to get the shape you want. So why do many of us avoid it altogether or invest in gym passes that only get used once every three months?

If you are committed to getting in shape and recognise that you are going to struggle to stay on course, try the following:

Start with a realistic regime. Since you have never been to the gym before and you are not getting married for nine months, how likely is it that you are going to go five times every week between now and then? Break yourself in gently – the most important thing is that you keep your word to yourself about anything you say you are going to do. Once you've managed that for a couple of weeks, then you can start to get a bit more ambitious.

Enjoy yourself. If you hate running, go swimming. If you suck at Step, join the ranks of Madonna and Sting and try Pilates or yoga. And you don't only have the option of going to the gym – walk to work, take the stairs, go to a dance class, go clubbing or de-stress at the weekends by taking a dog on a long country walk. Just because your new cycling shorts and sports bra are still in the cupboard doesn't mean that it doesn't count.

Take company. You are probably not the only one that wants to be in shape for the wedding. What about your family, your partner, bridesmaids or best men? But if you do 'buddy up' don't pick someone who is going to have less willpower than you – that's a subconscious cop-out. Ideally, it is great if your partner wants to exercise too, because apart from being a stress reliever, exercise reportedly makes you seem more attractive to the opposite sex (even if you're of the beet red, sweaty variety) and increases your sex drive. And then there is always the opportunity to sidle off for the odd steam room, sauna and massage. Marvellous.

Personal trainer. What a luxury. But then you are getting married. Hire your own Mr or Mrs Motivator and see if you can split the cost with someone else – that way you get a training buddy and it is cheaper overall.

Financial issues. Public leisure centres can be a lot cheaper than private gyms and sometimes the facilities are just as good. You just don't get the folded towels in the shower rooms. If that is still a bit of a stretch, you could either ask someone close to you for joint gym membership as an advance wedding present, buy a work-out video for home, play a team sport a couple of times a week or get outside and enjoy the fresh air. Lack of money is not an excuse for not exercising.

STRESS RELIEF

However good you feel you are at coping with pressure and however simple you are trying to keep your wedding, it is OK to admit to feeling a bit stressed out about it.

When it all gets a bit much, make time for yourself, time to be together and, most importantly, time away from the wedding mêlée.

Yoga. Sign up to a weekly class for a couple of months to have some respite and a reason to go and do something different. You don't have to be a bendy twig to do yoga and it has an amazing, calming effect. Get the hang of the basics with an instructor and then do a little bit at home each time you feel you need an escape.

Meditation. There are classes and books that will teach you the 'correct' way to meditate and to release your mind for a while, but simply closing your eyes and breathing right down into your abdomen will also immediately help you to feel calmer and more centred when things are running away with you.

Being together. Invest some quality time in each other and agree not to talk about the wedding. Make sure you don't forget why you want to marry each other in the first place.

Spa, pampering or massage. Either with your groom to have some relaxing time together or with your girlfriends or mum. Or if you are feeling decadent just sneak off by yourself and indulge.

Get your hair done. You might be putting it off to save money for the wedding and go overboard for the big day, but don't forget how great it feels to look good. Not to mention the sympathetic and expert ear of your hairdresser, who may well already have experience of more weddings than you will in a lifetime.

Laugh. As the saying goes, 'laughter is the best medicine'. It releases endorphins that rush around your body and melt away stress, so whatever is happening remember to have a good giggle. If you need a little help, rent a funny movie that you've seen a thousand times before or go and see some stand-up at your local comedy club.

Be realistic and flexible. Your plans will probably change along the way and with them, your budget. The trick is to make the best decision you can at that time, accept the consequences and get on with it.

Exercise. As previously mentioned, this is excellent for getting the endorphins and adrenaline flowing, both of which are depression- and stress-busters.

Life coaching. A life coach can help you to create the wedding you want by supporting you in setting and reaching staggered objectives. In the wedding whirlwind it can help to take time out with an outsider to stop things getting on top of you.

Camomile tea or a mug of good old-fashioned cocoa. To help you sleep.

Eat well. Stress, tiredness and anxiety can be brought on and made worse by having low blood sugar, so make sure you are balancing your diet with complex carbohydrates such as bread, brown rice and root vegetables. Try to avoid stimulants such as caffeine and alcohol as these will only make you more highly strung. Also think about taking a B-complex vitamin supplement, which is said to help support the nervous system. You can find B vitamins naturally in meat, fish, eggs and wholegrain cereal and bread. Consult a nutritional therapist for detailed information.

Keep a clear mind. We are at our most creative when our brain relaxes. This is often when we are lying in bed, just before we fall asleep, or when we have the chance to daydream. Keep a notepad and pencil by your bed and in your bag to capture those moments of inspiration. Then you can continue relaxing rather than feeling tense about the possibility of forgetting your brainwaves.

Natural remedies. To help the body to cope with anxiety. Pop into your local health store and ask someone in the know for more information and recommendations.

Be organised. A 'to do' list will help you prioritise your jobs, make the most of any spare time you have and give you a snapshot of what needs to be done. It is also very rewarding to be able to knock things off the list.

Hot bath with candles and relaxing bath oils. Lavender and geranium oils will turn your bath into a haven of relaxation with their calming properties. If you need a boost to your energy, citrus oils will revive you.

Give interfering folk chores to do. This will get them out of your hair and keep them happy.

Surround yourself with friends. Remind yourself of life before weddings.

Keep a diary. If you are the diary type, keep a record of your experiences. At the very least, write down all your frustrations in an effort to take the urgency out of them and stop yourself throttling your families. It might be best to keep this somewhere where your future mother-in-law won't find it!

Have plenty of sex. Make an effort to do this even if it is the last thing on your mind. A romantic or a rampant session can put right a lot of feelings of neglect, insecurity or doubt, so go for it.

Keep a sense of perspective. This is the start of your marriage. It is a celebration. It is not meant to be the most intense endurance test of your life to date. If you are finding that you are starting to employ SAS survival tactics, you're call-screening and stressing out about details that you had never even known existed at every other wedding you've been to, then take a step back and a deep breath. Whatever happens, it won't be the end of the world and your lasting memory of the day will be the feelings that you identify with it. Make sure that these are positive and don't let anything get on top of you.

GIFTS

Ooh! Presents!

> The traditional reason for a wedding list is to equip a young couple with all the basics they will need in their new home and future life. And if you are just moving in together then it can be a fantastic way to get you started. There's no need to feel awkward about having a list as long as you don't make present buying a prerequisite to come to the wedding or send the whole inventory out with your invitations. As long as you are humble about it, your guests will be grateful to know that they are buying you something that they know you want and need as opposed to them having to wander aimlessly round the shops the weekend before only to end up getting you your third cafetière that is going to be banished to the back of your kitchen cupboard until they come to visit.

CONVENTIONAL WEDDING LISTS

These can be obtained from most major department stores where you simply collate a list of everything that takes your fancy. In some stores you can do this by walking around with a barcode scanner and zapping everything that catches your eye, then the list is automatically drawn up for you. Pass your gift-list number and the name of the store onto your guests and then receive a lovely big pile of presents and a list of who bought them for you.

When you are compiling your list, remember to include choices for all budgets so that every guest feels that there is something they can buy you without breaking the bank. Work out how many guests you are inviting and how much per head you think they might spend, then have your gift list reflect this. And always have gift vouchers down as an option for those last-minute people who find themselves left with the £3,000 sofa or nothing. (Then you also get to have a spending spree when you return home from your honeymoon.)

Have a browse around the Internet, as there are an increasing number of companies that will make your and your guests' lives very easy. You draw up your private list and then your guests can simply log on from anywhere at any time or visit the store and buy a gift for you that will be wrapped up and delivered to your door. Try John Lewis, Marks & Spencer or Debenhams for first ports of call with the best of both worlds.

Also check out www.wedding.co.uk and www.thebottomdrawer.co.uk.

ALTERNATIVE IDEAS

If you have been living with your partner for a while you may not want to have a conventional wedding list. Perhaps you already have everything that you need, are on your second marriage or are a bit older and feel awkward asking your guests to kit you out. There is an ever-growing number of options for you to choose from. Remember that your friends and family may want to treat you to something or to make a gesture to mark the occasion of your wedding, so don't be afraid to give them at least one option.

GREEK-STYLE WEDDING

Instead of gifts, opt for the Greek-style wedding where the guests bring money in an envelope and pin it to the bride's dress. If you are hyperventilating at the thought of damaging your gorgeous dress in any way, then this is not for you!

'GIVING' GIFT LIST

If you are fortunate enough to feel you have everything you need or are just a generous soul, why not ask your guests to make a donation to your chosen charity? You can either give them the details of the charity (which may also be able to supply donation envelopes for you to include with your invitations) or go through a company such as Wedding List Giving (www.weddinglistgiving.com), which will co-ordinate the process for you. It works with charities such as Amnesty International, Oxfam,

Greenpeace, Friends of the Earth, Cancer Research, the Alzheimer's Society and Scope to make donating as easy as having a conventional list.

Other 'giving' gift-list companies include the World Vision Alternative Gift Catalogue, (www.worldvision.org.uk), The Woodland Trust, www.woodland-trust.org.uk) or for fair-trade gift check out the Traidcraft Catalogue (www.traidcraft.co.uk).

CHARITY HONEYMOON

Ever wanted to cycle or trek the Great Wall of China, Mount Kilimanjaro or the Inca Trail? Or maybe you've fancied doing an overseas bungy, parachute jump, adventure or aid work for charity but never been able to get around to raising the sponsorship to do it? This is your chance. Look at your favourite charity websites for inspiration.

ONCE-IN-A-LIFETIME HONEYMOON

Leading travel specialists are also beginning to offer a gift list service so that you can afford the trip of a lifetime for your honeymoon. Trailfinders has a minimum of £10 per gift (www.trailfinders.com/giftlist). If you want to arrange your honeymoon with another travel company, then find out if they will lay on the service for you, but be prepared for teething pains if it is not something that they usually offer.

CREATE YOUR OWN

Perhaps there is something big that you would like to buy, such as a piece of furniture, new kitchen or carpet? Ask people to contribute to the cause. Add a slip of paper in with your invitations to let everyone know your plan. If you are worried that people may like a bit more choice then give them two or three options.

If you have one store that is a particular favourite and they don't offer a wedding list service per se, ask to speak to the manager and see if they will hold a list at their branch especially for you. It is in their interests because they have got a list of guaranteed sales. If their products are on the Internet, then all the better.

POST-WEDDING SPENDING SPREE

If you do not have time to organise a gift list before your wedding or if you are about to move house and are not sure what you will need, then some stores now offer an account that your guests can pay into to let you have a spending spree after your wedding. In effect you are asking your guests for cash and this might grate on some of your more traditional invitees, but most people will be obliging if they can understand your reasoning and not just think that you are being penny-pinching. Check with your favourite stores, especially those with store cards, to see if they will set up an account for you.

DREAM HOUSE

In many Mediterranean countries, such as France and Greece, the emphasis of giving at a wedding is not just on furnishing a new home but on buying it too. If you fear that you will never be able to scrape together a deposit for a new house then you can ask the guests to contribute to your first marital home. With financial pressures being so great on newly married couples, people are more and more understanding of basic needs. After all, what good is a new towel set, dinner service and kettle and toaster combo if you don't have anywhere to live?

In this scenario, it is a very welcome touch to reflect this in your thank-you cards. Consider either having thank-you cards made up using a photo of the house you buy (if the timeframe is relevant) or have a card with a 'welcome' mat on it to let your guests know that their contributions will extend to an invitation to your new home when things have settled down. And when all these people have a stake in the bricks and mortar they might be willing to bring some generous house-warming gifts with them when they come!

DREAM GARDEN

Another new idea is to ask for your garden to be landscaped for your wedding present. Every time you look out of your window or sit out on a summer's day you will be reminded of your wedding day. Clearly this is going to be a big cost but The Bottom Drawer (www.thebottomdrawer.co.uk) have come up with a solution. They will send two or three landscape gardeners to you to provide quotes and once you have chosen your favourite design they will split the costs up into individual elements so that guests can buy, for example, a rose bush or part of the decking. The whole process can be completed online with guests choosing what to buy at their convenience and you can put photos of the finished product up on their website for your guests to admire.

PERSONAL TOUCH

Take a risk and ask your friends to use their imaginations. Ask them to buy you something that they think reflects your personality. This way you will end up with a whole host of weird and wonderful gifts that reflect your guests' personalities as well.

EXPERIENCES

If you feel that you have all the material possessions that you could desire then ask for experiences or adventures that you and your partner can enjoy together. Companies such as Red Letter Days (www.redletterdays.co.uk), and Virgin Experience (www.virgin-experience.co.uk) offer a whole range of exciting and indulgent choices from motor-racing days to pampering spa sessions, flying lessons to private yoga or dance classes, or even cookery classes.

Another option is to ask for experiences that you can indulge in on your honeymoon. Money for local attractions, a lavish meal out, an extra night in your luxury hotel, massages for the two of you in the hotel spa or even simply a couple of cocktails from a posh bar. Find out what's on offer in your honeymoon location and make a list of all those extras that will really make it truly amazing.

To show how much you appreciate people being willing to give you something untraditional and not tangible, send a photo of you doing the activity either with your thank-you card or as a postcard at a later date.

SOMETHING TO LAST THE YEAR

Choose a present that will last you all year so that you have a constant reminder of your big day. Ask for a subscription to your favourite magazines or membership of a wine club. Or how about fresh seasonal flowers once a month for a year?

DISTINCTLY DIFFERENT

If you want to take this opportunity for getting some really unique gifts that you would never buy yourselves then online gift companies have a range to make the mind boggle. How does an acre of the Moon, Mars or Venus, naming a star, owning a share in a racehorse, horse whispering or owning a vine in a vineyard sound?

All these and more from online gift companies like www.needapresent. com, www.iwantoneofthose.com and www.prezzybox.com.

WHEN IS IT PRESENT TIME?

 Traditionally, newly married couples used to open their gifts at the reception and put them on display.

Nowadays that is considered a bit ostentatious and not very practical. If you want to do it, go for it. But bear in mind that if you have a gift list at a store, they will deliver your gifts to your home and you might want to do this after your honeymoon. This can keep you elated for that little bit longer.

A very old tradition is for the father of the bride to give a pair of shoes to the groom at the wedding. This is because having a pair of shoes was the ultimate symbol of ownership for many people throughout the Middle Ages. And in giving the groom a pair of shoes this symbolised the passing of ownership of the bride from father to husband. There is still evidence of this today when you sometimes see shoes tied to the bumper of the wedding car.

GIFTS FOR EACH OTHER

You might want to give each other an additional token of your affection on your wedding day.

If your partner has got a burning desire to drive a sports car why not ease their nerves on the morning of the wedding and secretly hire one for their wedding transport – you can get the best man or bridesmaid in on the act so that everything runs smoothly. Or maybe one of you is web-friendly but does not have a digital camera. This would make a good gift to record the day and get carried away mailing digital photos of the wedding and honeymoon to all your guests.

GIFTS FOR THE WEDDING PARTY

Groomsmen. What about a yard of ale, tickets to see their favourite band, Scalextric or a Swiss Army knife? For these and more ideas check out www.firebox.com and www.drinkstuff.com.

Bridesmaids. If they are attending to you for most of the day, they will probably not have a chance to get the photos they would like. Rather than a piece of jewellery, offer to buy them a couple of the official wedding photos as a token of your gratitude. Or treat them to a meal for two in a swish restaurant.

Pageboys. Let the little ones have their own disposable camera to play with so that they can take their own pictures at the reception – boys love gadgets and being given control. Very grown-up.

Young bridesmaids. Buy a keepsake book along with a disposable camera for young bridesmaids. They can stick in wedding stationery, photos and diary entries to remind them of the day in years to come.

Mums. Bouquets of flowers are the old classic but how about a night at the theatre or a voucher for a spa day to thank her for all her hard work?

BUDGET OPTIONS

✓ If your guests are hard up, they do not know you very well or if you are having a very low-key wedding, you will need to make sure you have lots of low to mid-priced items on your list

✓ If paying for the wedding itself is more of a financial burden than you can stand, why not ask guests to give you the gift of them being able to attend your wedding by paying for themselves?

HEN AND STAG PARTIES

Although you don't need to think about your hen or stag night until about three months before the wedding, there's no reason why you can't start getting excited about it now!

> *My hen night was great because of the thought and preparation that went into it. I was touched by the lengths that my friends had gone to so that everything was tailored to suit me. The theme and forfeits gave focus and purpose to the evening's revelries, which beats wandering around aimlessly in a net curtain and a learner sign! Getting ready together really set the mood for the whole night and I'm glad I left it all to my friends because then everything came as a big surprise.*
>
> CLAIRE, 26

This is traditionally your 'last night of freedom' but is really a chance for your friends to give you a great send-off and also to let your hair down with your mates after all that endless wedding planning.

These days you don't have to settle for a night getting slowly more incoherent down the local but can expect a real occasion, hopefully somewhere other than your home town and possibly spanning an entire weekend rather than just the one night. Girls, if the idea of strippers and a net-curtain veil fills you with dread, and guys, if you don't fancy being tied naked to a lamppost, have no fear (well, maybe just a little bit) as hen and stag nights are thankfully evolving. With some imagination your send-off can be tailored specifically to your personality with a theme, forfeits, games and activities just for you. This is the point where you hand the responsibility over to your mates, make it clear that you are *trusting* them and hope for the best.

A BRIEF WORD TO THE BRIDESMAIDS, BEST MAN, CHICKS AND BUCKS

Avert your eyes brides- and grooms-to-be and hand the book over!

The most important thing about a hen or stag night is that it is created especially for your bride or groom. You can arrange a completely unique night just for them and that doesn't mean the whole affair has to be an entirely torturous and humiliating experience. Far from it. Strangely, we believe the whole point is that they should enjoy every minute of their sendoff (even if they do feel a bit ridiculous in the *Fame* outfit you have created for them) and be made to feel like the centre of attention throughout the whole thing. And contrary to popular belief, the big night doesn't *have* to be a raucous, drunken affair. If your hen or stag is more suited to a weekend of good food and fine wine in a country retreat then treat them to that instead – it's all about doing something for them that you will all enjoy.

THE DAY BEFORE
AND THE DAY AFTER

All that effort for one day?

Not likely. A wedding often stretches into a full weekend now, so this chapter looks at ways to keep the guests happy on the day before and after the main event. This is even more applicable if the wedding is abroad or friends and family have travelled long distances to be there for the big day.

THE DAY BEFORE

Traditionally, the bride and groom must not see each other after sunset on the day before the wedding. To be on the safe side, many brides and grooms do not see each other for the whole day before the wedding.

This is where the stag-do originated – to give the groom a send-off on his final night of freedom while the women prepared the bride to look beautiful for the next day. But after one black eye, shaved eyebrow and absent groom too many, this is pretty much a rarity nowadays.

Rehearsal dinner. You may need to have a rehearsal the day before your wedding because that is the only time you have everyone together in the lead-up to the day. In this case, organise a 'post-rehearsal dinner' like the Yanks do and kick off the celebrating early.

Wedding eve party. Are you likely to be completely organised with all the finishing touches in place early on the day before your wedding? Or is it more likely that you will be feeling like you are treading a fine line between being stressed and insane in your last effort to pull together all the final details? If you are the latter, then just concentrate on the job in hand. But if you have faith in your ability to be verging on boredom the day before your wedding, arrange a wedding eve banquet or cocktail reception for all your guests or maybe just close friends, especially if your wedding day celebrations are more about your families' tastes than yours. Go easy on the booze though if you are a victim of hangovers. And remember that your registrar or celebrant has the right to refuse to marry you if you seem to be inebriated at the ceremony.

A new you. Party or no party, if you are planning on some kind of physical transformation for your big day, you should still think about spending the night at different houses to let the sense of anticipation reach fever pitch before the ceremony and guarantee the desired wow factor.

> *When I was at the altar and the music started to signify that my wife-to-be had arrived, I felt so nervous. I turned to see her walking down the aisle and she looked so amazingly beautiful that I couldn't take my eyes off her. The whole thing was completely overwhelming and we both spent the ceremony choking back tears!*
> RICHARD, 31

THE WEDDING NIGHT

The bride and groom used to leave the wedding reception and go straight on their honeymoon, usually missing the end of their own party (heaven forbid).

Realistically, the last thing you need to worry about is packing for a three-week trip, let alone tackling a long-haul flight after a full and emotional day. And if one day with all your guests is likely to be enough, then you should consider having your first night in a different hotel, otherwise they may have the expectation that they will get to see you, if only briefly, the next day.

THE DAY AFTER

You might love the idea of spinning the celebrations out for another day. If you organise an activity in advance, people will know what they are doing and so the pressure on you to entertain either the masses or a select few will be alleviated to a large degree. And of course there is always the option of delegating to someone you think will be in a better state than you the day after your wedding.

Some ideas are:

Brunch. Keep it simple and wrap up the occasion.

A giant inflatable game. There are giant obstacle courses, bouncy castles and ball pits for children and human table football for adults available. Just look online.

It's A Knockout. To go all out, arrange to hold a family and friends *It's a Knockout* day. Try www.itsaknockout.net or www.itsaknockoutevents.com.

CELEBRITY SPOTLIGHT

To occupy guests on the day after the wedding, why not follow in Claudia Schiffer's shoes and organise a football match? German Claudia had the ideal premise, as her husband is English so an England–Germany rematch was on the cards. Miss Schiffer cheered her team on from the sidelines but it was to no avail as England defeated Germany 6–2.

Football match. Pit the two sides of the family against each other.

Activities. Arrange your own karting, 4x4 driving, clay-pigeon shooting or paintballing for your peers.

Tourists. Enquire with the local tourist bureau to find out if there are any activities in the region that might be suitable. Consider hiring a coach and taking everyone on a day trip – and it doesn't have to be sightseeing. Whether you are in the UK or overseas, you could take all your guests to a spa or to a vineyard for a pampering or hair-of-the-dog approach to getting over their hangovers.

Garden party, picnic or barbeque. The ideal might be something organised and run by caterers but after the expense of the wedding, a simple picnic of treats straight off the supermarket shelf, blankets and barefoot rounders is just as much fun.

Parent power. If you sense that your parents would like to own some decisions around your wedding but you are reluctant to have them involved with decisions about the day itself, put them in charge of hosting a post-wedding party.

Family day. This is an opportunity to involve children if you exclude them from your wedding day. But if families are travelling from further afield, unless they know babysitters near your venue, they may have left their children at home.

Dinner party. At a wedding it is not always realistic to spend the whole day talking to the people you really want to. Solve the problem by inviting a small number to a lunch or dinner party at your favourite restaurant the next day.

When you eventually head home, the groom should traditionally carry the bride over the threshold. This is from the old wives' tale that a bride should enter her house by the front door but should not trip or it will bring bad luck. So if she's carried, it avoids all complications. (Unless, of course, the groom trips and you both wind up in casualty.)

HONEYMOON

What kind of honeymoon is right for you?

One origin of the word 'honeymoon' is derived from the groom lying low with his newly kidnapped wife for one lunar month (or moon cycle) when they would drink a honeyed drink called mead, bestowing fertility and virility. The idea was that within the month the bride would be pregnant so her family would not contest the wedding, hence a 'honeymoon baby'.

A relaxing holiday on the white sandy beaches of a paradise isle could be right up your street. And for the restless adventurers, this is your chance to book the trip of a lifetime.

HONEYMOONS WITH A DIFFERENCE

You don't have to be porcelain-skinned and fry at the first sight of the sun to look into your alternatives to going on a tropical beach honeymoon. The world is an amazing place just waiting for you to discover it.

Reception-cum-honeymoon. Just because you are not up for getting married overseas does not mean that you can't follow your UK ceremony with a blessing and reception abroad to kick off your honeymoon.

All-inclusive honeymoon. These are popular for the obvious reason that once you get there, you need to part with very little money and there is a great atmosphere because of that. But because all-inclusive resorts need to allow for heavy drinkers, eaters, smokers and sporty people, if you are planning on being completely inactive and not overdoing the indulgences after the wedding, then there are more economical ways of doing things.

Extended honeymoon. If you are willing to budget and are happy to take the career break, the money you would spend on a conventional honeymoon would get you a long way around the world with your backpacks.

Delayed honeymoon. Don't feel you have to go straight away. If it's not a convenient time or you can't afford it along with the wedding, then consider it as something to look forward to.

Adventurous honeymoon. This depends on your definition of adventurous. You can nearly always find a package holiday of some description to any 'adventurous' destination, whether it involves trekking, a safari, extreme sports, culture, jungle and rainforest trips, island hopping, climbing volcanoes or remote romantic hotspots. It will undoubtedly make life easier for you and very enjoyable, but if you are willing to leave the tourist trail you can also have some unique experiences and might even save some money.

For a really random destination, close your eyes and stick your finger on the map. Start investigating this place first for your honeymoon.

Island honeymoon. Rent a private island for you and maybe even take some friends along. Choose from beautiful desert islands in the Caribbean to the fresh waters of Nova Scotia. Check out Vladi Private Islands for more information (+49 40 33 89 89, www.vladi-private-islands.de).

Themed honeymoon. If you have enthusiastically carried your theme throughout your wedding, why not carry it on for the honeymoon? You can stay in Bedouin-style tents in the desert, an underwater hotel in Florida, visit New Orleans for a jazz flavour, or Hawaii to really top a Hawaiian theme off in style.

Honeymoon at home. This is especially pertinent if you have just bought a new house. Then you could justify spending the amount you would usually spend on your honeymoon on a luxury you would otherwise have to go without. Plus, remember that getting married can be a stressful experience and some relaxing time at home to conserve energy and funds might be just what you need. If you have kids and your home is usually completely chaotic, think about packing them off to their other parent or grandparents so that you can enjoy your home as a sanctuary.

Group honeymoon. Invite other people with you if you are not bothered about having all your time to yourselves. Just because you are married does not mean you have to be joined at the hip to the exclusion of all others.

Last-minute honeymoon. There is just no telling any more if you will get a good deal if you book a last-minute honeymoon. If you are open to a variety of possible places where you might end up then it is worth considering, either to be spontaneous or to try to save money. But you are unlikely to go to very unusual destinations because the routes that tend to have availability are the popular package destinations, although these do include places like Jamaica and Mexico. If you can't get the last-minute package you want, then look for last-minute flights from any of the main operators or Teletext and book your room separately.

Aid/voluntary work. Amazing locations but you may need to raise a certain amount of money to be considered.

Shipwrecked honeymoon. Stay on Robinson Crusoe Island, just off Chile, where Alexander Selkirk was marooned for over four years. Now a national park and Unesco World Biosphere Reserve, it is home to 500 inhabitants and is definitely not a mainstream holiday destination. The scuba diving, bar and swimming pool might just make it a little more bearable than it was for Selkirk!

Treasures close to home. Few places can offer such diversity in so small an area as the British Isles. If you have not really explored these shores to date you will be absolutely blown away by what you will see – you don't have to go to New Zealand for snowcapped mountains and lakes or the Caribbean for long deserted stretches of beach (albeit freezing). For an activity-packed holiday you can also look into country-house hotels that offer clay-pigeon shooting, 4x4 driving experiences, walks in the country, spas, golf, pampering, balloon flights, falconry, archery and horse trekking.

OUR TOP 10 ROMANTIC HOTSPOTS OF THE WORLD

✓ Viewing the sunset at the edge of the Grand Canyon

✓ Sunning yourselves in a gondola on the canals of Venice

✓ Strolling beside the Seine in Paris

✓ Watching the giraffes take their first drink of the day at sunrise from the top of a lookout tower in the Etosha National Park, Namibia

✓ Romantic seclusion, lazing on a pure white sand beach in Zanzibar

✓ Curled up in each other's arms in front of a roaring log fire after a day's skiing in Whistler, Canada

✓ A windswept walk through the dramatic Highlands of Scotland, topped off with a hot toddy

✓ Watching the Northern Lights, cosied up on a sled in Norway

✓ Wandering around the ancient lost city of Machu Picchu in Peru before the other tourists are even awake

✓ Waking up on your very own secluded private island off the coast of New Zealand

HELPFUL TIPS

To get more from your honeymoon, think about the following:

Package details. Check out what your honeymoon package includes if you book with a tour operator. Sometimes the little extras that you would usually struggle to afford are thrown in as part of the service.

Treat yourself. If holidays are important to you, don't scrimp on this one because this really is the time that you can justify a bit of luxury as opposed to the usual one-, two- or three-star places you end up in. A great view, romantic surrounds, luxurious rooms and excellent facilities are all ways you can pamper yourselves. And the pound will go a lot further in some countries than others – before you dismiss an option out of hand as too expensive, work out what your actual costs when you are there are likely to be, combined with your flights. You might be pleasantly surprised.

Milk it. Don't be overtly greedy but do let people know you are on your honeymoon and you might be able to get free upgrades on flights, in hotels and even the odd glass of champagne. To increase your chances for flight upgrades, dress smartly and dump your tatty suitcases for something a little classier. Take a copy of your marriage certificate and wield it where you can.

Timing. Travelling on your wedding day is traditional, but that was back when couples did not really go overseas for their honeymoon. If possible, let the whirlwind settle for a day or even three, so that on the morning of your wedding you only have to think about being a gorgeous bride and sexy groom.

Make it last. Holidays are about relaxing but they are also about new experiences and memories. Make sure that your honeymoon stands out from your other holidays by creating some special memories – surprise each other, romance each other, keep a memento and take trips or do new things that will cast you back to your dream location and newlywed feelings whenever you remember them.

Standards and services. As mentioned in the **Getting Married Abroad** chapter, standards and services vary in different countries. If you want guaranteed luxury and excellent service then book a five-star hotel. If you are willing to have a honeymoon with more character and surprises, then take less than five-star and travel to exotic locations. The whole experience will be an adventure and more than likely be luxurious too – and if you avoid developed countries you can enjoy the height of luxury for a much more reasonable price. Also, remember to book a double bed because in some places, twin beds are standard in a 'double' room rather than one double bed.

Practicalities. For basics to bear in mind when booking your honeymoon, see the 'Practicalities' section in the **Getting Married Abroad** chapter.

ADVISORY RESOURCES

FOREIGN AND COMMONWEALTH OFFICE

For the official line on destinations and links to consulates, embassies, safety warnings and advice, contact the Foreign and Commonwealth Office (www.fco.gov.uk) before you travel – if only to ensure that there are no severe warnings so that you can check that your travel insurance is valid. The FCO will tend to err on the side of caution, particularly these days, but if your insurance company is still willing to insure you anyway, then you should be safe enough – these companies are profit orientated after all and will have assessed the degree of risk to ensure that their investment in you is commercially justifiable.

IF YOU SKI

A holiday provider, they also have an information service for ski resorts around the world. If your ideal honeymoon involves snow then check them out (www.ifyouski.com).

MAGAZINES

Again, the old favourite bridal magazines rear their head. Every month they feature different honeymoon destinations and real-life honeymoon tales for you to look to for inspiration. But a lot of the articles tend to focus on deluxe destinations – if you want to experience something a little less cosseted then you should branch out into travel magazines and the Sunday paper supplements. Keep looking and asking around until you come across something that really appeals to you both.

TRAVEL GUIDES

One of the best known series is probably *Lonely Planet*, the backpackers' bible. While your backpacking days might be behind you, don't dismiss them out of hand because they are travel guides without the gloss. They give you information on the history, culture, customs and wildlife of a country, plus interesting fact files, travel and visa advice, health precautions, everyday phrases and are a great starting point for hotels, restaurants and entertainment for all budgets. Using these guides to supplement your trip, rather than define them completely, you can have a unique experience with the peace of mind that the book is a good 'hand holder' should you need it. They also have an informative website with an overview of each destination they cover at www.lonelyplanet.com.

Other guide series include; *Rough Guide, Footprint Handbook, Let's Go, Eyewitness Guides* and *Time Out*. In the more hectic moments of your wedding planning, seek out the solitude and indulgence of a coffee shop within a book shop, gather up all the guides you are interested in and work out which one will suit you best.

TRAVEL OPERATORS

If you want more ideas then contact Trailfinders (0845 050 5926, www.trailfinders.com), Travelbag (0871 703 4698, www.travelbag.co.uk), Quest Travel (0845 263 6963, www.questtravel.com) or other specialist travel companies that will help you to create your perfect and unique holiday as an independent traveller. Their staff are generally well travelled and should be able to give you some inspirational ideas based on your requirements. If not, then move on to the next operator!

Both Trailfinders (0845 050 5926) and Quest Travel (0845 263 6963) have a gift-list wedding service, which means that you can ask your guests to contribute to the cost of your honeymoon.

VIRTUAL TOURIST

This content comes from people's real experiences and they post it themselves. See through the marketing bumph and get great insider tips on things to see and do off the beaten track (www.virtualtourist.com).

THANK YOUS AND
AFTER THE WEDDING

 In your post-marital bliss (or chaos) don't forget to send out thank-you cards or letters to all your guests. You need to thank everyone for joining you in your celebration and for any personal or present contribution that they made as well.

In terms of timings, it is reasonable to send them within a month of returning from your honeymoon. The main thing is to show your guests that you appreciate them and have not stopped making the wedding effort once you have what you want.

ALTERNATIVE THANK YOUS

See the **Invitations and Stationery** chapter for the practicalities of printing wedding stationery.

Postcards. If you are going on an extended honeymoon, send people postcards as thank-you cards. It is traditional to send an official thank-you note, but if you did not send official invitations and had an informal wedding then this is more in keeping with the tone you have set to date.

Photo card. Get a photo that really embodies the day for you. If you are a whiz with computers, you can scan the photo to create your own thank-you cards that a printer will print out en masse for you. Alternatively, most print shops will have graphic designers that will sort the whole thing out for you. But remember to check the proofs before you accept a full print run.

Theme. If you had a strong theme running throughout the day, include this in the thank-you notes.

Email. Think twice about sending email thank yous and no posted cards or notes at all. If people have made the effort to spend the time and money coming to your wedding, be prepared that they may well get the hump if you send them an email rather than a personal note. You also have to have a pretty high-tech bunch for it to suit everyone. Email should only be a last resort and you might be able to claw back some credibility if you've included a link to your website (see below).

Website. Set up a flickrpage (www.flickr.com) and upload a selection of photos from the day. That way, everyone gets to see the photos in one handy place rather than waiting until the next time they see you. Facebook (www.facebook.com) is another option but you may not want your entire extended family to have access to your page and the hen and stag photos you don't really want to share with your new in-laws!

Party. Consider having all or some of the guests over for a get-together a month or so after the wedding. It is a chance to say another thank you, avoid a complete anticlimax, share your photos, anecdotes and memories, and if you ask them all to bring a dish or a bottle it needn't break the bank.

MISS, MS OR MRS?

There is no reason why either of you has to change your name. Anyone over the age of 16 can choose to be known by whatever name they wish. But to change your name officially on legal documentation, you either need to produce a marriage certificate or go about having your name changed by deed poll. If you have children, you can also change their names but need the consent of their other parent if you were married at the time of their birth. Otherwise, consent is only required from the parent with legal custody. Consult a solicitor for further information.

Options for the two of you include:

✓ Bride takes groom's surname – traditional, and the most common

✓ Groom takes bride's surname

✓ You both take on a double-barrelled name

✓ Bride keeps her surname but officially changes her title to 'Ms' by deed poll

✓ Bride keeps her own name for professional purposes but takes her husband's name for all other legal purposes

If one of these appeals, you need to send a copy of your marriage certificate along with your request for the specific name change to all the authorising bodies for the documentation you will need updated. The documents you need to remember to change are:

✓ Passport

✓ Current account, savings account, credit cards, store cards

✓ Shareholder certificates

✓ Pension plan

✓ Tax and National Insurance records

✓ Human resources and Payroll and any other records held at your place of work

✓ Professional membership bodies

✓ Driver's licence

✓ Car registration, insurance and other motor policies

✓ Household insurance (buildings and contents), holiday insurance, mortgage insurance and payment protection and any other insurance you hold

✓ Mortgage and deeds documentation

✓ Council tax and electoral registry at your local borough council

BEATING THE POST-WEDDING BLUES

While you are planning your wedding, you probably can't wait for the big day to come. But have you given any thought to what it is going to be like when it is over? After having so much to think about for so long, you might not know what to do with yourself, so take it easy and let your life come back into balance in it's own time. But that doesn't mean you have to stop having fun.

Here are some ideas to keep you entertained and enjoy your first months of marriage together:

Save your presents. Open them when you get back from your honeymoon.

Spick and span. Make sure your home is not left in a mess before you leave.

Easy does it. Ideally, have ar least two days in your home together before you have to go back to work.

Photo memories. Develop the films from the disposable cameras.

Soirées. As soon as you get back, arrange a couple of nights out to look forward to or invite the best man, adult bridesmaids and their partners round to dinner to thank them for everything they've done and reminisce about the day. And make the most of visits to the family to show them your photos.

Take it in your stride. If you do feel a bit down, accept that it is OK for now and give yourself a break. Work out what would make you happier and get a date in the diary to do it. Stagger your post-wedding treats so that you always have something to look forward to.

Fresh air. A windswept day in the countryside will make you feel alive.

Activity days. From racing cars to falconry, parachute jumps to rock climbing or gliding. If you organise these directly with the venues yourself, they tend to be cheaper than going through an 'experience' company. But if you've included Virgin Experiences or Red Letter Days on your gift list then you don't need to worry about the expense at all. Result.

Time out. Know when enough is enough and set some time aside for just the two of you to enjoy being together and doing something that you love. Take the phone off the hook, switch off your mobiles, do not answer the door and don't change your plans for anyone.

New goals. Give yourself a two- or four-week limit to think about what your next objective or project might be; a holiday, house improvement, course, job or even planning a family perhaps ...

A 12-MONTH WEDDING PLANNER

Your own wedding checklist will be personal to you, especially if you plump for something really alternative or decide to get married abroad.

But here are a few common pointers to get you started or just to remind you that if you have your heart set on specifics you will need to book early to avoid disappointment.

TWELVE TO SIX MONTHS BEFORE

Announce your engagement! And enjoy this moment before you get swept up in the whirl of planning.

What to do. Decide how and where you would like to get married – try to focus on what would please you and your partner.

Set your budget. And make a pact to do your best to stick to it!

Set the date. Or at least a provisional date, as this may change as you start to investigate what you want to do.

Venue. Narrow down your list of preferred venues for your ceremony and reception and book as soon as possible – popular ones go fast!

Speak to your registrar or celebrant. When you book your ceremony double-check that you meet all the requirements to get married, whether you choose to marry in church or a civil venue.

Suppliers. If you want professionals book them early as they will also get booked up well in advance. This applies to your:

✓ Photographer and/or videographer

✓ Music and entertainment

✓ Caterers

✓ Florist

✓ Transport

Insurance. Check out your options and arrange this at an early stage.

Choose your colour scheme or theme. Think about the style of wedding that will suit you. Having a general colour or theme in mind will help you to decide on everything from now on. The advantage to deciding so far in advance is that you can snap up this year's bargains as they go out of season ready for next year.

Guest list. Draw this up early so that you have time to make changes, trim it down if you have to and get to grips with what you are dealing with.

Hold the date. If you are not ready to send out your invites but think you have chosen a popular date then send out 'hold the date' cards to let everyone know to keep your wedding date free.

Ladies' outfits. You may want to start shopping for outfits at this stage for you and your bridesmaids, or at least looking around for ideas. If you are having a dress made allow as much time as you can to account for fittings and alterations and, to be on the safe side, give them a date a month in advance of your actual day.

Choose your bridesmaids, best man, ushers and witnesses. Maybe hold a dinner party or have drinks to ask them all together.

Get in shape. If it's important to you, start a sensible eating and exercise plan so you can look your best on your big day.

Stationery. Look at your stationery options and order now to allow for delivery time, especially if you are having it tailor-made.

Prenuptial. Speak to a solicitor if this is something you are interested in.

BETWEEN FOUR AND TWO MONTHS BEFORE

Marriage licence. Meet with your celebrant or registrar and arrange to give notice of your impending wedding either in the form of a public notice or banns.

Wedding rings. Buy your wedding rings together and make an occasion of it.

Gift list. Decide what you want to do about gifts and, if you need to, register your list with your chosen supplier.

Invitations. Send out invites to all your guests about six to eight weeks before your wedding with gift-list information and any other bits you feel people need, such as directions to the venue, accommodation information or details of any dress code.

Honeymoon. Unless you are booking a last-minute deal you should have yours booked by now. And don't forget any vaccination requirements or travel insurance.

Cake. Choose what you would like, place your order and discuss delivery.

Gents' outfits. If you are hiring outfits for the guys make sure they are fitted and booked.

Favours. Decide what you would like to have (if at all) and start buying or creating.

Ceremony content. Decide on which readings, songs and music you would like included in your ceremony and clear these with your officiant. If you are writing your own vows you should be thinking about these now.

Roles and responsibilities. Make sure all these are delegated.

ONE MONTH BEFORE

Reconfirm your bookings and catering requirements. Give all your suppliers a call and reassure yourself that you are happy with all your arrangements.

Hen and stag nights. Take a night (or weekend) off from all that planning. Go and let your hair down – you will more than deserve it by now.

Hairdos and make-up. Have a trial run to make sure you are happy with your choices.

Chasing guests. Put a call in to those you haven't received RSVPs from so you can confirm your numbers.

Seating plan. You will have most of your replies by now so get started on a seating plan if you are having one.

Gifts for the wedding party. Buy and wrap these early to save you dashing around at the last minute.

Flowers. Make sure your plans for flowers are finalised and that you know how they are going to be delivered on the day. If you need someone to pick them up then nominate this person now.

ONE WEEK BEFORE

Rehearse. Most venues will allow you to have a rehearsal a few days before the event, which is bound to get your bottom lip quivering in anticipation.

ON THE DAY

Get ready. Allow yourselves plenty of time for this so you can get ready in a leisurely fashion and enjoy a glass of your favourite tipple to set the tone for your day.

Relax and enjoy your wedding day. Let everyone else do the hard work!

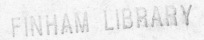

GET MARRIED IN THREE MONTHS

What if you want to avoid a whole year of expectations and planning madness?

Well, set your mind to it and you can get married as quickly as you like. After all, now you are engaged, what's stopping you? All you need to do is cover all the basic requirements and the rest are optional extras.

There are obviously issues with this and you will need to be either very flexible or not particularly pernickety about some aspects of your wedding. Availability and costings can work against you if suppliers know that you are desperate to make a last-minute booking. Also, you may not be able to hire the venue you want and some guests might not be able to make it at short notice. But three months is enough time to find somewhere to wed and give your notice of marriage, to choose your outfits and send out your invitations.

At a real push, you could even get married in a month – you only need to give 15 days clear notice to have a civil ceremony in the UK.

Alternatively, it is feasible to arrange an overseas wedding through a tour operator in three months as long as you are quick off the mark. Or you can organise it yourselves. Provided you have all the right paperwork prepared in advance you can get married in some countries, like Australia, the day you step off the plane.

WEDDING SHOWS

Wedding shows tend to be held in either January/February or September/ October.

Check for a venue near you and any updates or new locations from the organisers. At the time of going to press, the larger shows were:

NATIONAL WEDDING SHOW

London, Manchester and Birmingham.
See: www.nationalweddingshow.co.uk

THE UK WEDDING SHOWS

Newcastle, Birmingham, Liverpool, Cardiff and Manchester.
See: www.theukweddingshows.co.uk

THE WEDDING AND LIFESTYLE SHOW

This Harrogate-based wedding fair is the largest in the north of England and has around 150 exhibitors.
See: www.weddingandlifestyle.co.uk

THE SCOTTISH WEDDING SHOW

Glasgow.
See: www.thescottishweddingshow.com

OTHERS

Keep an eye on local press, in the bridal magazines and bridal shops for events in your area. They might not be as big as the national shows but you should still be able to pick up a bargain and some great ideas and it can be a fun way to while away the hours with your husband-to-be, mum or bridesmaids.

> We would definitely recommend trying out a wedding show if you can. They sound like a nightmare but you can pick up good discounts. We got a 15 per cent discount on our wedding rings from a voucher we picked up at the show, saving about a hundred pounds.
>
> MARIE AND ANDY, 29 AND 30

APPENDIX – NOTABLE UK DATES

Some dates to consider when booking your wedding are listed below.

This is just to provide you with an approximate guide and you should double-check all dates against a calendar for the year you are getting married because some can vary annually.

JANUARY

1st – New Year's Day bank holiday (UK)
2nd – Holiday (Scotland)
5th – Birth of Guru Gobind Singh Ji
6th – Epiphany
25th – Burn's Night
27th – Holocaust Memorial Day

FEBRUARY

Shrove Tuesday and Ash Wednesday (but these may fall in March)
Chinese Lunar New Year (may fall in January)
14th – St Valentine's Day
Rugby Union – Celtic League Final, various Irish and Scottish venues (www.rfu.com)
Rugby Union – Six Nations; Paris, Dublin, Edinburgh, Twickenham, Cardiff, Rome (www.rfu.com)

MARCH

1st – St David's Day (Wales)

17th – St Patrick's Day (Northern Ireland)

Mothering Sunday (may occasionally fall in April)

Jewish Purim (this can also fall in February)

Hindu Holi

British Summer Time begins on the last weekend in March

Football – League Cup Final (www.thefa.com)

Horse Racing – Cheltenham National Hunt Festival and Gold Cup, Cheltenham (www.cheltenham.co.uk)

Rugby Union – Six Nations; Paris, Dublin, Edinburgh, Twickenham, Cardiff, Rome (www.rfu.com)

APRIL

21st – Queen Elizabeth II born 1926 (public buildings and services might not be available)

23rd – St George's Day

Easter weekend (UK, but this can also fall in March)

Jewish Pesach/Passover (this may fall in March)

Sikh Baisakhi

Athletics – London Marathon, London (www.london-marathon.co.uk)

Horse Racing – Grand National, Aintree (www.aintree.co.uk)

Horse Racing – Irish Grand National, Fairyhouse (www.fairyhouseracecourse.ie)

Horse Racing – Scottish Grand National, Ayr (www.ayr-racecourse.co.uk)

Rowing – Boat Race, London (www.theboatrace.org)

Rugby Union – English Cup Final, Twickenham (www.rfu.com)

MAY

First Monday in May bank holiday (UK)
Spring bank holiday (UK, but can also fall in June)
Football – FA Cup Final, Cardiff (www.thefa.com)
Football – Champions League Final, various European venues
(www.uefa.com)
Rugby Union – European Cup Final, various European venues
(www.rfu.com)
Rugby Union – Principality Cup Final, Cardiff (www.rfu.com)

JUNE

Jewish Shavuot/Pentecost (this may fall in May)
Queen's Official Birthday (falls on a Saturday and public buildings and
services might not be available)
Father's Day (always a Sunday)
Sikh Martyrdom of Guru Arjan Dev ji
Horse Racing – The Derby, Epsom (www.epsomderby.co.uk)
Horse Racing – Royal Ascot, Ascot (www.ascot.co.uk)
Tennis – The Championships, Wimbledon (www.wimbledon.org)

JULY

4th – Independence Day, USA
Athletics – London Grand Prix, Crystal Palace (www.uka.org.uk)
Cricket – Twenty-20 Semi-finals and final (www.ecb.co.uk)
Formula One – British Grand Prix, Silverstone (www.formula1.com)
Golf – British Open Championship, various UK and Ireland courses
(www.opengolf.com)
Rowing – Henley Royal Regatta, Henley (www.hrr.co.uk)

AUGUST

Islamic Eid ul-Fit (dates vary annually)
First week – bank holiday (Scotland)
Last Monday in August – bank holiday (UK except Scotland)

SEPTEMBER

Jewish New Year/Rosh Hashanah
Jewish Yom Kippur/Day of Atonement (can also fall in October)
Jewish Succot/Tabernacles (can also fall in October)
Gaelic Football – All Ireland Finals, Croke Park, Dublin (www.gaa.ie)

OCTOBER

British Summer Time ends on the last weekend in OctoberIslamic
Laylat Al Isra wa Al-Miraj
Jewish Simchat Torah
Hindu Navratri (sometimes in September)
31st – Halloween
Rugby League – Super League Grand Final, (www.superleague.co.uk)

NOVEMBER

5th – Guy Fawkes' Night
11th – Remembrance Day. This is noted on the closest Sunday for the
Remembrance Sunday services
30th – St Andrew's Day (Scotland)
Hindu Diwali (dates vary annually)
Sikh Martyrdom of Guru Tegh Bahadur ji

DECEMBER

25th – Christmas Day (UK, if this falls on a weekend, the bank holiday rolls over)

26th – Boxing Day (UK, if this falls on a weekend, the bank holiday rolls over)

31st – New Year's Eve

Islamic New Year/Al-Hijra (varies annually)

Islamic Ashura (varies annually)

Jewish Hanukkah (sometimes begins in November)

In addition to these, events that run every four years rather than annually are:

Football – World Cup (2010, 2014)

Football – European Championships (2012, 2016)

Rugby – World Cup (2011,2015)

Rugby – British Lions World Tour (2013, 2017)

Cricket – World Cup (2011, 2015)

Olympics (2012, 2016)

Winter Olympics (2010, 2014)

For fixtures that run at various times throughout the year, check out the sporting calendar on the BBC website at www.bbc.co.uk or http://news.bbc.co.uk/sport.

Who knows? If you are both keen sports fans perhaps you can plan far enough in advance to purposely coincide your wedding with one of these fixtures for a unique theme. If the event is overseas then you could get married in that country instead.

INDEX